The Release 12 Primer

Shining a Light on Release 12

Published by Solution Beacon

ISBN: 978-0-6152-3844-9

Solution Beacon, LLC
14419 Greenwood Ave N #332
Seattle, WA 98133
Phone 206 366-6606
http://www.solutionbeacon.com

Meet the Authors

If you have questions about Release 12, send a note to Solution Beacon's Release 12 Team at Release12Team@solutionbeacon.com

Our authors and their areas of expertise are:

Alyssa Johnson – Financials

Alfredo Pantaleon – E-Business Tax, Oracle Projects

Lance Reedy – Java, Fusion Middleware

Montella Alston – CRM

Anthony Della-Croce – CRM

Susan Behn – Integration Repository (*i*Rep), Workflow

Karen Brownfield – Workflow

Paul Cyphers – Procurement, BPEL

John Faucher – Resources

Daryl Geryol – Master Data Management, the Swan Interface

Chuck Kennedy – Security, Supply Chain Management

Randy Giefer – Security

Rob McMillen – Fusion Middleware

Naren Thota – Business Intelligence

Lon White – Technology

John Stouffer – Fusion Middleware, Technology

Barbara Matthews – Team Lead

Real Solutions for the Real World®

Give us a call when you're ready to implement or upgrade to Release 12! We have the knowledge and experience that you need. We are Your Trusted Advisors.

Dedication

The Solution Beacon Release 12 Team donates all proceeds from the sales of this book to the Solution Beacon Foundation. The Solution Beacon Foundation is a charitable organization whose mission is: "Feeding Children's Bodies and Minds" by delivering aid and assistance to others less fortunate.

http://www.solutionbeaconfoundation.org/stevepeifer.htm

Solution Beacon's Release 12 Team is a group of functional and technical experts who investigate the inner workings of Release 12. The team installs and tests multiple Release 12 environments. They also research problems reported by users of Solution Beacon's free Release 12 Vision Instances and our clients' Release 12 installs and upgrades.

As preparation for this book, team members developed a set of presentations about topics covered in each of the chapters. The team presented these presentations as live webinars and workshops around the country at various OAUG venues. You can see all of Solution Beacon's presentations, including those about other topics, at www.solutionbeacon.com

Special Thanks

The Release 12 Primer is a collaborative effort between Solution Beacon and the Oracle Applications User Group. We appreciate OAUG's support in helping us publish this book.

We offer special thanks to all those who contributed, particularly our reviewers, including:

Brian Bent, Melanie Burns, Geordie Coates, Don Driggs, Anurag Goel, Hope Malone, Tim Sharpe, and Cathy Sumeracki of Solution Beacon

Ron Batra, Jeannie Dobney, Mark Farnham, Nancy Fox, Kathy Hohenstreiter, Jerry Ireland, Michael Moscatello, Anthony Pennington, Elke Phelps, Floyd Teter, Mike Towery, Henry Y Yee

Special thanks to Alysha Behn, who assisted with editing.

TABLE OF CONTENTS

Introduction

With 18 new products and over 2400 enhancements, describing the features and functionality of Release 12 of Oracle's E-Business Suite of Applications could fill several books. Major architectural changes were made in this release in order to support the new products and enhancements required by Release 12.

The purpose of this book is to highlight areas where users will receive the greatest return on investment. It is not intended to be an exhaustive analysis of Release 12, but rather a look into the features and functionalities that will be of interest to a wide audience. This book describes the features that will increase processing efficiency, reduce errors, speed data flow, improve auditing visibility and give company decision-makers the most accurate and timely view of the data. It is not the purpose of this book to compare and contrast earlier releases of the Applications with Release 12. We want the book to be of use to anyone considering Release 12, without requiring experience with Release 11*i* or other Applications releases.

The book is divided first by product family and includes Chapter 2, *Financials Product Family*, Chapter 3, *Procurement Product Family*, Chapter 4, *Supply Chain Management Products*, Chapter 5, *Customer Relationship Management (CRM) Products*, and Chapter 6, *Projects Product Family*. While not a comprehensive list of all the product family changes, these chapters will give users a glimpse into the power of Release 12.

Once one understands the functional highlights of Release 12, the remaining chapters cover the rest of the story. Chapter 7, *Technology*, provides a description of the technical architecture of Release 12. Chapter 8, *Security*, describes the security issues technical staff must be prepared for in order to secure a company's data. Chapter 9, *Resources*, describes the resources that a company will need to support the Release 12 environment. Certainly, Release 12 is no less complicated than Release 11*i*, so organizations should anticipate even more specialized skill sets will be required to maintain the Applications environment. Finally, the Release 12 Primer will wrap up with Chapter 10, *Fusion Middleware*, which details the aspects of Fusion that are currently available, what is coming, and what organizations should start doing now to prepare for the upcoming changes that Fusion is sure to bring.

We hope that this Primer will give users some basic Release 12 knowledge and will inspire them to find out more.

RELEASE 12 – THE GLOBAL BUSINESS RELEASE

Oracle terms Release 12 as "The Global Business Release". This may prompt the questions - "What does this mean to our business? Do I have to be a Global operation?" The Global Business Release does not imply that organizations must be global or do business globally. The idea is that the applications and technologies of Release 12 facilitate global thinking. Another definition of global is "being comprehensive, all-inclusive, or complete" and as you will see in this book, the different applications are positioned to enable that strategy for your business needs.

Oracle's Release 12 theme is "Think Globally, Work Globally, and Manage Globally". Release 12 fulfills that vision with the following features:

Think Globally – Business decisions will only be as good as 1) The data they are based on, and 2) If the data is correct, the representation of that data. To facilitate data integrity and a single source of the truth, Release 12 uses both the hub/spoke architecture and data repositories in several key areas of data storage. Users will also find enhanced tools to present data to management including XML Publisher, Daily Business Intelligence (DBI) and most recently, Oracle Business Intelligence Enterprise Edition (OBIEE).

Work Globally – To improve the user experience, Oracle has made a concentrated effort to enhance the user interface. This results in increased productivity and reduced need for training and support. Release 12 has an improved visual style through the new Swan Interface (Figure 1). With this new interface, pop-ups and duplicate screens have been greatly reduced.

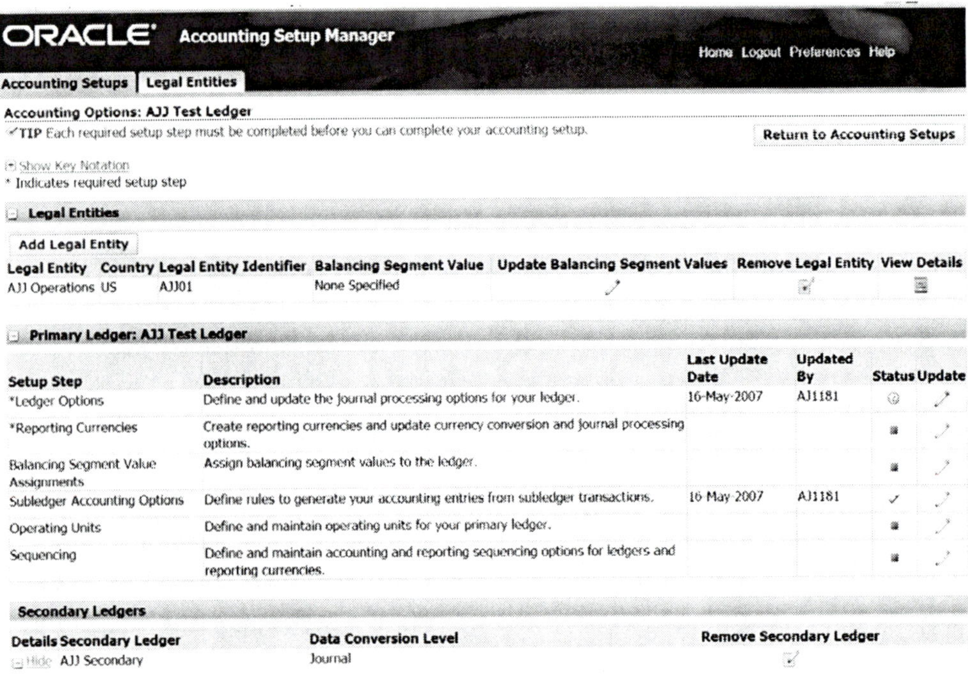

Figure 1 – The new Accounting Setup Manager is an example of the new Swan Interface

Another new feature that improves a company's ability to work globally is Multi-Org Access Control (MOAC). By using MOAC, companies that operate Shared Service Centers are able to perform tasks across multiple organizations. This streamlines processing, reporting and access across operating units.

Manage Globally - As Oracle expands both technically and functionally, it becomes even more vital that tools are in place to manage the complete E-Business Suite. A key component to global management is security. Both technical and functional users will want to be sure to read Chapter 8, *Security*, for an in-depth discussion of the security features available in Release 12.

Furthermore, in many instances, users can leverage the Release 12 configuration capabilities to personalize without relying on additional customized programming. This can be accomplished through Flexfields, folders, workflow, OA Framework personalizations, Professional Forms personalization and XML Publisher.

With the increase in the number of interfaces, both inbound and outbound, a tool has been developed that describes all of the Oracle interface endpoints and API definitions whether they are Business to Business (B2B) or Application to Application (A2A). With the Integration Repository (*i*Rep), users can both view and deploy the interfaces as needed. This tool should help to speed the development process by giving the developer a single place to look for interface information. The Integration Repository is described in more detail in Chapter 7 - *Technology*.

Before moving into the product family details, three areas that affect all of the products will be discussed here. As mentioned before, in order to make valid business decisions, data must be well managed and well represented. This has led to the development of the Master Data Management concept and data representation tools such as XML Publisher, DBI, and most recently OBIEE. Also, the new Swan Interface is so prevalent throughout Release 12, it warrants further mention because this is a point of data entry into the system.

MASTER DATA MANAGEMENT

Every system has a core set of data. Whether your system is used for manufacturing or core financials data, data exists that determines the accuracy of almost every transaction. This core set of data is called Master Data. Without Master Data, your enterprise would be "up the river without a paddle".

Master Data within the Oracle E-Business Suite includes the following key entities: customers, suppliers, products, locations, assets, employees, and chart of accounts. These are the foundation of nearly every business process or transaction from sales, procurement, financial reporting, service and supply chain. Now that we know the key entities, we can review what makes them so important, and how they are managed within the E-Business Suite of Applications.

Why is Managing Master Data Important?

Poor or nonexistent Master Data management can lead to the following risks:

- Compromised business decisions

- Inaccurate financial reporting
- Decreased overall system integrity and decreased user adoption
- Loss of revenue or increases in costs and expenses due to issues in shipments, billing, payments or accounting
- Loss of effectiveness and time wasted by the user
- Increased overhead costs to support the E-Business Suite environment

A typical example of a Master Data issue is the existence of duplicate supplier or customer records. When this happens, it can cause confusion during the sales or procurement process, along with issues in collections, payments and reporting. Prevention and remediation are the two methods for dealing with Master Data issues. Remediation can be accomplished by running standard concurrent programs to merge records – the "Vendor Merge" or "Customer Merge" concurrent programs. These programs should be run periodically to keep these master files "clean".

To make ongoing remediation quick, simple, and more easily managed, a good prevention policy and process should be introduced. Some of the applications have standard controls or checks to help manage duplicates. For instance, the Applications include simple checks for duplicates during record creation. This is not foolproof, as normal spelling errors, differences in capitalization, spacing or punctuation will create unique entries. Additional controls can be created to look for patterns or force additional lookups, making it harder to create duplicates. Simply creating easily defined and implemented rules, like using forms personalization to enforce uppercase (after making all records uppercase, of course), will eliminate one way of creating duplicate data.

Effectively Managing Master Data

With good controls in place, Master Data can be managed more effectively and can be relied upon as a company's single source of truth. To accomplish this, well-defined processes and controls must be in place for the three main activities required for Master Data: creating records, managing changes to records, and terminating records.

A good starting point is to review your business processes and separate them according to the seven key entities (customers, suppliers, products, locations, assets, employees, and chart of accounts) and the three main activities (creating records, managing changes to records, and terminating records). Prioritize the data by the impact on the business, reporting or cost.

Access Control

Access control is imperative. Separation or segregation of duties is not only required but is also a good control to apply regardless. The traditional security best practice guiding principle usually works best: "If a user has access, there is risk". To begin, review which forms and functions are used for each of the three activities and identify which responsibilities have access to them. Do not focus on the users until the last step. Removing non-required or inappropriate functions will have the greatest overall impact and cause less overall work. Remove inappropriate functions by excluding them from responsibilities if they are not required or appropriate for those responsibilities.

Once responsibilities have been modified, review those users assigned to be sure they have the correct responsibilities and do not have excessive responsibilities based upon their job role. This is a remediation exercise and it will take some time. A prevention mechanism is to perform a thorough manual or automated review of each user's job responsibilities prior to actually assigning roles. Implementing user provisioning, User Management (UMX) and Role Based Access Control (RBAC), or other software packages offering these features can be very helpful if they are certified for use with the E-Business Suite of Applications. The implementation of the Role Based Access Control (RBAC) model is recommended because it is an ANSI standard that reduces the cost of administering user access, streamlines setup and implementation of security policies, and structures user access control based upon users' job roles instead of individual identity.

Data Creation/Change

The next focus is on the creation of data and the management of changes to that data. If a user or group of users has access based on job roles, what is the best way to create or manage Master Data? First, with regard to creating data, we need to look at any situation where users are only allowed to create data conditionally. For example, within a group of users, only a few might be intended to create suppliers of "type" employee. However, once any user is granted access to the functions allowing new supplier creation, any type of supplier can be created, so there is risk that an unauthorized user might create employee suppliers. To limit users through an application, more advanced application controls or rules are required. These rules, called business rules, need to provide conditional security or control based on specific business requirements. To implement such rules there are options like forms personalization and workflow, data security, custom.pll modifications, third-party applications, customization (not preferred), and using manual controls. The last option, using manual controls, is always available but not preferred for obvious overhead and maintenance reasons. To control or manage the change of data, the focus is the same. The options, however, increase to include adding approval processes and auditing.

As an example, let us say that a group of receivables clerks has access, as part of their job function, to increase credit limits, but someone has mistakenly changed the credit limit from $10,000 to $100,000. To remediate the problem, audit controls could be set up so that any changes are recorded. With audit controls, it is imperative that review processes are in place to review reports often enough to notice issues. A more proactive and preventative approach is to force users to enter reasons for the change so that there is a recorded reason for the change. Another option would be to implement an approval process to prevent the change prior to a secondary approval, thus making this a two-step or "two-touch" process. Approval controls do add another step or additional oversight to a process but could be well worth the cost given the risk of some changes. Another control that should be considered is continuous control monitoring to issue an alert or notification when certain changes occur. It is wise, and not unheard of, to implement redundant controls for certain types of data. Whether to do so is a question of the level of risk acceptable to the business for the given data.

End-dating or Terminating Data

There are regulations that impact the period of time required to keep data. The amount of "old" data retained will contribute to decreasing reports and forms performance, increasing overall user dissatisfaction, and increasing space requirements as the amount of data stored increases dramatically over time and Applications releases. This data may show up on reports or system forms and mistakenly end up being used in transactions.

Solution Beacon Recommends: *Take proactive and continuous steps to end-date records where appropriate. Create methods to identify obsolete and inactive data. Institute purges or archive programs that adhere to corporate and industry data retention standards or regulations.*

There are applications to assist in archiving data while still providing seamless end user access so that the user will not even know that the data has been "archived". It is worthwhile to research the value of these applications for your environment. Most of these applications also maintain controls on who can manage the data that is inactivated, archived or removed and who can run programs to remove data.

Summary

Fortunately, Release 12 has made some aspects of Master Data Management easier. Customer, Suppliers and Master Items all include improvements to help manage Master Data. As we move through the chapters watch for details outlining these improvements.

Control and management of Master Data is important to the business in many ways. Master Data should be secure, controlled, and accurately maintained. Controls may be automated or manual. Establishing Master Data groups to manage the data is also a good idea. Master Data groups can be set up in a variety of ways, all of which make sense as long as process and control is emphasized. The idea is to centralize much of the management of the data. Without centralization, individual users may not know the impact of a credit rule they are setting up or the ramifications of changing an Item category. The processes for data management should take into account regions and time zones where applicable. The control or process for end dating or inactivating Master Data should be tightly controlled and reviewed on a regular basis. These steps can significantly improve the quality and accuracy of reports and users' effectiveness, as well as reduce costs in many areas, while providing for a healthier E-Business Suite environment for the enterprise.

DATA REPRESENTATION

Even as a single source of truth comes closer to becoming a reality, the focus on data representation is equally intense, so that robust data can be reported to decision makers in a way that supports the very best decisions. Three tools – XML Publisher, Daily Business Intelligence, and Oracle Business Intelligence Enterprise Edition are available in Release 12 to assist users in achieving this goal.

XML Publisher

XML Publisher has been available in Release 11*i*, but is becoming more pervasive moving into Release 12. Its impact is felt across all product families. As you read, bear in mind that all this flexibility brings an increased need for security and change control for reporting. Oracle's goal is to convert all remaining Oracle Reports to XML Publisher by the end of the Release 12 Application cycle. The design of XML Publisher consists of the following components: a data and/or metadata extract is performed and merged with an XML template to generate output in a variety of available formats that are then delivered in a variety of methods (see Figure 2).

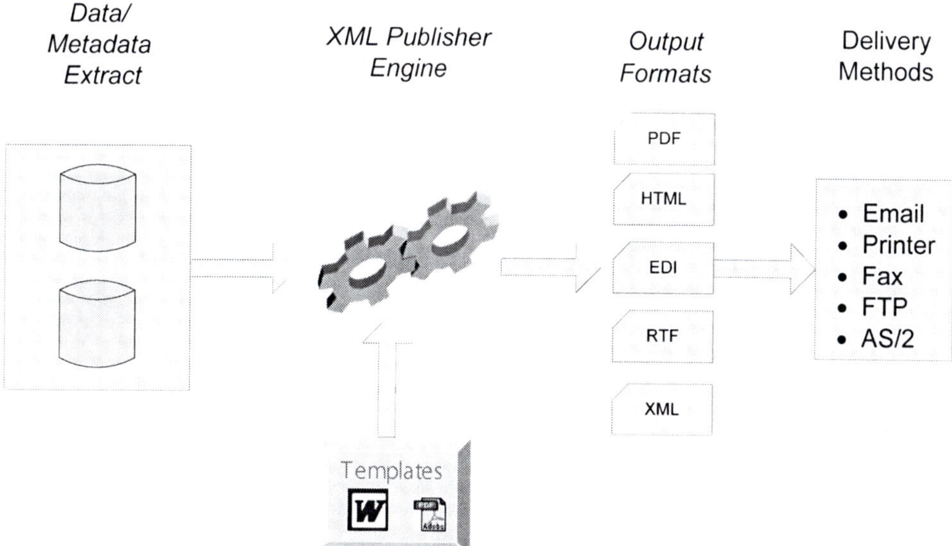

Figure 2 – XML Publisher flow

Many data extracts and templates are available out of the box in Release 12. Data extracts are large; containing all columns that Oracle thought could possibly be required in a report. Also, over 855 templates are currently available in Release 12. Users are not constrained to use only out of the box reporting. Developers can create custom data extracts. Templates are easy to create and maintain because they are saved as Word or Acrobat files. Excel templates will be available in the future. In fact, the goal of XML Publisher is to enable business analysts to modify existing templates to save development time. One application that has many templates – 120 at last count – is Payments. The large number of available templates are used to support multiple payment methods. Figure 3 is the Microsoft Word document template for a standard check. Notice the fields in gray. Many of these are column names that can be removed or added, as required. If companies would like their logo on the check, since it is a Word document, a simple cut and paste will accomplish the change.

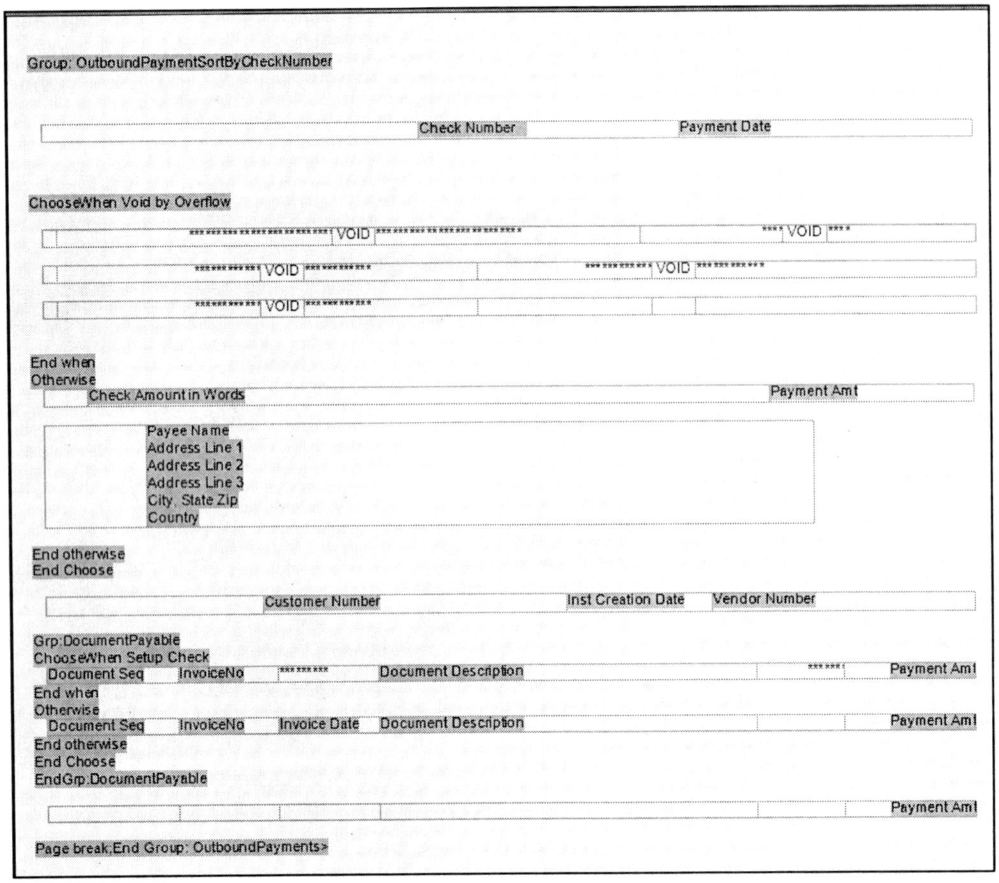

Group: OutboundPaymentSortByCheckNumber

Check Number Payment Date

ChooseWhen Void by Overflow

*********************** VOID *********************** **** VOID ****

*********** VOID *********** *********** VOID ***********

*********** VOID ***********

End when
Otherwise
Check Amount in Words Payment Amt

Payee Name
Address Line 1
Address Line 2
Address Line 3
City, State Zip
Country

End otherwise
End Choose

Customer Number Inst Creation Date Vendor Number

Grp:DocumentPayable
ChooseWhen Setup Check
Document Seq InvoiceNo ******** Document Description ****** Payment Amt
End when
Otherwise
Document Seq InvoiceNo Invoice Date Document Description Payment Amt
End otherwise
End Choose
EndGrp:DocumentPayable

Payment Amt

Page break;End Group: OutboundPayments>

Figure 3 – XML Publisher Standard Check template in Payments Application

Electronic file outputs are as easily maintained. Figure 4 represents a Positive Pay file. The record is mapped and the columns are defined in a Word document so changes can be made more quickly than modifying a standard Oracle report.

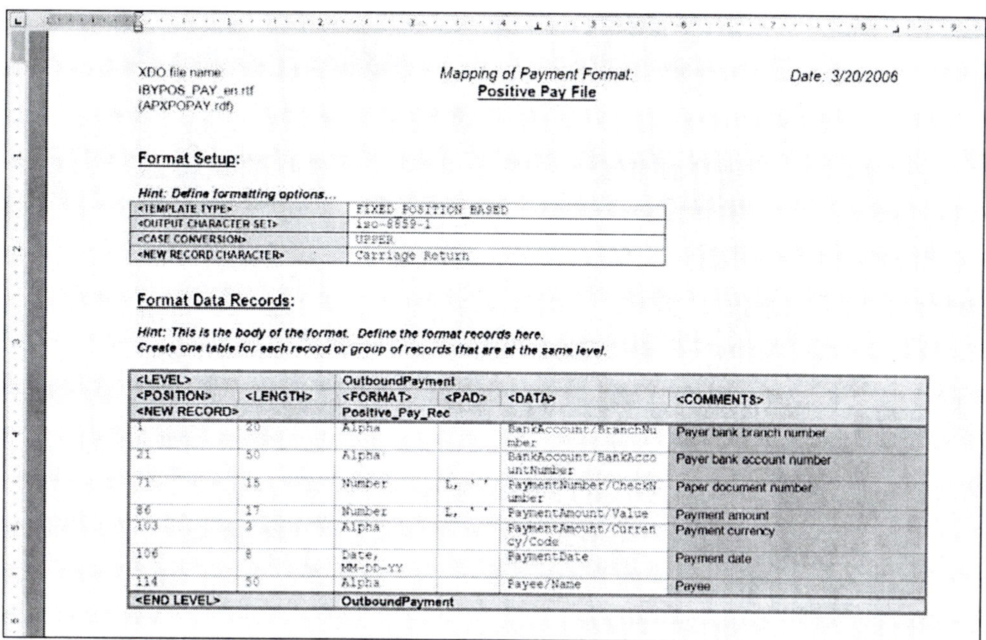

XDO file name
IBYPOS_PAY_en.rtf
(APXPOPAY.rdf)

Mapping of Payment Format:
Positive Pay File

Date: 3/20/2006

Format Setup:

Hint: Define formatting options...

<TEMPLATE TYPE>	FIXED POSITION BASED
<OUTPUT CHARACTER SET>	iso-8859-1
<CASE CONVERSION>	UPPER
<NEW RECORD CHARACTER>	Carriage Return

Format Data Records:

Hint: This is the body of the format. Define the format records here.
Create one table for each record or group of records that are at the same level.

<LEVEL>		OutboundPayment			
<POSITION>	<LENGTH>	<FORMAT>	<PAD>	<DATA>	<COMMENTS>
<NEW RECORD>		Positive_Pay_Rec			
1	20	Alpha		BankAccount/BranchNumber	Payer bank branch number
21	50	Alpha		BankAccount/BankAccountNumber	Payer bank account number
71	15	Number	L, ' '	PaymentNumber/CheckNumber	Paper document number
86	17	Number	L, ' '	PaymentAmount/Value	Payment amount
103	3	Alpha		PaymentAmount/Currency/Code	Payment currency
106	8	Date, MM-DD-YY		PaymentDate	Payment date
114	50	Alpha		Payee/Name	Payee
<END LEVEL>		OutboundPayment			

Figure 4 – XML Publisher Positive Pay template in Payments Application

XML Publisher integrates with OBIEE and as such, the terminology is moving toward calling this tool BI Publisher.

Daily Business Intelligence (DBI)

While this product has been put on maintenance mode as of July 2007 with no new releases available, there have been expansions in Release 12. Currently, the Daily Business Intelligence solution extends to 19 Modules with 60 Dashboards, more that 350 Key Performance Indicators (KPI), and over 900 Reports. DBI has pre-built role-based content that gives executives a graphical representation of important data with cross-functional and drill down analytics. The dashboards are easy to use and interactive. Figure 5 illustrates the Procurement DBI dashboard. While the tool is extensible and customizable, it can be a rigid application in terms of development effort. That is why with the acquisition of Siebel, Oracle is moving to OBIEE as the solution of choice.

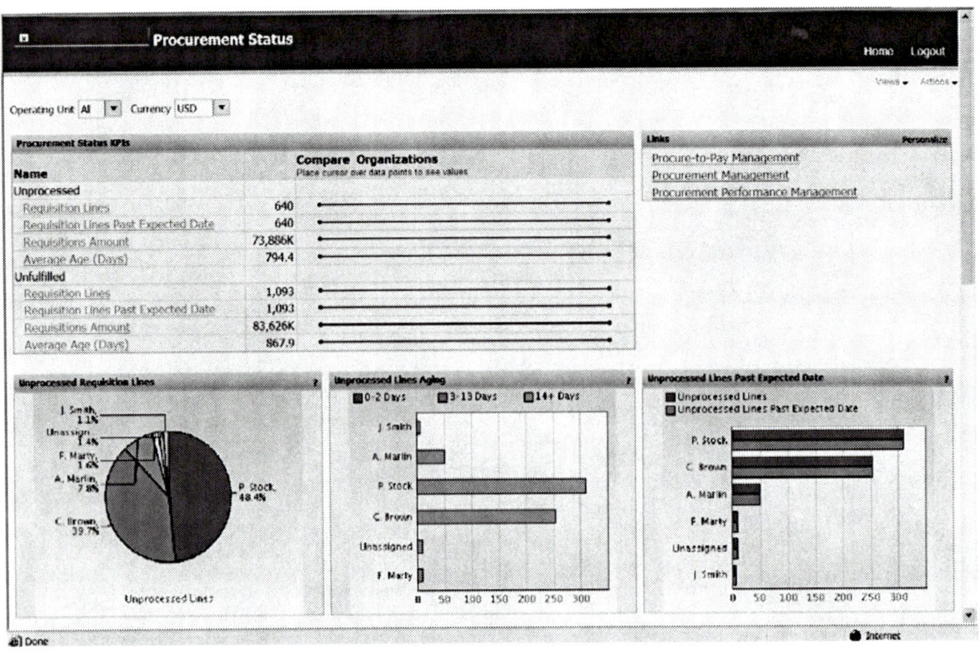

Figure 5 – The Procurement Daily Business Intelligence Dashboard

Oracle Business Intelligence Enterprise Edition (OBIEE)

OBIEE is the Business Intelligence and Analytical reporting interface for interactive dashboards and ad hoc query reporting. The application, although not completely integrated with Hyperion yet, does include certain components of Hyperion's Key Performance Indicators and Dashboards, and therefore the latest release of OBIEE is now called Oracle Business Intelligence Extended Edition Plus. One of its key features is the ability to connect with multiple data sources on any of the major platforms, including SQL*Server, Teradata, file systems, XLS files, XML files, as well as the Oracle database. The product suite includes pre-packaged External Data Warehouse Adaptors including Extraction-Transformation-Load logic (ETL), and Star Schemas (Facts and Dimensions) for Oracle E-Business Suite (Release 11*i* and Release 12), Siebel, PeopleSoft, and SAP. Content includes answers, reports and interactive dashboards. For Release 11*i* and Release 12 of Oracle E-Business Suite, content can be licensed by Business Area (e.g., Finance Analytics, Supply Chain Analytics, etc.) or by module (e.g., GL and Profitability Analytics, Payables Analytics, Receivables Analytics, etc.)

Oracle also offers a scaled down version of OBIEE, referred to as Oracle Business Intelligence Standard Edition1 (OBISE1), targeted towards smaller businesses that do not need a data warehouse as a solution. This solution is expandable to OBIEE in the future. It includes the ad hoc query reporting and interactive dashboards as well as BI Publisher.

THE SWAN USER INTERFACE

Not all of the navigation in Oracle is new, but if you are a hardcore Oracle forms user, look out. POW! BANG! BOOM! Oracle's use of the Swan Interface has some differences that many will like and others will simply love. The user experience is quite different in the Swan

Interface. As many of the features noted earlier state, data is more accessible and drill downs are more abundant.

New Concepts

If you've been using keyboard shortcuts in Oracle forms, you'll find them of no use in the Swan world. Pressing CTRL-L will no longer pop a List of Values (LOV). However, some nice additions make this change less of a loss.

Process Train

The process train may show up in different areas of your screen. In Figure 6, the process train is on the top. Very often, it will be on the top right of the screen. The process train shows users where they are in a process. At times, the process train is more interactive and will act as a shortcut or Locator Link to other areas in a process. Users can use the Locator Links to move through a process much more quickly.

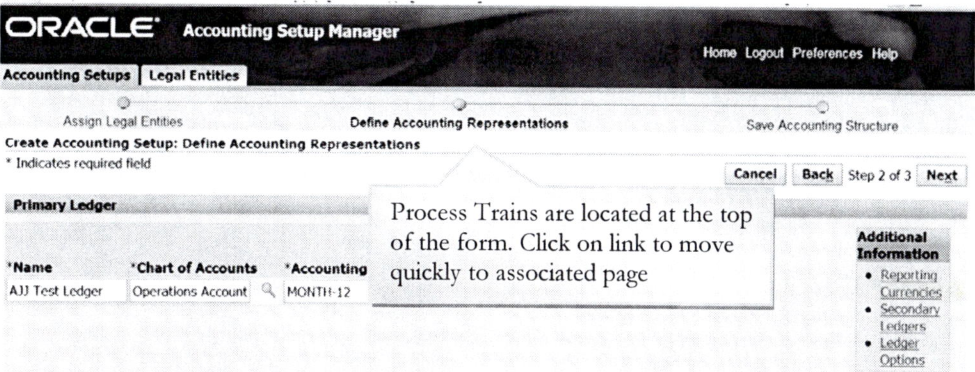

Figure 6 – Process Train to set up Accounting Structure

Global Links

Global Links work to give you a way home. Have you ever found yourself lost, in trouble or just plain in need of a way to return to somewhere more familiar? While the E-Business Suite doesn't have ruby slippers, you could use the Global Links much like a yellow brick road. Some of the links rarely change, such as Help Diagnostics and Preferences. Some of the other links change based on the application or form you are using. The links tend to bring you back to a starting point. Figure 7 shows examples of Global Links.

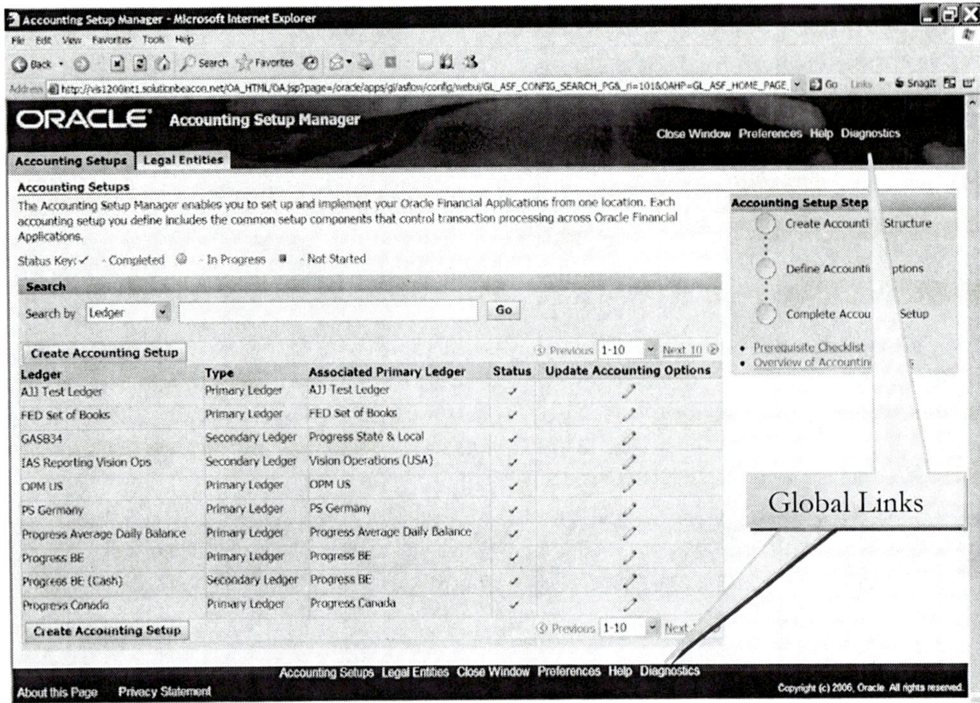

Figure 7 – Examples of Global Links

Date Picker

The date picker is not much of a change from using the calendar in forms. Users should have no trouble getting used to it. What is quite nice is the point Oracle developers made in making the date picker different from a standard List-of-Values (see Figure 8)

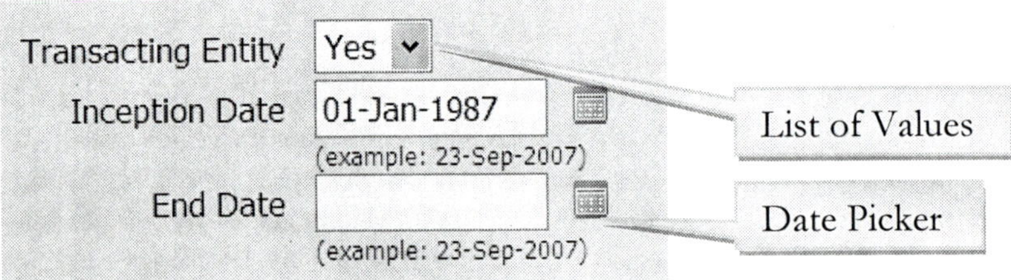

Figure 8 – Difference in List of Values and Data Picker

List of Values

The List of Values (LOV) has been a popular tool in the Applications. Until Release 12, when you landed on certain fields, you could press the CTRL-L keys to choose from a list of valid values. With the Swan Interface, Lists of Values are in drop down lists or as Quick Selects. If the user clicks on the Quick Select icon, the value will populate immediately into the form (see Figure 9).

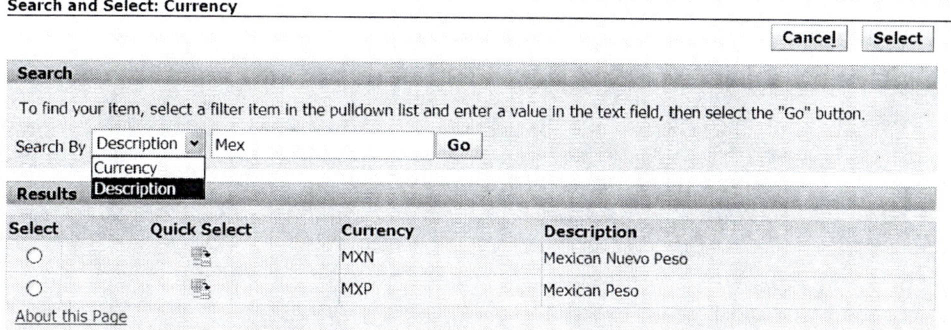

Figure 9 – List of Values for Currency and Quick Select icon

Edits and Updates

Edits and updates tend to be represented as a pencil icon. The pencil will open a new window putting the current record in edit mode. Users will sometimes see more data in edit mode as well. "Save", "Done" or "Apply" buttons are on the form when in edit mode so changes can be applied. In Figure 7, if the pencil icon is clicked, an update screen opens and the user can make changes to updateable values.

Navigation Techniques

In earlier releases of the Applications, many users spent their days using the mouse and the keyboard to move through the forms. Prior to the mouse and keyboard, with pre-Release 11*i* versions of the Applications, we had character screens that had other shortcuts. While you can still highlight a value and execute the CTRL-C to copy the data, or use the CTRL-X and CTRL-P key sequences, other shortcuts have been eliminated or replaced by new features in the Swan Interface.

Query operators and wild cards are an essential part of working in Oracle forms. Many of the operators are not as critical. These operators, shown in Figure 10, still function in forms, but they provide no value in the Swan Interface. The only exception to this is the % wildcard operator, which can still be used.

Operators	Meaning	Example
%	Wild Card	Vis%Ope
=	equals	= 'Visi'
!=	is not	!= 'Visi'
>=	at least	>= 50
<=	at most	<= 99
<	less than	> '01-JAN-07'
>	greater than	> '01-JAN-07'
#BETWEEN	between two values	#BETWEEN 1 AND 1000

Figure 10 – Query operators and wild cards

Navigating records and forms is much easier in the Swan Interface. To navigate through record sets, look for the "Previous" and "Next" labels at the top and bottom of records. You can jump from one record set to the next or use the drop list to jump record sets. See Figure 11 for an example.

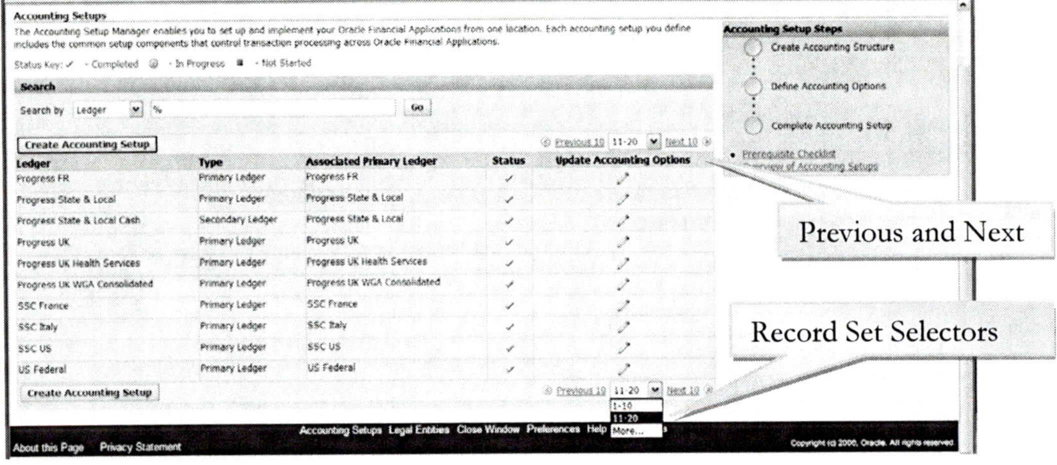

Figure 11– Click on Previous or Next to see more records, or see even more records using the Record Set Selectors

SUMMARY

Even with all the changes, the Global Business Release should be looked at as an opportunity. Many of the new features necessitate adjustments in the way you manage your enterprise's data and security. Any new implementation or upgrade to Release 12 will give enterprises a chance to improve their business processes and how they use the Applications. Changes in the user interface for many of the forms will require some learning by seasoned Oracle users, but the return will be worth the effort. If you currently employ good processes for managing Master Data and security, you have a great start. You should review those processes to make certain your transition to Release 12 brings no surprises with it. Don't forget about any bolt-ons or third party software that you use. In the following chapters our goal is to guide you through some of the key features of Oracle Release 12 and point out the areas relevant to "Global Thinking" that have the most potential to add value to organizations. Now, let's look first at the functional enhancements in the Financials product family.

Financials Product Family

The Financials product family was a primary focus for the Release 12 design teams. Five of the 18 new products can be found in Financials. The Global Business Release theme is at the forefront of many of the enhancements and moves the Applications toward the goal of global financial management.

Before diving into the Financials product family itself, our first stop will be at the HRMS application, because one of the foundational pillars of the functional processing in the Financial Product Family is the organizational structure a company chooses. Many of the functional products and features are ultimately tied to this model. A good understanding of both the structure and the terminology will benefit the user during the design of the organizational structure, in order to fully leverage the financial features. Furthermore, keeping the structure at the forefront during maintenance and expansion planning will support good decision-making and efficiency of change. The organizational structure in Figure 12 is a very simple example that highlights the various classifications that can be assigned to the nodes of an organization. Several features discussed throughout this chapter will reference this structure and will give the user insight into how to implement an organizational structure that will best meet their business needs.

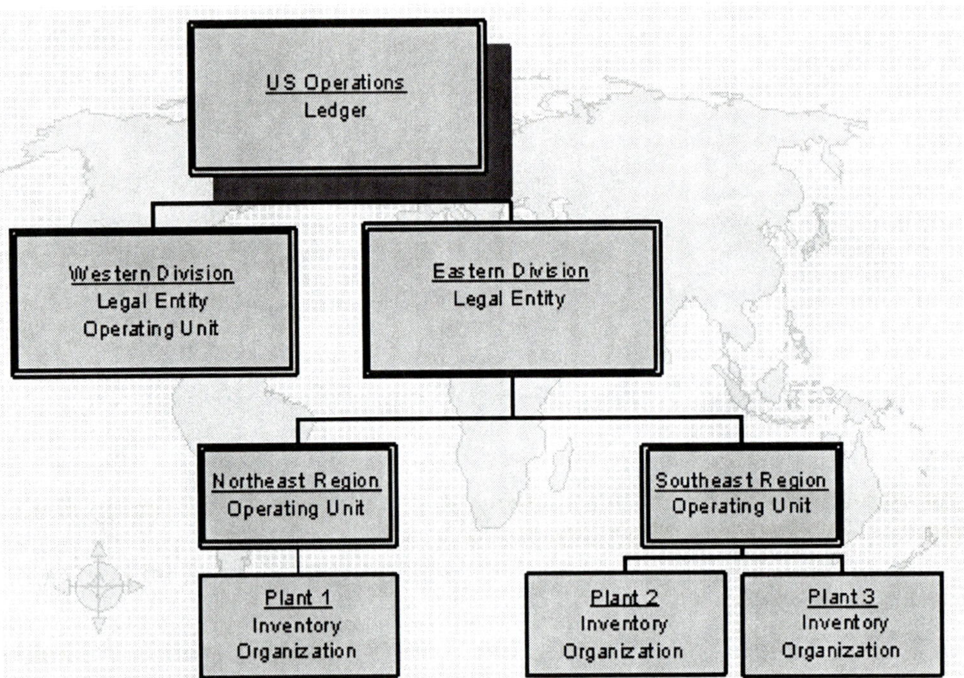

Figure 12 – A sample organizational structure

Analyzing the structure from the top down from a financial point of view, the ledger is the view of the financial data of the business group as a whole. Multiple ledgers can share the same business group, if they have the same business group attributes. The term "Set of Books" in Release 11*i* has been replaced by the term "Ledger" in Release 12. A ledger is made up of one or more legal entities. A Legal Entity represents the legal corporate structures, or companies, within a business group. These are the organizations that are specified for fiscal or tax reporting. Next, the Operating Unit represents an organization that uses any of the Oracle subledgers, such as Order Management, Purchasing, Payables, Receivables, and Cash Management. In terms of the business operations, an operating unit may be, for example, a division, a region, a sales office, or a department and is used to segregate data. Operating units are no longer associated with the legal entities. Instead, they are assigned to ledgers and a default legal context. Multiple Operating Units and multiple Legal Entities can be assigned to the same Ledger. Finally, the Inventory Organization tracks inventory transactions and balances. It can also be an organization that manufactures or distributes products. Examples include plants, warehouses, and distribution centers. Notice in this example, the Western Division functions as a Legal Entity and an Operating Unit. This type of flexibility is allowed and enables users to accurately represent their business in the system.

Now on to the Financials product family. Figure 13 illustrates the flow of data through the Financials system and will be used throughout the discussion.

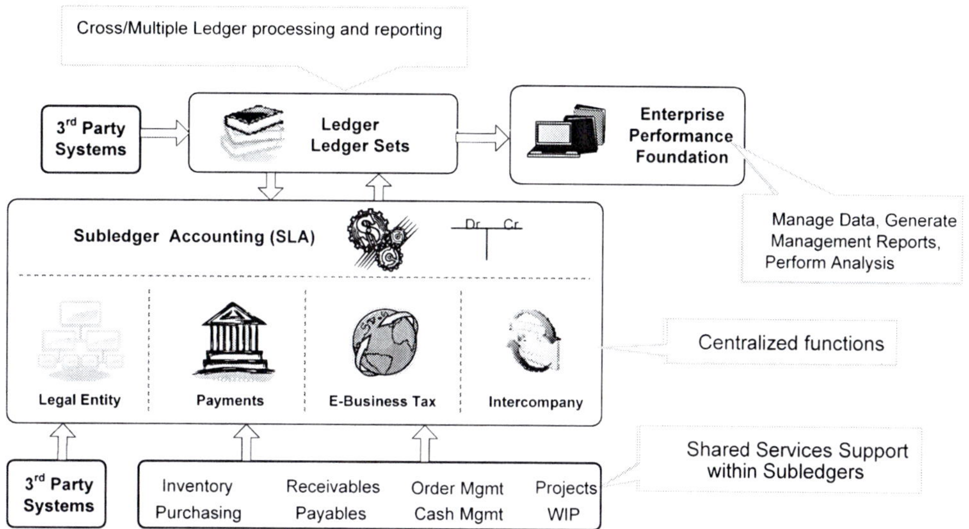

Figure 13 – Global Financial Management

Shared Services Support

One objective of the Release 12 initiative was to increase the effectiveness of the Shared Service Center. In prior releases, a separate responsibility was required for processing in each operating unit. Users were required to switch between these responsibilities in order to perform tasks for different organizations (i.e., operating units). For example, a receivables clerk would need three separate responsibilities – one to process transactions for Vision Operations, one for Vision Services, and one for Vision Communications.

Improving the efficiency of processing within subledgers enables employees to focus on their job responsibilities without stopping to manage the multiple operating units within the business model. Multi-Org Access Control (MOAC) is the functionality that achieves this goal. Users can now access multiple operating units from a single application responsibility. They can enter transactions, process data, view information, and run reports for and across multiple operating units. For the purposes of our example, a single responsibility (e.g., Receivables Clerk), instead of three, could be used to manage all three operating units. This increases the effectiveness of Shared Service Centers while still maintaining security across operating units. Even for companies not currently employing shared service centers, processing efficiencies can be improved by using Multi-Org Access Control.

Multi-Org Access Control is available across several modules. The following subledgers can leverage MOAC: Receivables, Payables, Purchasing, Order Management, Inventory, Projects and Work in Process (WIP). Multi-Org Access Control is used to designate Inventory Organizations only to the extent that users can view and process Inventory Organizations that are under the operating units to which they have access.

On an upgrade from Release 11*i*, Multi-Org Access Control is not enabled. Each responsibility has access to the operating unit assigned to it prior to the upgrade. This puts the control in the hands of the users and lets them make a conscious decision to leverage MOAC.

Enabling Multi-Org Access Control

Three Profile Options control the functionality of operating unit processing. During an upgrade, the MO: Operating Unit profile is seeded with the default operating unit from the previous release. At this point, Multi-Org Access Control is not enabled. Figure 14 describes the available profile values. The profile values can be assigned at both the responsibility and the user level.

Profile Name	Description
MO: Operating Unit	Access to only one operating unit. Seeded on upgrade with responsibility's operating unit
MO: Security Profile	Access to multiple operating units that are assigned to a security profile name
MO: Default Operating Unit	Default operating unit for responsibilities with access to multiple operating units

Figure 14 – Available profile values

The first step is to identify the groups of operating units that each responsibility should have access to based on the company's operations. This is also a good time to evaluate current processes and procedures to identify areas where modifications could leverage MOAC to an even greater extent.

Creating Security Profile Names

After the groupings of operating units have been identified, the first step to enabling MOAC is to create a Security Profile Name. This function can be accessed through the HRMS Superuser Responsibility: Security – Profile navigation. Figure 15 shows an example of how to create the security profile.

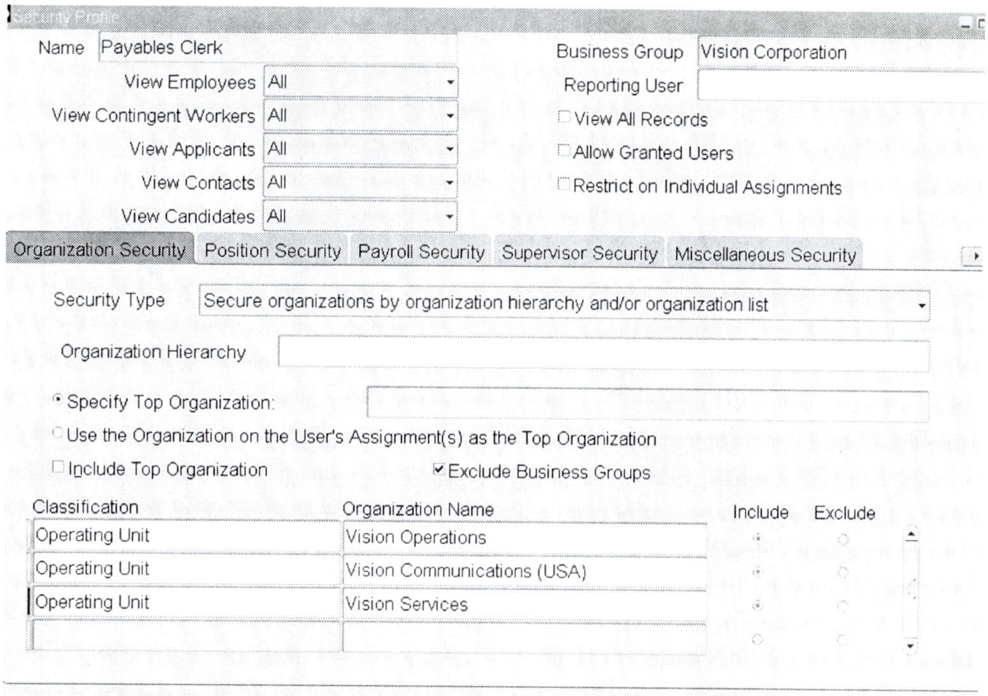

Security Profile

Name: Payables Clerk
Business Group: Vision Corporation
View Employees: All
Reporting User:
View Contingent Workers: All
View All Records
View Applicants: All
Allow Granted Users
View Contacts: All
Restrict on Individual Assignments
View Candidates: All

Organization Security | Position Security | Payroll Security | Supervisor Security | Miscellaneous Security

Security Type: Secure organizations by organization hierarchy and/or organization list
Organization Hierarchy:
Specify Top Organization:
Use the Organization on the User's Assignment(s) as the Top Organization
Include Top Organization
Exclude Business Groups

Classification	Organization Name	Include	Exclude
Operating Unit	Vision Operations		
Operating Unit	Vision Communications (USA)		
Operating Unit	Vision Services		

Figure 15 – An example of how to create the security profile for a Payables Clerk

To create the security profile, enter the new Security Profile Name in the required name field. Enter the Business Group this security profile operates in the business group field. Select the Security Type of "Secure organizations by organization hierarchy and/or organization list".

If all of the operating units for this security profile are underneath a specific node of the organizational hierarchy, users can choose to enter the organization hierarchy name in the "Organization Hierarchy" field. Then they can specify the top organizational node the security profile will use (e.g., from Figure 12, if a security profile was created for the Eastern Division, the top organization node could be specified as the Eastern Division and all operating units underneath that node would be part of this security profile). Users can include the top organization by checking the associated box. In this example, this box would be unchecked because the Eastern Division is not classified as an operating unit.

However, if the operating units for this security profile are across organizational branches, the organizational hierarchy can be left blank and individual operating units can be specified regardless of their location on the organizational structure.

Run Security List Maintenance

Once the security profile name has been created or modified, the next step is to run the concurrent program "Security List Maintenance". In the context of operating units, this concurrent program generates the list of operating units that the security profile can access. The list of values for the "Generate Lists For" required parameter that will enable the created security profile are "All Security Profiles", "All Security Profiles in One Named Business Group", and "One Named Security Profile". If the user is creating or updating a single security profile, the "One Named Security Profile" parameter will result in the greatest processing efficiency.

Assign Profile Values

Now the security profile name can be assigned by the Applications System Administrator to the appropriate Profile Option - "MO: Security Profile" - at the responsibility or the user level. A default operating unit can also be assigned to the "MO: Default Operating Unit" Profile Option.

All operating units will be listed in this list of values. If an operating unit is assigned as a default operating unit that cannot be accessed by the security profile, then the default operating unit will not be enabled for this user.

At this point, the "MO: Operating Unit" Profile Option is ignored as the system now uses the security profile for the given responsibility or user combination.

Multi-Org Access Control Functionality

Once MOAC is enabled, users can view data, process transactions, and run reports for and across the operating units to which they have access. This improves processing efficiency and gives users a global view of the data related to operating units assigned to their security profile name.

Query

Figure 16 shows an example of the query functionality across operating units. Notice that this Purchasing user can view transactions for both Vision Operations and Vision Services. Now the user does not have to change responsibilities in order to view or perform actions on their incomplete orders.

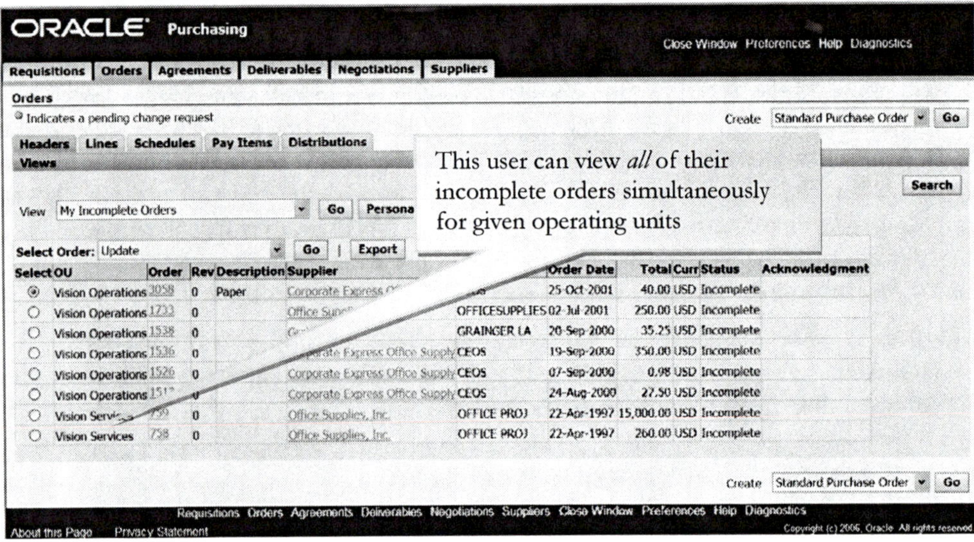

Figure 16 – An example of the query functionality across operating units, thanks to MOAC

Data Entry

All of the operating units assigned to this security profile can be used by this Payables user for entering invoices (see Figure 17). If a default operating unit is specified in the Profile Option "MO: Default Operating Unit", then that operating unit will populate the field initially.

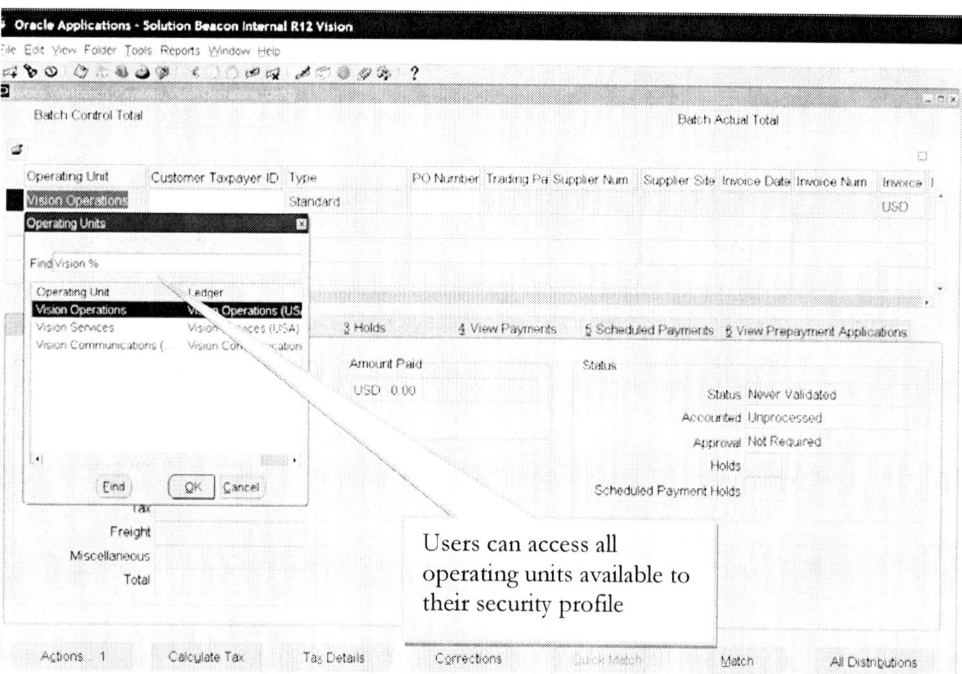

Figure 17 – Users can access all operating units available to their security profile

MOAC enabled forms may have the operating unit visible or hidden inside of the folders. If the field is not visible, right-click your mouse and select "Show Field" to get a list of fields to add to the form. The operating unit field can be added and saved to the default folder for the form.

Concurrent Programs

Concurrent programs are divided into two categories: those that can only be run for a single operating unit and those that can be run for and across multiple operating units.

Single-Org

A new field has been added to the Submit Request form to facilitate submitting requests for a single operating unit. When a concurrent program is identified as a single-org program, then the operating unit is a required field as shown in Figure 18. Single-org programs can only be run for one specified operating unit at a time.

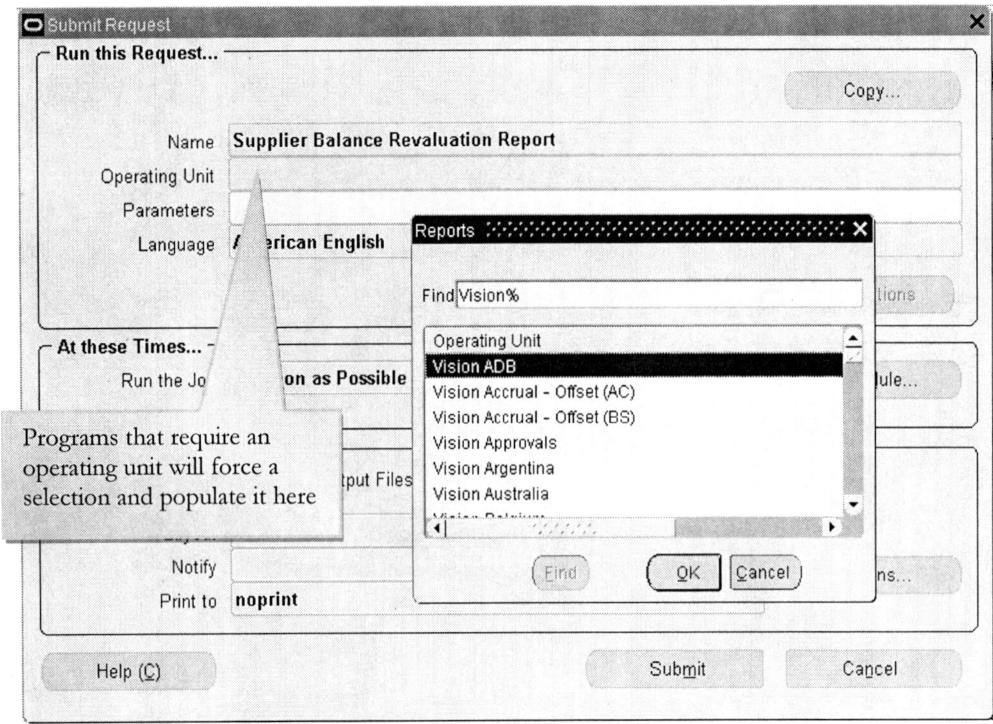

Figure 18 – With MOAC enabled, programs that require an operating unit will force a selection

Multi-Org

Over 400 concurrent programs have been re-designed to leverage Multi-Org Access Control. For some concurrent programs, this increases processing efficiency and for others it actually gives users a global view of data across operating units. For example, the Invoice Validation concurrent program has been designated as a multi-org concurrent program. When users submit the program for execution, they can specify one single operating unit or they can leave the operating unit parameter field blank and the program will validate invoices for all the operating units for which the user has access. This speeds the validation process because the user is not required to submit separate concurrent requests for each operating unit. Notice in Figure 19 that the operating unit is not required.

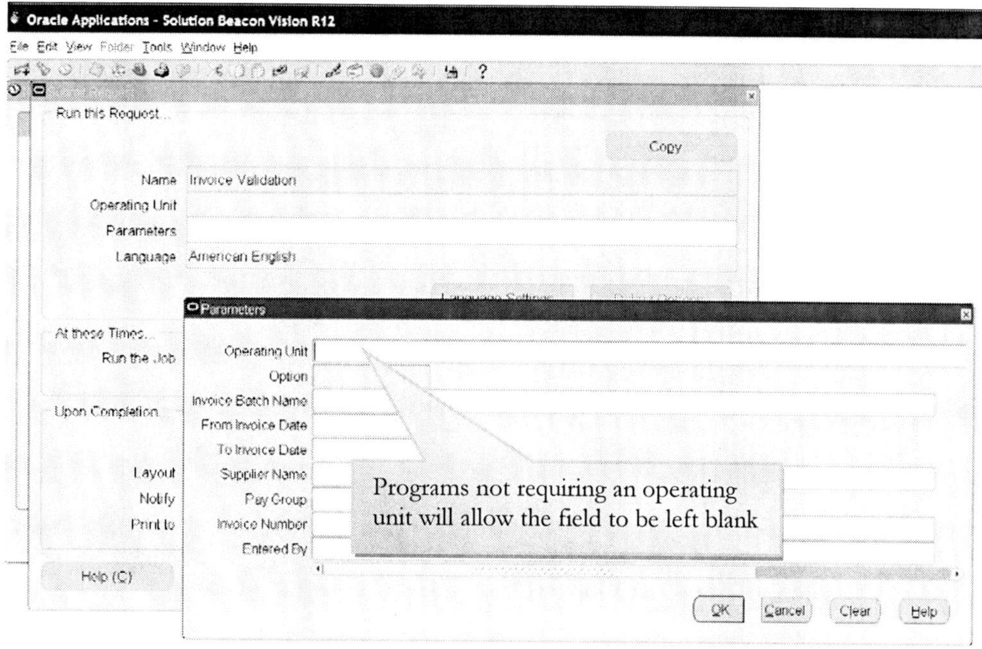

Figure 19 – If a program doesn't require an operating unit, you can leave the field blank

Table Changes to Support Multi-Org Concurrent Programs

In order to support processing concurrent requests for multiple organizations (operating units), a change was made to the `FND_CONCURRENT_PROGRAMS` table. A new column, `MULTI_ORG_CATEGORY`, was added that can have a value of Null, "S" (for Single-Org processes), or "M" (for Multi-Org processes). During an upgrade, the values for this column are populated based on Oracle designations for each concurrent program. If the concurrent program definition has been customized, this column will not be auto-populated and the value in this column will be Null. If this column is Null, a concurrent process will not execute. The following update script will populate the column with the correct value:

```
UPDATE FND_CONCURRENT_PROGRAMS
SET MULTI_ORG_CATEGORY = {'S' or 'M'}
WHERE CONCURRENT_PROGRAM_NAME = '{Program Name}'
```

Solution Beacon Recommends: Always test prior to and after a direct update is made. The update script above is only a sample of what must be done. Alternatives may be created to update all programs that need to be updated.

User Preferences Form

Users can now update their own Multi-Org Access Control user preferences without assistance from an Applications System Administrator. The function "FNDMOPREFS" can be added to any user menu to enable users to access the Multi-Org Preferences form in Figure 20.

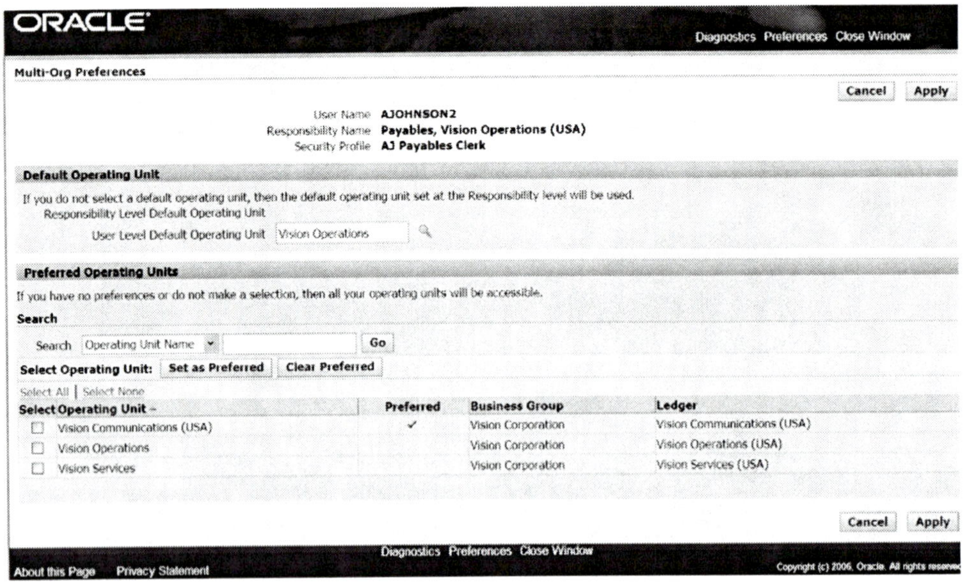

Figure 20 – The Multi-Org Preferences form

First, users can set their default operating unit to be any of the operating units accessible through the security profile assigned to them by the System Administrator. Secondly, users can designate preferred operating units. This functionality is beneficial when the user has been given access to many operating units by the System Administrator, but only needs to access a more limited number for a period of time. The user can select one or more operating units by checking the box next to the operating unit and clicking on the "Set as Preferred" button. The "Preferred" column will then be updated with a check mark. When accessing forms, only those operating units set as preferred will be displayed in the list of values. By limiting the list of values, the user can more quickly complete their processing tasks.

Impact on Custom Code and Supporting Applications

As with any upgrade, attention must be paid to custom code or supporting applications that use the Multi-Org Architecture. In Release 11*i*, the organization context was set with the "CLIENT_INFO(Org Context)" function. Release 12, however, leverages the Virtual Private Database (VPD) feature, making the "CLIENT_INFO" call obsolete. All custom forms and reports need to be initialized to secure access through the security profile.

The following custom code updates are required in order to access the desired organization (i.e., operating unit)

Release 11*i* script to access data by org_id

```
begin
dbms_application_info.set_client_info('&org_id');
end;
/
select * from po_headers
/
```

Release 12 updated script to request access through the Security Policy in the database

```
begin
 mo_global.set_policy_context('S', &org_id);
end;
/
select * from po_headers
/
```

MetaLink Doc. ID: 420787.1, "Oracle Applications Multiple Organizations Access Control for Custom Code" includes more detailed instructions on updating custom code to use MOAC.

Solution Beacon Recommends: *Always review supporting applications to be sure they are certified with the latest release. Check if testing was done on applications in which MOAC was implemented for only some users. This approach should help ensure you do not run into any surprises if you intend to enable MOAC features to limited users.*

CENTRALIZED PROCESSING

In Release 12, Oracle has either enhanced or completely redesigned several key areas of centralized processing. These include the expanded use of the Legal Entity, the new Payments system, the new E-Business Tax Engine, the Advanced Global Intercompany System (AGIS), and last, but certainly not least, the new Subledger Accounting Engine. Subledgers can leverage each of these systems to provide for more consistent and efficient processing, greater transparency and auditability, and greater flexibility and user-definability to meet each customer's unique business needs. The sections below will provide an overview of each of these new centralized features.

Legal Entity (Schema XLE)

The Legal Entity organization classification was available in Release 11*i*, but it was little more than a placeholder compared to the functionality that now exists with Release 12. A legal entity represents the legal corporate structure (or companies) of an enterprise and is vital to leverage the full functionality of some of the new Release 12 modules. The Legal Entity designation is used by accounting functions in the Subledger Accounting Engine, the E-Business Tax Engine, the Advanced Global Intercompany System, and is now the owner of the bank accounts.

The Legal Entity definition consists of the name, identification, address, establishments, registrations, contacts and intercompany parties. Legal Entities are designated as Parties in the Trading Community Architecture. The Legal Entity can be set up in two locations through the Accounting Setup Manager in the General Ledger Responsibility, or through the Legal Entity Configurator, which is a separate responsibility (Figures 21 and 22). The new user interface is the same in both the Accounting Setup Manager and the Legal Entity Configurator, except for one difference. The balancing segments for the Legal Entity can only be assigned in the Accounting Setup Manager, but not in the Legal Entity Configurator. This supports the standardization of the setups because the balancing segment is an accounting consideration and therefore resides under the ownership of the Accounting Setup Manager.

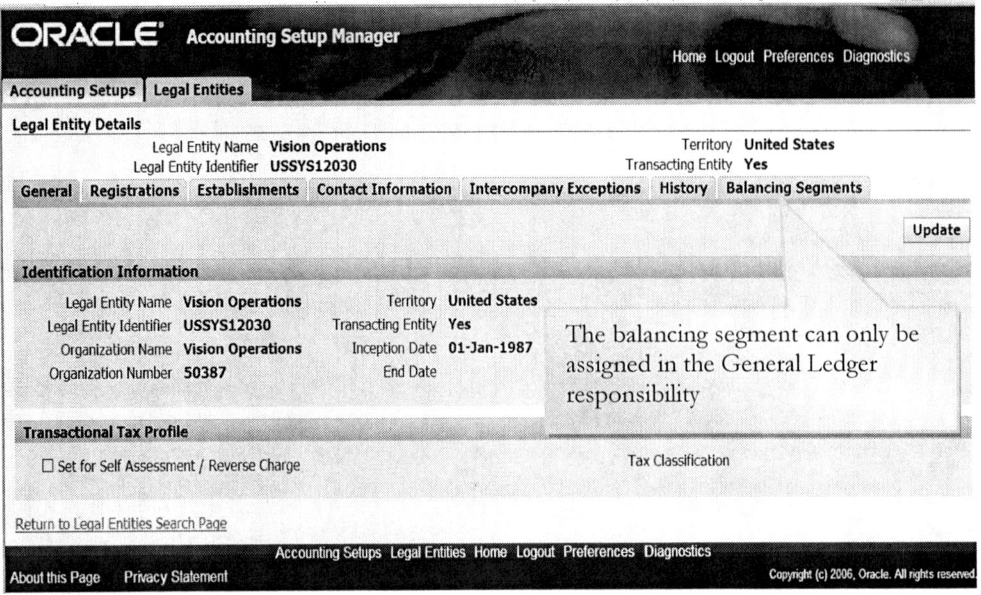

Figure 21 – The legal entity can be set up in the Accounting Setup Manager in the General Ledger responsibility.

ORACLE Legal Entity Configurator

Home Logout Preferences Diagnostics

Home | Legal Entities | Setup

Legal Entity Details

Legal Entity Name **Vision Operations**
Legal Entity Identifier **USSYS12030**
Territory **United States**
Transacting Entity **Yes**

General | Registrations | **Establishments** | Contact Information | Intercompany Exceptions | History

Create Establishment | Change Main Establishment — Previous 1-10 Next 10

Name	Registration Number	Registered Address	Territory	Main Establishment	Active	Registered Activity	View Details
Vision Operations	SYS12204	475 Park Avenue, New York, US, United States, US	United States		Yes		
W4 - Belmont Distribution	SYS12348	2347 Old County Road, Belmont, US, United States, US	United States		Yes		
Project Operations	SYS12290	90 Fifth Avenue, New York, US, United States, US	United States		Yes		
Future Use Organization 4	SYS12288	1000 East Blvd, Atlanta, US, United States, US	United States		Yes		
Defective Warehouse	SYS12300	393 Berkeley Street, Boston, US, United States, US	United States		Yes		
Field Service Technicians	SYS12299	5476 216 Ave, Seattle, US, United States, US	United States		Yes		
Discount SuperStore-Atlanta	SYS12296	395 Peachtree Road, Stone Mountain, US, United States, US	United States		Yes		
Vision Eastpoint Discount Store	SYS12294	626 Plum Street, Central Valley, US, United States, US	United States		Yes		
W3 - Houston	SYS12277	15011 Mississippi Street, Houston, US, United States, US	United States		Yes		
W3 - Houston	SYS12278	15011 Mississippi Street, Houston, US, United States, US	United States		Yes		

Create Establishment | Change Main Establishment — Previous 1-10 Next 10

Return to Legal Entities Search Page

Figure 22 – The legal entity can also be set up and maintained from the Legal Entity Configurator responsibility. Notice, however, the Balancing Segment cannot be assigned through this responsibility.

Setup Tips

When the general required information is saved for the legal entity, the main establishment and registration are created and the information is defaulted from the required information. This feature saves the user time in set up, reduces entry errors and data discrepancies.

The Profile Option "XLE: Generate Legal Entity Identifier" controls whether the Legal Entity Identifier is set by the system or the user. If this profile value has been set to "Yes" then the Legal Entity Identifier is automatically set by the system and the field does appear on the data entry form. The system-generated value is comprised of the International Organization for Standardization (ISO) code of the country (e.g., US for United States Legal Entities) plus the registration number of the identifying jurisdiction (e.g., the EIN/TIN number for United States Legal Entities). A "No" value is the default and requires this value be entered manually by the user.

When creating the Legal Address, an existing address can be used to reduce errors. If a new address is created, the address fields are not validated, so care should be exercised in entry. The values can be updated after the Legal Entity has been saved.

Payments (Schema IBY)

The new Oracle Payments system combines Funds Disbursement and Funds Capture into one centralized payment engine. Enterprises can generate payments across multiple organizations, currencies and regions, increasing straight through processing rates. Because processing centralization can provide real-time visibility to cash inflows and outflows, companies can achieve better capital management. From an auditability standpoint, improved control and a full audit trail are available to a single point of payment processing. Oracle Payments also manages the interfaces between E-Business Suite products and financial institutions such as banks and credit card processors. With several seeded transmission protocol/formats to choose from, implementation of an interface solution can be quicker and the total cost of ownership can be lowered.

One Payment Processing Solution

By centralizing the payment processing into one payment engine, multiple applications can leverage the same functionality (e.g., credit card payments, direct debits). Previously, in Release 11*i*, the same functionality would be an element of several different products (see Figure 23).

Receivables	Bills Receivable Remittance	Direct Debits			
***i*Payment**	Bills Receivable Remittance	Direct Debits			Credit Card Payments
Global Financials	Bills Receivable Remittance	Direct Debits	Check Printing	EFT Payments	
Payables			Check Printing	EFT Payments	

Figure 23 – Release 11*i* Payment functionalities and the applications that leverage them

This created redundancy between the systems and was an ineffective use of resources. Now, with Release 12, products leverage a single payment processing solution (see Figure 24).

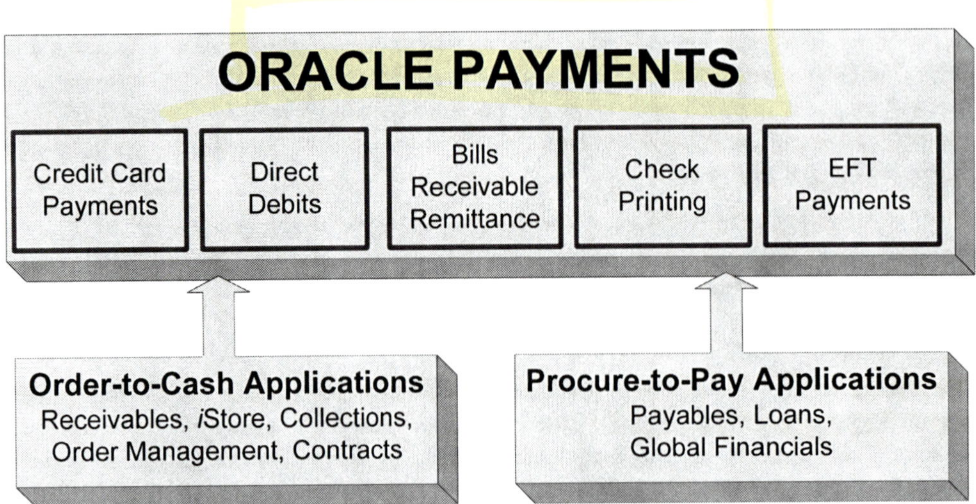

Figure 24 – With Release 12, products leverage a single payment processing solution

This centralization also extends to the creation and management of bank accounts. In Release 11*i*, bank account management is separate for each application. Cash Management, Payables, and Receivables access the Payables bank accounts, Payroll accesses the Payroll bank accounts, and Treasury accesses the Treasury bank accounts. The management of these accounts is separate, so the data is replicated even if the banking information among these three bank account systems is the same. Now, in Release 12, all of the bank accounts are associated with the Legal Entity and retained in the Trading Community Architecture (TCA). This poses significant time savings and control advantages for the data (see Figure 25).

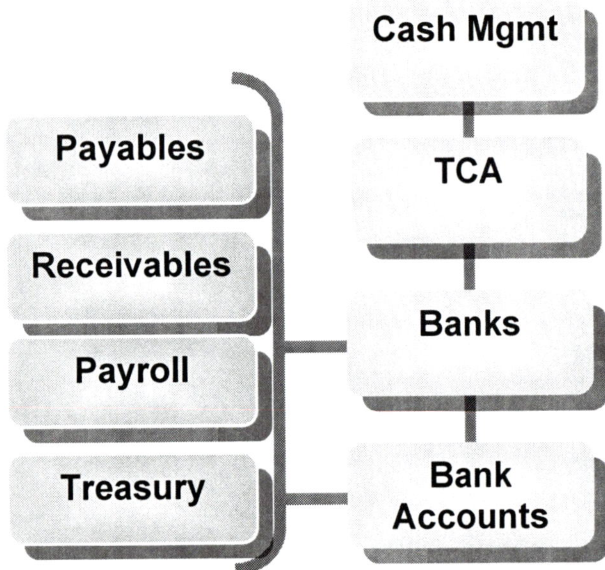

Figure 25 – In Release 12, all bank accounts are associated with the Legal Entity and are retained in the Trading Community Architecture.

Bank information is now maintained through one form (see Figure 26). The bank, bank branch, and bank account information is accessed via links where it can be created and maintained more efficiently. Users can also manage the payment documents from the bank account form.

ORACLE Cash Management

Close Window Preferences

Manage Bank Accounts

Bank Accounts

Simple Search

Advanced Search

Account Name | Alternate Account Name

Short Account Name | Account Number

Account Owner | Currency

Bank Name: bank of america | Branch Name

Go | Clear All

Select Account | Update Account | Manage Payment Documents | Create

Previous 1-10 Next 10

Select	Account Name	Alternate Account Name	Short Account Name	Account Number	Bank Name	Bank Number	Branch Name	Branch Number
○	US Main A/C-204			10271-17621-789	Bank of America	163281189	New York	7361982736
○	Primary Checking Account-202			1233349-484877	Bank of America		San Francisco	
○	BofA-EUR-204			999-665-00	Bank of America	163281189	New York	7361982736
○	BofA - Comms-1733			10271-78681-146	Bank of America	163281189	New York	7361982736
○	Do Not Use-204			922-112-00012	Bank of America	163281189	New York	7361982736
○	Cash Account-202			8222-29887	Bank of America	163281189	New York	7361982736
○	BofA-204			10271-17621-619	Bank of America	163281189	New York	7361982736
○	BofA-458			716247142-2647	Bank of America	163281189	New York	7361982736

Figure 26 – The Bank Maintenance form

Funds Disbursement

A business can choose to use funds disbursement in three different ways, depending on its business needs. This provides the user with the opportunity to leverage the most powerful payment solution while retaining the flexibility to select a solution that best fits the company's business processes. Following are the three payment processing solutions:

- **Decentralized Processing** – In this processing scenario, a user or team would perform all of the payment functions from selecting invoices to be paid, making payments, and resolving issues in the payment process. The Payables Payments Dashboard makes this a very efficient process for the user.

- **Centralized Processing** – In this processing scenario, one user or team owns the Payables functions such as invoice selection and payment process request submission and would use the Payables Payments Dashboard. Another user or team would be dedicated to payment processing. These users would likely use the Funds Disbursement Process Dashboard because users cannot select invoices or submit payment process requests from this dashboard and this would ensure segregation of duties.

- **Payment Factory Processing** – This is the most powerful and efficient payment solution. Payments are combined from multiple batches submitted by the Payables team to form a single payment. The Funds Disbursement Process (FDP) Dashboard would need to be used for the processing option. Figure 27 shows the Payment Factory model.

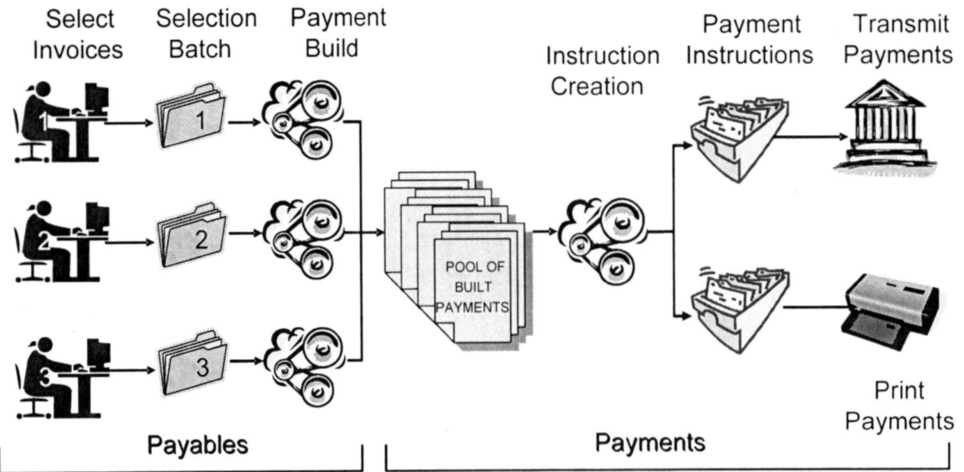

Figure 27 – The Payment Factory model generates payments from a pool of built payments for the most efficient payment processing.

Payables Payments Dashboard

Use the Payables Payments Dashboard (see Figure 28) to begin the payment process. Users begin by submitting payment process requests (i.e., Build Payment Batch in Release 11*i*). For regular payment process requests, users can save templates which default all of the criteria needed in order to build the payment. The dashboard home page gives users information regarding the day's processing including links to all payment process requests, shortcuts to standard processing functions and a list of process requests needing action.

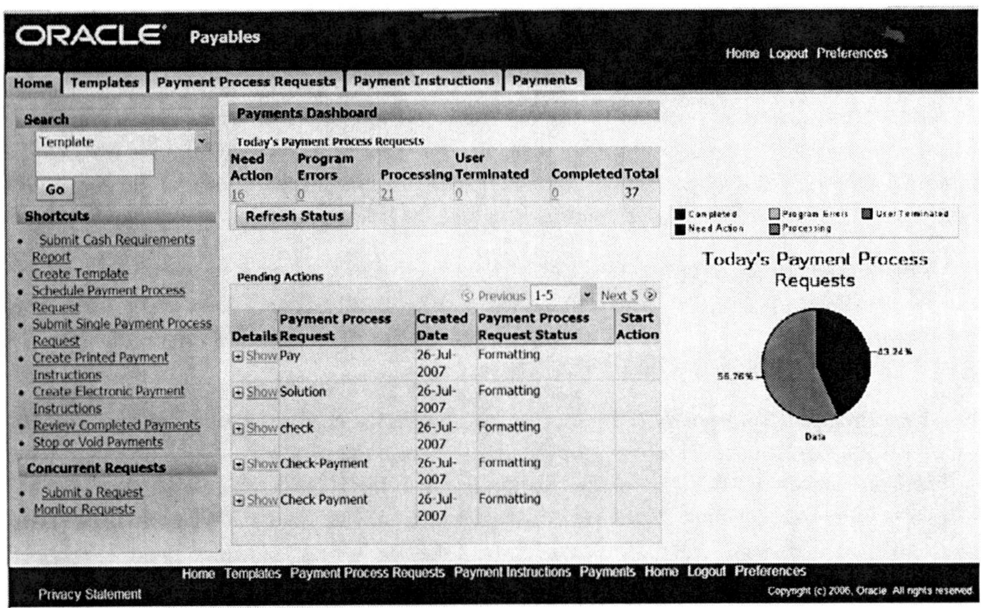

Figure 28 – Payables Payments Dashboard

Funds Disbursement Process (FDP) Dashboard

The Funds Disbursement Process (FDP) Dashboard (see Figure 29) manages the creation of payment instruction and generation of payments and reporting, such as payment instruction registers. Users can monitor the payment instruction process and take action when required including the confirmation of the payment. The form includes quick searches, links to standard processing functions, a list of payment instruction pending actions, and a list of payment process requests that have been completed with Quick Links to submit payment instruction registers and separate remittance advice. Users are able to drill down to payment details from the home page. Finally, graphical metrics are also included on the dashboard detailing the straight through processing rate and error count for the previous year.

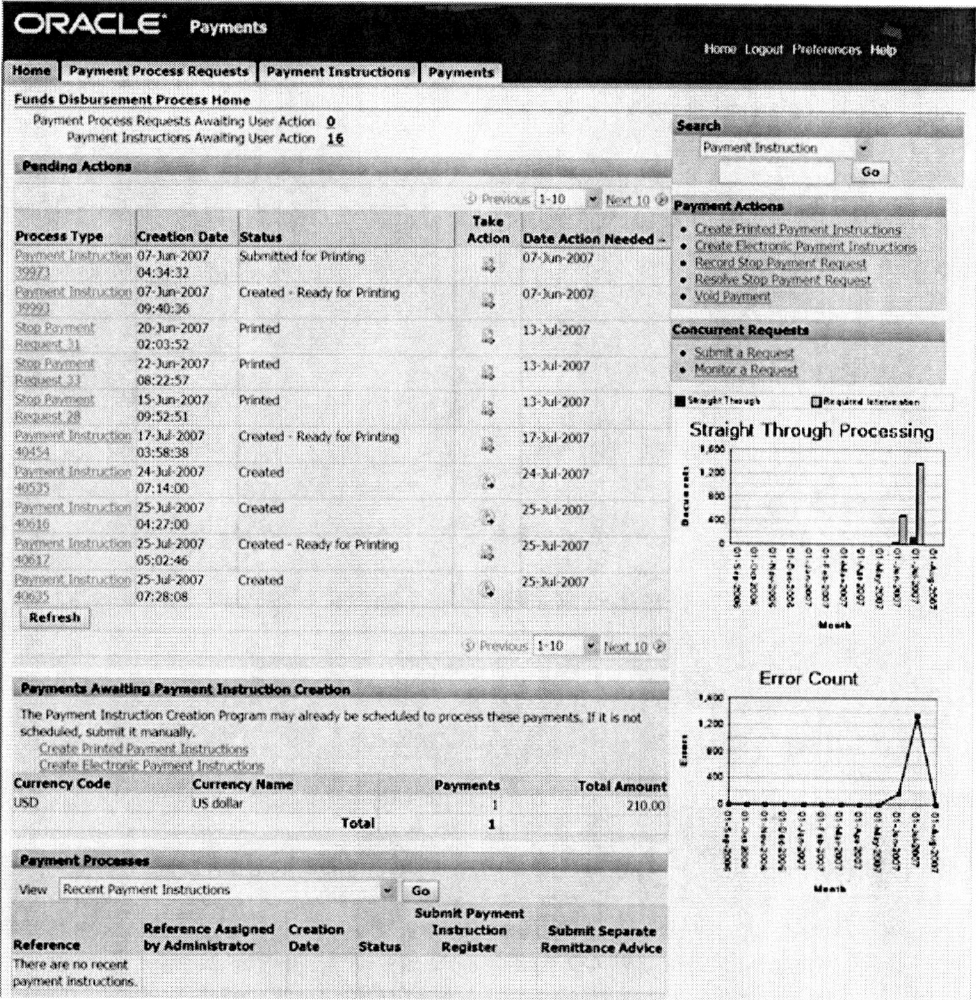

Figure 29 – Funds Disbursement Process Dashboard

Funds Capture

While Funds Disbursement is the payment of monies from the organization, the Funds Capture process represents bringing monies into the company. The end-to-end processing of the funds capture begins when an Oracle source product creates a transaction (which captures necessary payment information) and requests authorization from Oracle Payments. Payments then authorizes the transaction. Routing rules determine how the transaction will be processed and which third party payment system will be used. On the settlement side, Receivables sends a request for settlement and the payment engine manages that request and sends it to the payment system. The Payments application also queries the payment system for an acknowledgement that the transaction was processed successfully. On a side note, the new Payment module replaces the functionality of *i*Payment in Release 11*i*, therefore making it obsolete in Release 12. Figure 30 illustrates the funds capture flow.

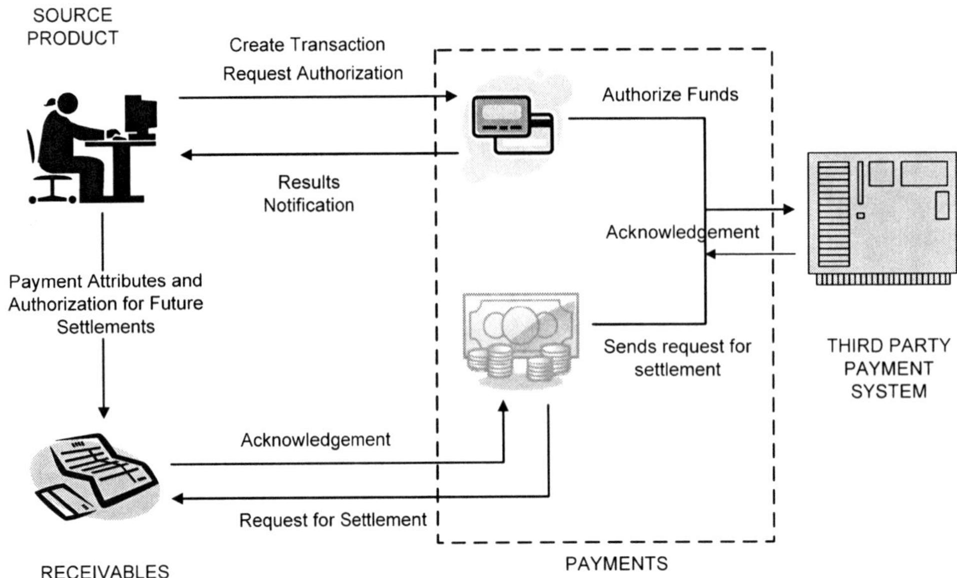

Figure 30 – Funds Capture Process Flow

Oracle Payments integrates with the following source products to facilitate funds capture:

Collections	Service
*i*Receivables	Service Contracts
*i*Store	Lease Management
Order Capture	Receivables
Order Management	Student System

Figure 31 identifies the third party payments systems that are supported out-of-the-box in Release 12, along with the payment instruments for each system. Several transmission protocols are also supported out-of-the-box to help to speed implementation, including FTP, Secure FTP, HTTP, HTTPs, and AS/2.

	Credit Card	Purchase Card Level 2	Purchase Card Level 3	PINless Debit Card	US ACH
Paymentech	●		●	●	●
Concord EFSnet	●		●	●	●
Wells Fargo	●	●			●
First Data (North Platform)	●	●			
CyberSource	●	●			
VeriSign	●	●			

Figure 31– Third Party Payment Systems and Payment Instruments supported out-of-the-box. Note: Purchase Cards are also known as Procurement Cards.

Purchase Card Level 2 transaction data consists of data such as tax amount and order number in addition to basic credit card data and Purchase Card Level 3 transaction data consists of specific purchase information such as item description, quantity, unit of measure and price, in addition to the information from Level 2. PINless Debit Cards facilitate electronic transfer of payment amounts from a customer's bank account to the payee's bank account.

Funds Capture Process (FCP) Dashboard

The Funds Capture Process (FCP) Dashboard (see Figure 32) is the one location that processors can go to manage the funds capture process. Included on the home page is quick search functionality, links to standard processing functions, a list of recent successful settlement batches, as well as recent failed operations. The Transaction Testing tab can be shown or hidden using menu functions. This tab enables users to perform transmission testing when a new protocol or third party system is coming on line.

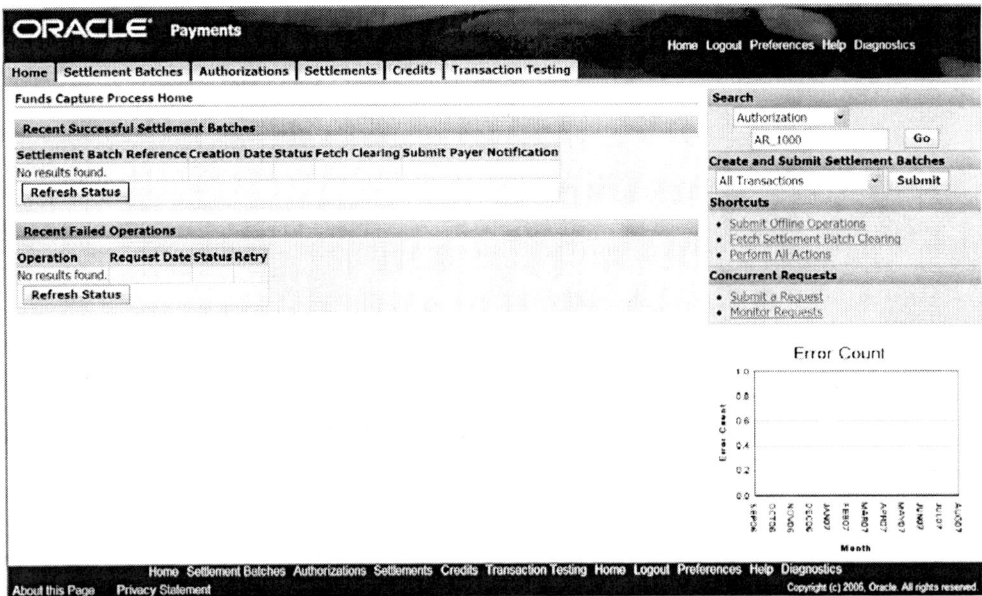

Figure 32 – Funds Capture Process Dashboard

Setup

Payment processing for both funds disbursement and funds capture can be set up through one form, the Payments Setup form. This setup form is shown in Figure 33.

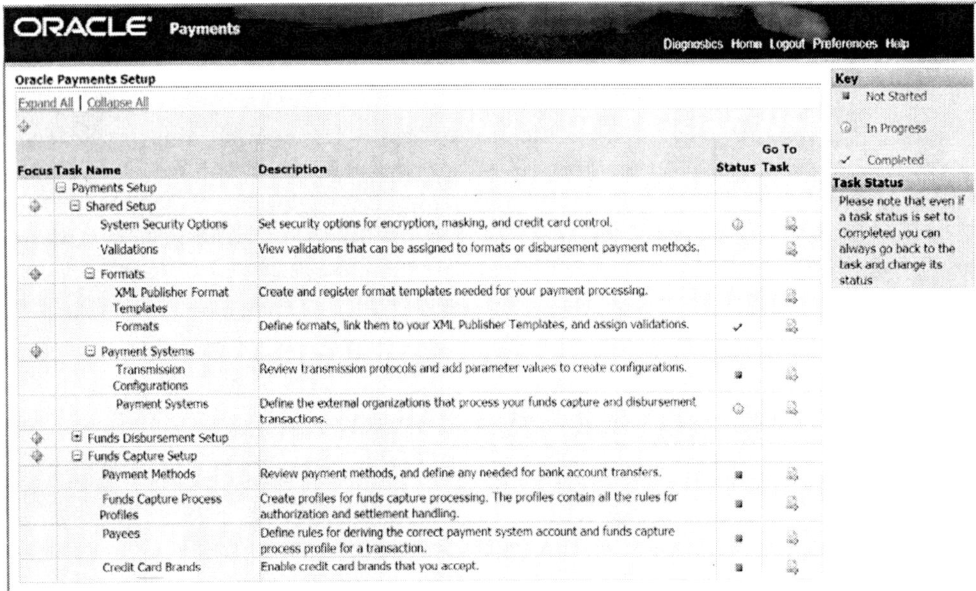

Figure 33 – Payments Setup Form

Shared Setup includes the ability to set up security options such as credit card control. Both pre-defined and user-defined validations can also be assigned in the shared setup. Since Payments relies heavily on XML Publisher, format templates can be created and maintained for payment processing. Transmission configurations and third party payment systems are also defined here.

Funds Disbursement Setup includes payment methods and codes. It can also create and maintain payment process profiles that contain the rules about how payments are created and disbursed. Finally, maintain disbursement system options include payment processing options such as how the system handles validation failures and payment overrides.

The Funds Capture Setup enables the user to create and maintain payment methods, create profiles for funds capture processing, define rules for deriving the correct payment system account and enable the accepted credit card brands.

Advanced Global Intercompany System (Schema FUN)

The Advanced Global Intercompany System (AGIS) enables users to create, settle and reconcile both intercompany and intracompany transactions. Intercompany transactions are transactions that occur between two related legal entities. Intracompany transactions occur between groups in the same legal entity. By the definition alone, you can see the role the Legal Entity plays in intercompany transactions. This system integrates with both the Receivables and Payables modules to provide a complete intercompany solution. A single user-friendly form makes it possible for the user to set up, process, and report on intercompany activity from one centralized location (see Figure 34).

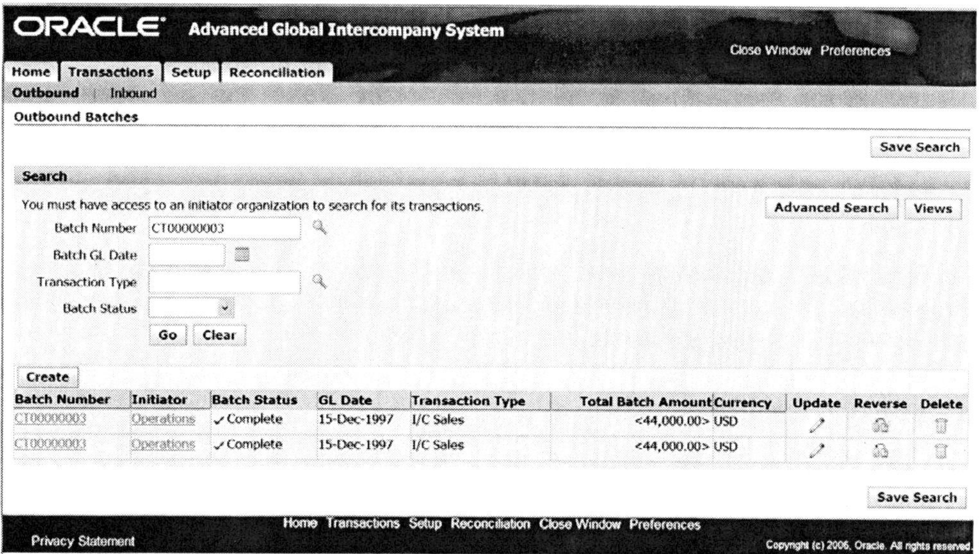

Figure 34 – The user can setup, process and report on intercompany activity from one centralized location

Home Tab

To speed processing, the Home tab displays the most recent transactions requiring user action, a summary of open notifications, and the five most recently received transactions. Users can also perform quick searches for transactions by inbound or outbound batch number, or navigate to the "Create Batch" page to create an intercompany transaction.

Transactions Tab

Users can process both outbound and inbound transactions from the Transactions tab.

Flexible Approval Rules

Once an intercompany receivable transaction is completed, the receivables invoice number is used and a mirror-image invoice is created in Payables.

AGIS supports importing transactions from an external source via the Intercompany Open Interface Tables and from Excel using Web ADI. It also supports the manual entry of transactions through the form. A single batch of transactions can be applied to multiple recipients and across different ledgers. Distribution amounts can be automatically prorated based on the recipient transaction amounts. When a recipient transaction is deleted or rejected, the distribution amounts can be adjusted by prorating them.

Setup Tab

The Setup tab gives the user one place to go to perform the setups necessary for the AGIS. Users can set up periods, accounting, organization, security, invoicing options, transaction types, and system options.

The period status functionality provides you with a central point to control the timing of intercompany transaction processing independent of General Ledger, Receivables and Payables through the "Intercompany Periods" page. In the Accounting tab, users can input both intercompany and intracompany balancing rules. To assist the user while setting up new rules, the order of precedence in which rules are evaluated is detailed on the entry form. This is just another example of the improved usability of forms in Release 12.

After accounting setup is complete, organizations must be defined and associated with the appropriate Legal Entity. If invoices are required, the organization must also be associated with an Operating Unit. Intercompany organizations are defined in the Trading Community Architecture (TCA) and ultimately represent the initiators and recipients in an intercompany transaction.

Through MOAC functionality, users can access multiple organizations through a single responsibility. However, for intercompany processing, users must still be assigned access to each organization through the Security tab (see Figure 35).

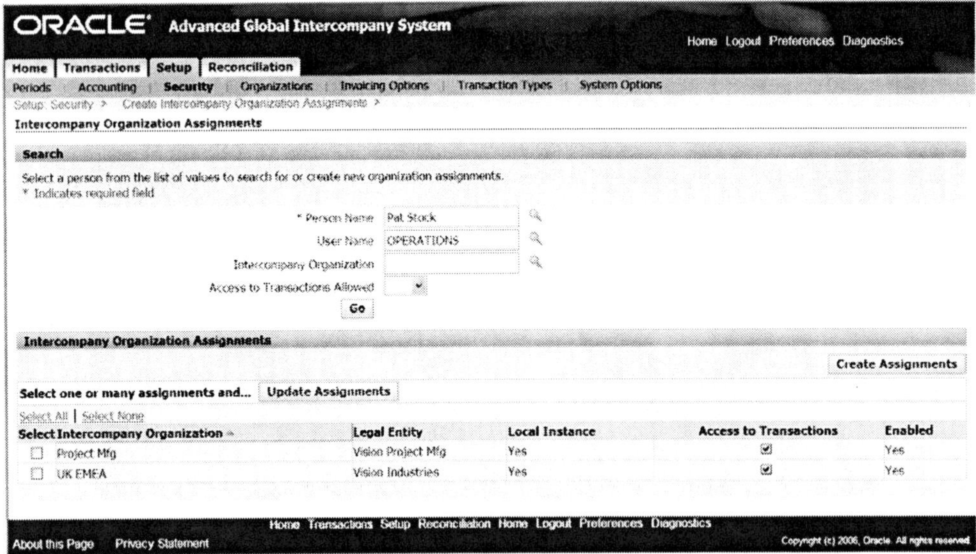

Figure 35 – The Security tab allows users to set up access to intercompany transactions by organization

Reconciliation Tab

The reconciliation process for intercompany transactions has been improved by using the XML Publisher tool. The Reconciliation tab enables the user to run the "Intercompany Reconciliation Data Extract Program" and then view the results from the Reconciliation tab using an HTML template. Links are available on this report to drill down to transaction details to speed the reconciliation process.

E-Business Tax System (Schema ZX)

The new E-Business Tax System provides users with a single point of management for tax with the E-Business Suite. The new self-service user interface extends control for products-based tax. It further provides country-specific tax content and simple to complex country-specific legislations. It supports cross-border transactions, as well as local compliance requirements. E-Business Tax users can easily modify tax content to keep up with constant tax changes by local jurisdictions, legislation, rates and exceptions. The tax configurations have also been simplified to ease manageability.

New Features

Several new features are now available and provide improvements in functionality for users.

- One addition is the "Tax Repository". All tax transactions are stored in this repository, providing a single source of transactional tax information (tax lines). This supports tax reporting, tax accounting and tax reconciliation processes. The repository further provides an underlying infrastructure for users to view and/or modify (override) tax lines.

- E-Business Tax also supports a "Self-Assessment/Reverse Charge". A self-assessed tax is a tax calculated and remitted for a transaction, where tax was not levied but is deemed as due. The purchaser is responsible for calculating and remitting tax. An example: a consumer/purchaser receives an invoice for $100, which is due to be paid to the supplier. Tax A (10%) was not charged on the invoice, however the purchaser is deemed responsible to pay Tax A. The purchaser would "self-assess" the $10 and remit it directly to the taxing authority for Tax A.

- The new "Tax Zone Type" is used to define, identify and group correlated tax zones. For example, an Iowa Sales Tax Zone Type will include the handful of Iowan cities that actually have a city level sales tax rate. It can be whatever pertinent rate levels exist at the particular authority.

- "Tax Formulas" can be used to provide special calculations not covered by the standard calculations available in the system. Users can now define formulas to calculate taxable basis, set up complex compounding rules and tax amounts. Release 11*i* users could define open PL/SQL formulas to accomplish this, but that functionality will no longer be supported in Release 12 because of the addition of Tax Formulas.

- "Tax Condition Sets" are used in tax rules and are a group of tax conditions, defined for a "Tax Determining Factor Set". Several "Tax Condition Sets" can be defined for the same "Tax Determining Factor Set". A Tax Determining Factor Set identifies certain factors to consider when evaluating a tax rule.

- Finally, the "Tax Simulator" provides a mechanism for users to simulate tax calculations based on "what-if" scenarios. It can be used to replicate standard transactions such as purchase orders, invoices, and invoices matched to purchase orders that are typically integrated with the tax lines interface. A parallel audit trail is generated to review which Tax Rules have been satisfied. This tool is a quick way users can enter transactions to perform "what-if" scenarios on tax calculations, but not perform normal validation in the application forms.

Setup

Figure 36 represents the E-Business Tax setup form. The Setup Tasks are found in this one location and are quite easy to navigate. The user has a global view and control of all tax related setups. Notice there is a column that specifies to the user whether the particular setup step is required or optional. Quick Links to the detailed setup task are also available with a click of the button. All of this functionality speeds up implementation and eases maintenance tasks for the user.

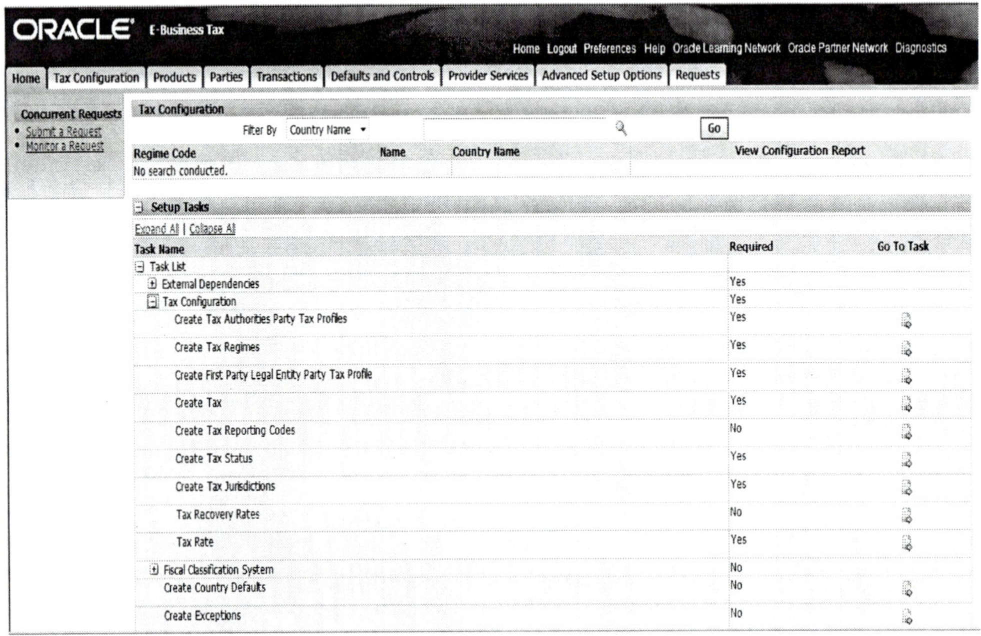

Figure 36 – These are the individual configuration steps of the E-Business Tax System

Service Oriented Architecture

The Service Oriented Architecture of the E-Business Tax System is detailed in Figure 37. A detailed description of each of the areas appears after the diagram.

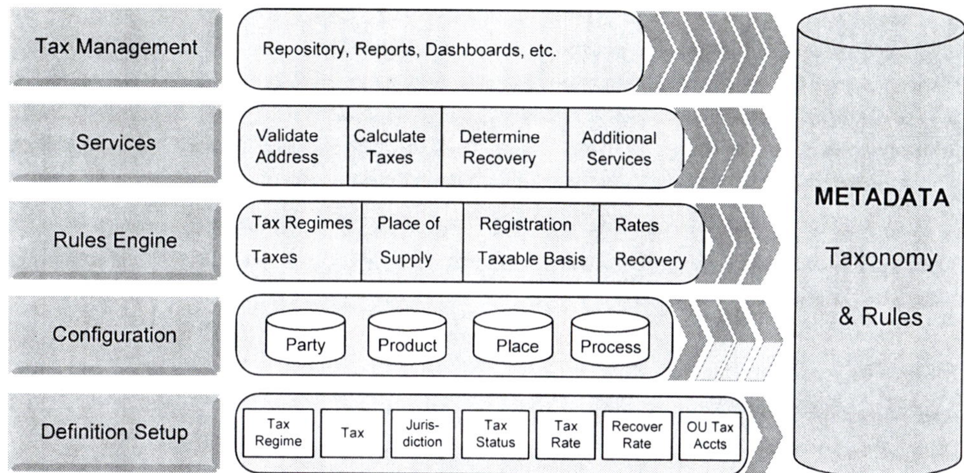

Figure 37 - E-Business Tax Service Oriented Architecture

First, definitions are set up including the tax regimes, tax, jurisdiction, tax status, tax rates, recovery rate, and operating unit tax accounts. Next, users define configurations including tax profiles and dates for a basis of tax determination. The 4Ps (Party, Product, Place, and Process) are the determining factors or "key building blocks" of tax rules. Users can also define geographies on the types of transaction for goods and services sales transactions.

The Rules Engine is based on a set of tax rules based on factors that can be applied to calculating tax on a transaction, especially when default values do not work for a particular tax regime. To use the Rules Engine, you must first determine the Tax Regime and Candidate Tax. Once you have that information, you can determine where the supplier is located for each candidate tax. If E-Business Tax cannot find the tax for jurisdiction of that location type, no tax is applied and the tax is removed from the tax transaction.

Services are module integrations using key business flows. There are two types:

- **P2P** - Purchasing, Oracle Internet Procurement, Consignment Inventory, Oracle Internet Expense, Oracle Payables
- **OTC** - Oracle Order Capture, iStore, Quoting, Oracle Order Management, Oracle Trade Management

Currently, services are not provided for Payables withholding tax, Latin American Receivables transactions, and India transaction taxes. Tax Management contains the Tax Repository, reports, and dashboards. This is an area that will heavily use XML Publisher.

Third Party Integrations

The E-Business Tax System supports integration with third party tax software systems. Support structures for both Vertex and Taxware are pre-bundled with Release 12. Separate licensing is required to use this functionality, which supports only US State and Local taxes within the Order-to-Cash cycle. The systems are certified prepackaged in Release 12. If an existing server-side version exists, then auto upgrade is available, and certification, if necessary, is performed on the more recent versions.

The Third Party integration then follows a specific path, which includes installing scripts, modifying Profile Options, creating lookup codes (tax exemption reasons), creating provider-specific tax regimes and taxes, installing the client-side tax software whether it is Vertex or Taxware, and loading sales tax rates. Then users set up tax accounts (liability), enable address validation (make sure to do so before creating new addresses), add jurisdiction codes, then finally validate/test the provider implementation via test cases.

The business processes provided by the third party vendors are service provider codes definitions (Vertex=Geocodes, Taxware=Jurisdiction Codes), the handling of exemptions, reconciliations and procedures.

Process Flow

Figure 38 outlines the flow through the E-Business Tax System.

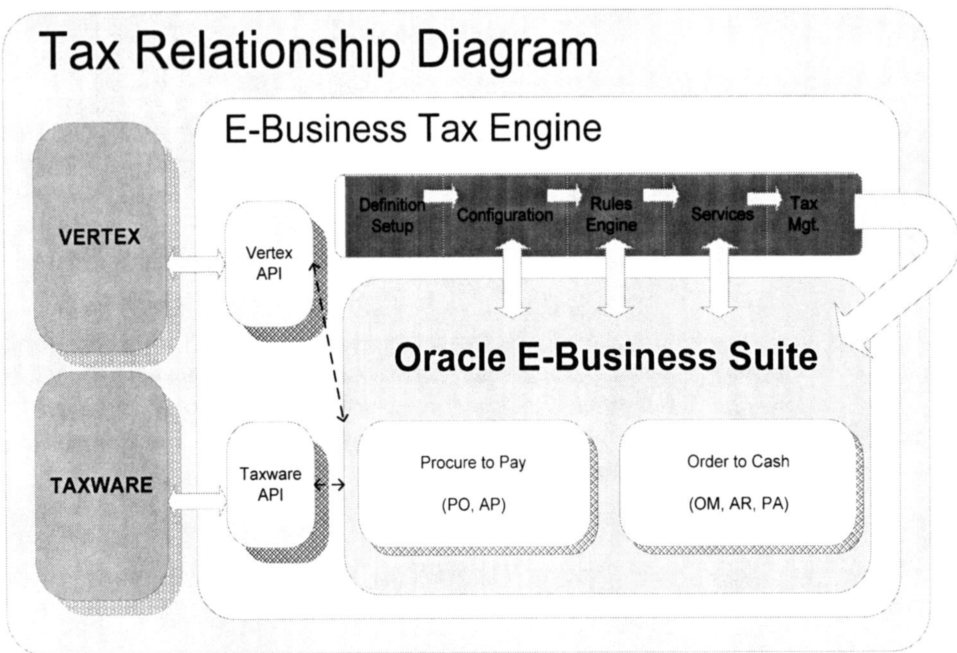

Figure 38 – The E-Business Tax relationship with Oracle Applications and Third Party Tax Software

Benefits

Some of the benefits derived from the E-Business Tax System are:

- Greater efficiencies through automated processes
- Improved consistencies using global tax rules, allowing the business to conform to governmental requirements both foreign and domestic
- Allows better control of the decision-making process through increased global visibility of the enterprise
- Ease of configuration and usage

- Ability to test/pre-determine taxable scenarios

Subledger Accounting Engine (Schema XLA)

The new Subledger Accounting Engine represents a major shift in architecture for the accounting component of the Financials product family. In prior releases, the accounting events were stored within individual subledgers. Now a new schema (XLA) exists and the accounting events for each subledger are retained within one data model. Figure 39 outlines the new accounting flow.

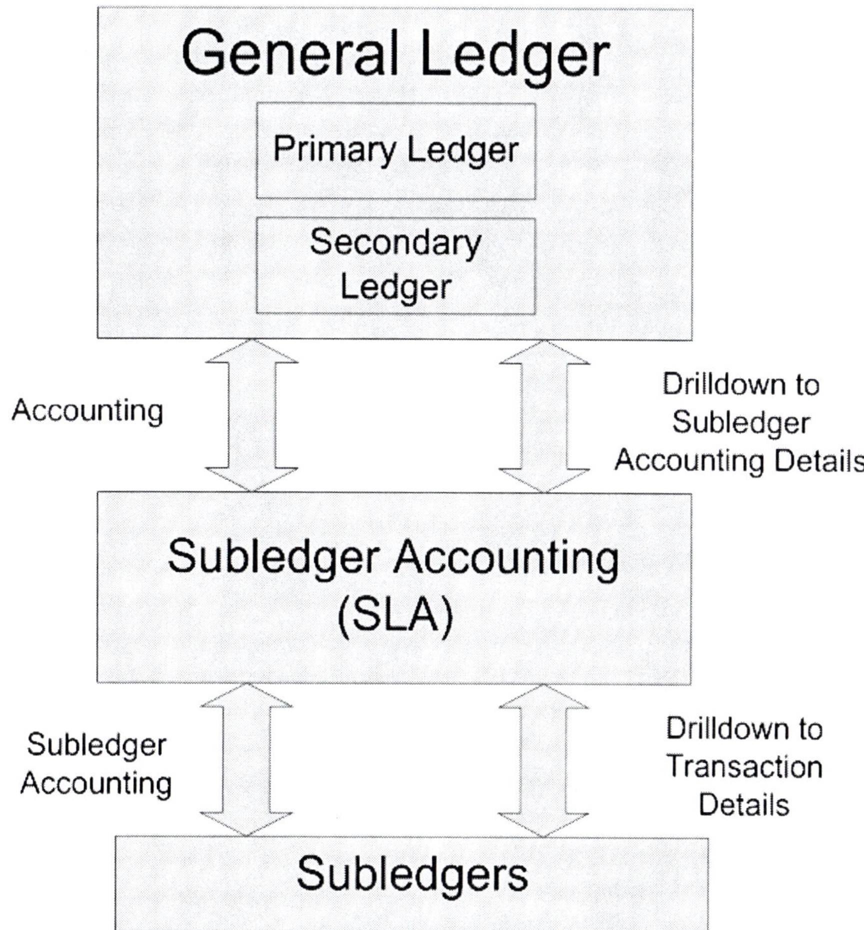

Figure 39 – The accounting events for each subledger are stored within one data model.

The following subledgers use the Subledger Accounting Engine when accounting entries are generated:

Purchasing	Assets	Receivables
Payables	Cash Management	Intercompany
Cost Management	Process Manufacturing	Projects
Payroll	Loans	Lease Management
Property Manager	Public Sector/Federal	Globalizations

Figure 40 – These subledgers use the Subledger Accounting Engine when accounting entries are generated

This new rules-based accounting model provides several benefits, including the standardization and consolidation of the accounting. Previously, the "Create Accounting" process was not standardized throughout the subledgers. Now, in Release 12, because the accounting is generated in a central location, there is consistency across the subledgers. This will help make the transfer to GL and month-end close processes simpler.

Of course, SLA supports shared service centers by leveraging the Multi-Org Access Control. It supports multiple operating units assigned to one ledger and is able to manage the associated accounting.

Because the accounting entries are all stored in one centralized repository, companies will realize improved control and transparency of their accounting. A definite shift has occurred in that the processing of the transactions is separated from the accounting associated with transactions. Also, because of this centralization, balancing can now occur at the subledger level. Finally, the bottom line is that this centralization streamlines reconciliation and results in a faster close.

Accounting Methods Builder (AMB)

Another benefit of the new Subledger Accounting application is the ability to create and maintain user-defined accounting rules through the Accounting Methods Builder. This provides the user with great flexibility while maintaining necessary control. Users can also more easily comply with multiple geographic, legislative, or industry requirements. By putting accounting rules in place, manual journal entries and customizations can be reduced. An added benefit is that because these user-defined accounting rules are created and maintained through the forms, all user-defined accounting rules will be retained in subsequent upgrades.

When defining a ledger (see Figure 41), notice that one of the fields is the Subledger Accounting Method (or convention – the 4th C). Release 12 comes seeded with five Subledger Accounting Methods: Accrual with Encumbrance Accounting, Cash with Encumbrance Accounting, Standard Accrual, Standard Cash, and US Federal Accounting. If any of these methods can meet your accounting needs, no user-defined rules are required and the user can just assign this default accounting method to the ledger. However, if special accounting rules are required, users can define them using the Accounting Methods Builder (AMB).

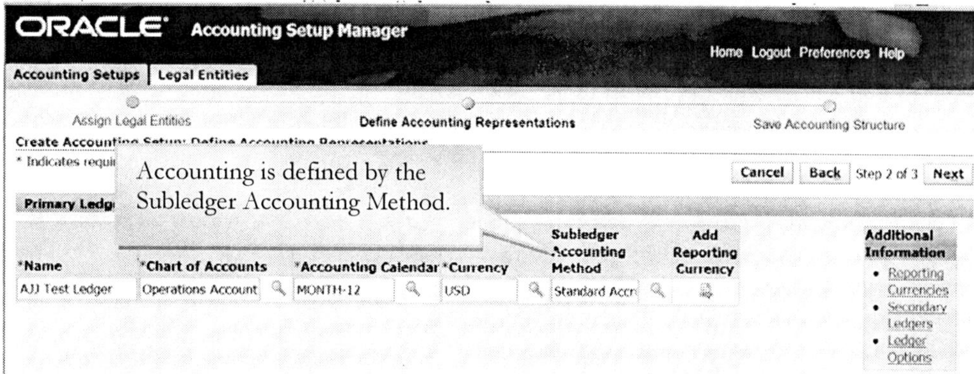

Figure 41 – Assigning a Subledger Accounting Method

The Subledger Journal Entry Inquiry Form (see Figure 42) illustrates areas that can be customized using the AMB to meet a company's business needs.

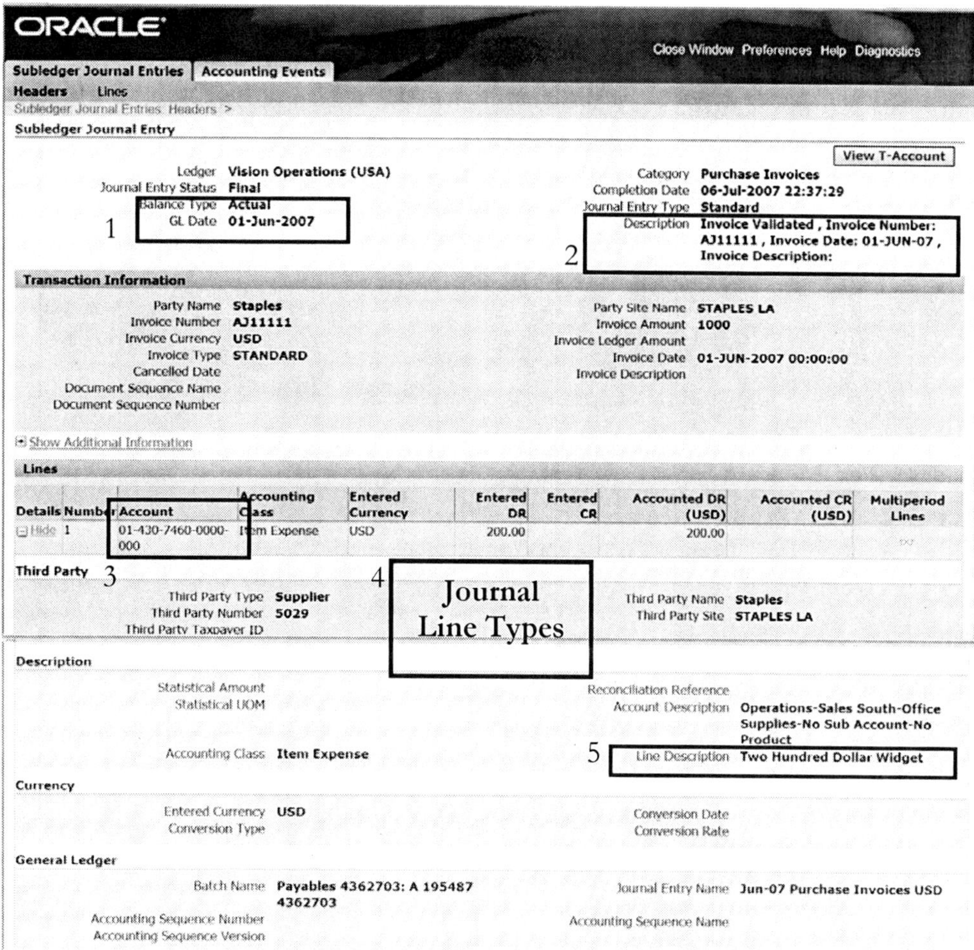

Figure 42 – Journal Entry components that can be customized with AMB

Users can create user-defined Journal Header Assignments (1) and Header Definitions (2). Account Derivation Rules can also be formulated that given a certain set of conditions derive a different account combination (3) than the account combination entered at the transaction level. Users can also define Journal Line Types (4) and the Journal Lines Description (5).

To customize an accounting method, users must create a user-defined Subledger Accounting Method. A Subledger Accounting Method is composed of multiple Application Accounting Definitions. For example, the Standard Accrual Subledger Accounting Method is made up of the following Application Accounting Definitions: Asset Standard Accounting, Cash Management Standard Accounting, Load Standard Accrual, Cost Management, Accrual Basis (which is the Payables definition), Process Standard Accounting, Projects Standard Accounting, Property Manager Normalized Accounting, and Receivables Default Accrual. Notice these represent the different subledgers that will create accounting entries in the General Ledger. Figure 43 represents the structure supporting each of these Application Accounting Definitions and the components that make up a complete accounting method. Note: these correspond to the sections identified in Figure 42.

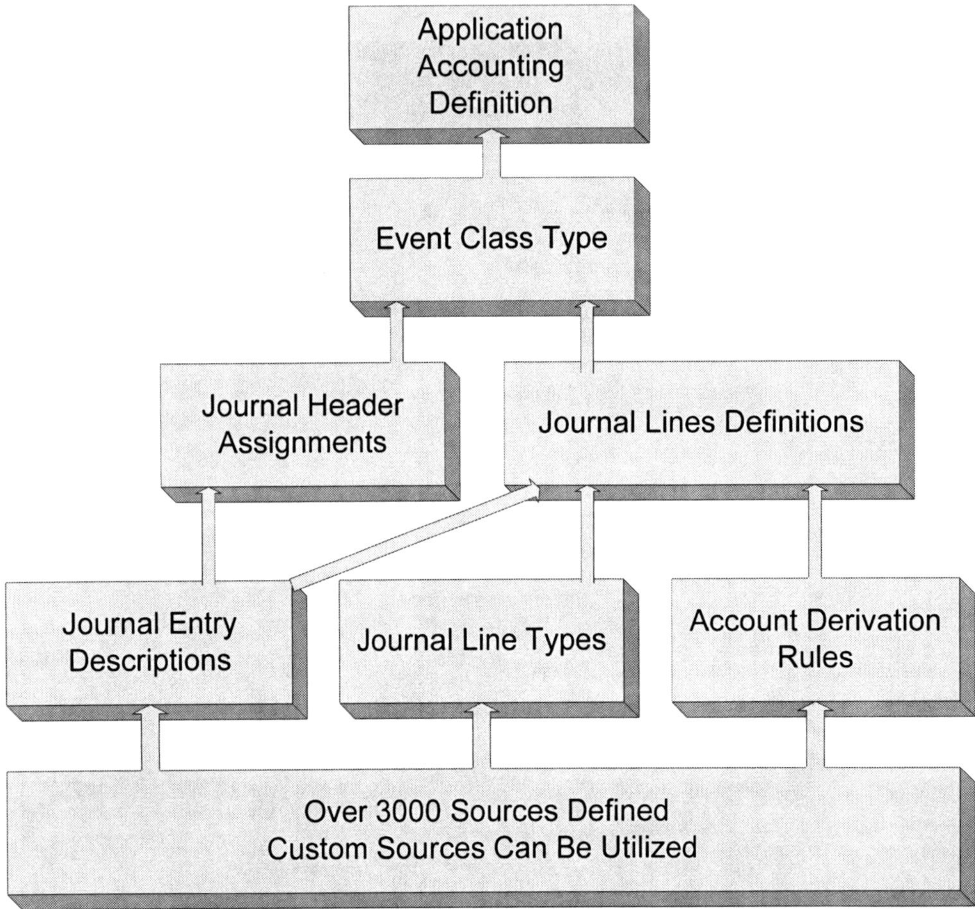

Figure 43 – The structure supporting each of the Application Accounting Definitions and the components that make up a complete accounting method

Each of these definitions except sources can be copied and modified from the Oracle seeded definitions to meet your accounting needs. Sources are the components of a transaction such as a supplier or distribution line. If a user needs a customized source then a developer must develop custom code but it can be plugged into the list of sources.

Creating Accounting

Fortunately, the introduction of the Subledger Accounting Engine and the ability to define accounting rules is, for the most part, transparent to the end user. The Create Accounting program still exists and functions in much the same way it did in earlier releases. Figure 44 shows the parameter list for the "Create Accounting" concurrent program, with the addition of the Ledger (which is the Set of Books) and the Mode (which enables Draft Accounting and straight through posting to the General Ledger). The Subledger Accounting Engine uses the Subledger Accounting Method that has been assigned to the Ledger to generate the accounting entries.

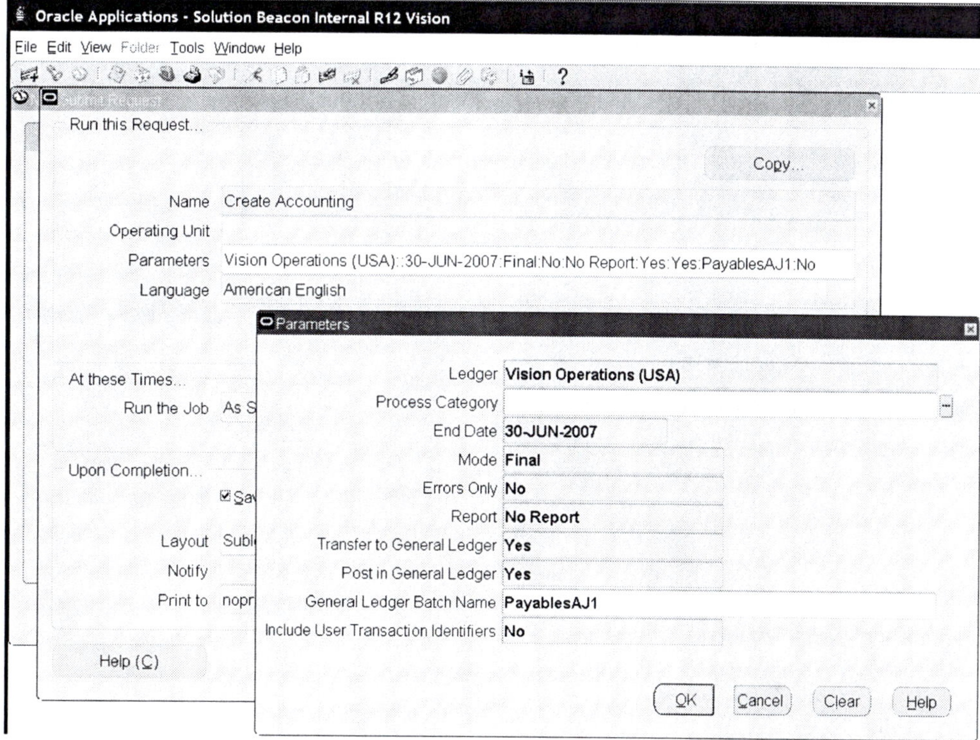

Figure 44 – The parameter list for the "Create Accounting" concurrent program.

On-line Inquiry Forms

While keeping the Create Accounting process very similar, new online Subledger Journal inquiry forms will make life easier for the end user when it is time to research and reconcile accounting entries. These forms – Accounting Events, Journal Entries, and Journal Entry Lines – are available to each individual subledger responsibilities in the Subledger Accounting submenu.

Accounting Events Form

The Accounting Events form enables the user to view accounting entries queried based on user-defined search criteria. Users can Save Searches for quick access, view related Transactions, and view related Journal Entries with one touch of a button. Note: Figure 45 has only the simple search fields. An advanced search gives users even more searching capabilities.

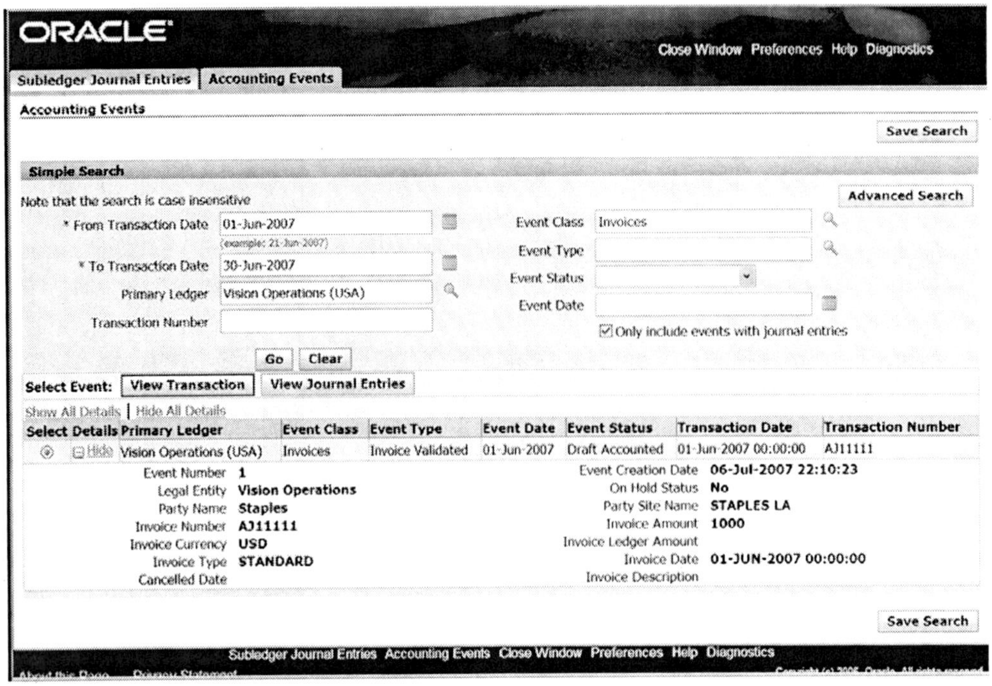

Figure 45 –View Accounting Entries based on search criteria

Subledger Journal Entries Form

The Subledger Journal Entries form enables users to view all journal entries that have been generated in the subledger accounting entries repository. Users are also able to create journal entries to transfer to the General Ledger. Notice that in Figure 46 not only the accounting information but also the transaction information is displayed on the same page. Users also can drill down to each individual line level detail. Users can also click on a button to view the T-accounts in the General Ledger. Searches can be saved for quicker access to data for searches that are performed regularly.

Figure 46 – Both the accounting and transaction information are displayed on the same page.

Subledger Journal Lines Form

Figure 47 shows the Subledger Journal Lines form. In addition to viewing information regarding the journal lines, users can also view related transaction information and the associated journal entry with the click of a button. Note that users can switch between querying header and line information by clicking on the links at the top of the form.

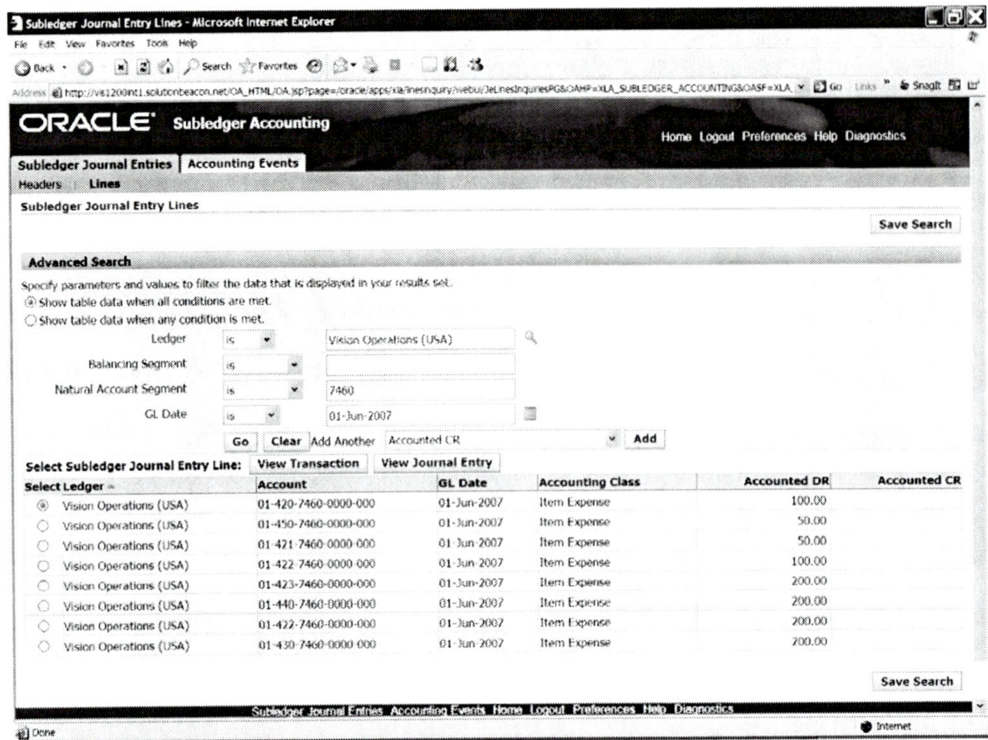

Figure 47 – The Subledger Journal Lines Form

As you can see, the addition of the Subledger Accounting Engine represents a major shift in how accounting is performed. No longer do businesses have to account by exception. Clear ownership of ledgers and configurable accounting rules support automated processing instead of manual journal entries. Customizations to handle specialized accounting can be greatly reduced. Reconciliation has been streamlined with visibility to transaction details, robust reporting and drill down capabilities, and integration with XML publisher. Finally, period close processing has been improved with online accounting and straight-through processing.

LEDGERS

The transactions have been entered, the accounting entries have been generated by the Subledger Accounting Engine, and now the journal entries are ready to be posted. Ledgers have replaced Sets of Books from Release 11*i*. Along with the change in terminology comes enhanced functionality. A single transaction can be booked to multiple ledgers using the subledger accounting engine and secondary ledgers, alternate reporting currencies can be assigned to primary ledgers to facilitate multiple reporting currencies, and ledger sets can be created with one or more ledgers for reduction of errors and faster processing, including period close.

Ledger Definition

Ledgers are defined by a Chart of Accounts, a Calendar, a Currency and a Subledger Accounting Method. The Chart of Accounts, Calendar, and Currency are required fields when defining a ledger. The Subledger Accounting Method is an optional field but is necessary to leverage the accounting rules established in the Subledger Accounting Methods Builder. Once the Chart of Accounts, Calendar, and Currency have been assigned to a Primary Ledger, these values *cannot* be updated. Ledgers are defined in the Accounting Setup Manager (see Figure 48).

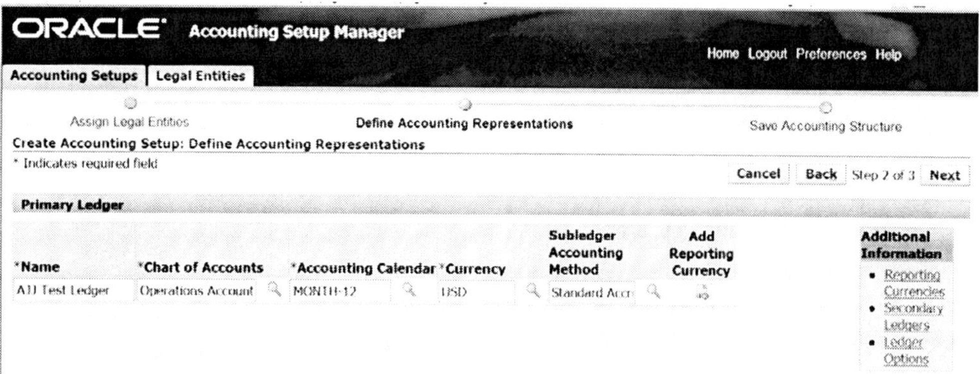

Figure 48 – Once the Chart of Accounts, Calendar and Currency are assigned to a Primary Ledger, the values cannot be updated.

Primary and Secondary Ledgers

The Primary Ledger is the main accounting representation of the financial system. A Secondary Ledger or Ledgers can be associated with a Primary Ledger and can serve several purposes. A Secondary Ledger can serve as an alternate accounting representation for geographic, legislative or industry requirements; or a consolidated accounting representation; or an adjustment ledger. The data in a secondary ledger can be stored at several different levels depending on the data conversion level selected by the user. The following data conversion levels are available:

- **Subledger Level** – data is converted for the subledger journal entries, general ledger journal entries and the balances. Both the Subledger Accounting and the General Ledger Posting concurrent programs perform these conversions. This would be the most detailed representation of the data.

- **Journal Level** – data is converted for the general ledger journal entries and the balances. These conversions are maintained using the General Ledger Posting concurrent program. Every time a journal is posted in the primary ledger, the same journal can be automatically replicated in the secondary ledger for those journal sources and categories that are set up for this behavior.

- **Balance Level** – data is converted for the balances only and requires the Oracle General Ledger Consolidation program to transfer primary ledger balances to the secondary ledger.

- **Adjustments Only Level** - stores only the adjustment data in the secondary ledger. Secondary Ledgers using this data conversion level must share the same accounting structure as the associated primary ledger. To obtain a complete secondary accounting representation that includes both the transactional data and the adjustments, ledger sets must be used.

Alternate reporting currencies can be assigned to the Primary Ledger. An alternate reporting currency can be used instead of a secondary ledger when the only part of the ledger that is different is the currency.

Ledger Sets

Multiple ledgers can be associated to form a ledger set as long as each of the ledgers in the ledger set have the same chart of accounts and the same calendar. A ledger can belong to multiple ledger sets (Figure 49). A ledger set can also be composed of ledger sets. The user has a great deal of flexibility in representing the enterprise operations with ledger sets. The following actions can be performed for ledger sets:

- Open/Close Periods
- Create Journals
- Translate Balances
- Reporting
- View Information

Because these functions can be performed simultaneously across multiple ledgers, reliability, consistency, and transparency are increased. A higher level of data security is also in place and the auditability of ledger data is improved.

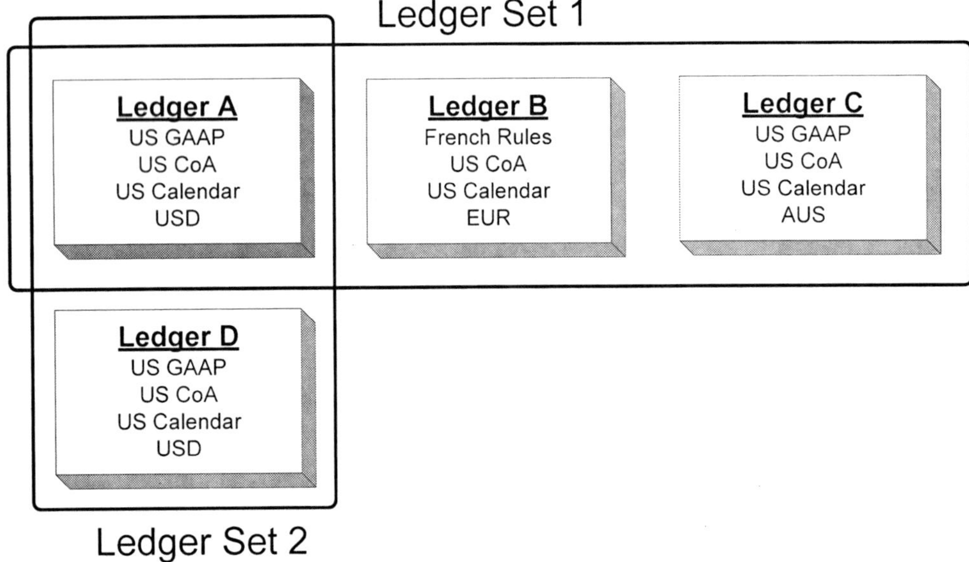

Figure 49 – Ledger Sets consist of Ledgers with the same Chart of Accounts and Calendar

HIGHLIGHTS BY SUBLEDGER

Many new features can be found throughout the individual subledgers in the Financials product family. The following features are not comprehensive but give a sense of the changes that can be found within Release 12.

General Ledger

Accounting Setup Manager

One of the enhancements to the Financials product family as a whole is the new Accounting Setup Manager tool, referenced earlier in this chapter. In one centralized location, accounting setups can be entered and maintained. In Release 11*i*, setups spanned multiple tabs and pop-up windows. Now the user can find all that functionality arranged in a user-friendly progression in the Accounting Setup Manager. This tool is found under the General Ledger Super User responsibility with the navigation path of Setup – Financials – Accounting Setup Manager – Accounting Setup and leverages many of the features of the new user interface. This tool is used to set up legal entity, primary ledgers, secondary ledgers, and accounting options. The setups are segmented into three components: setup of the accounting structure, defining the accounting options, and completing the accounting setup (see Figure 50).

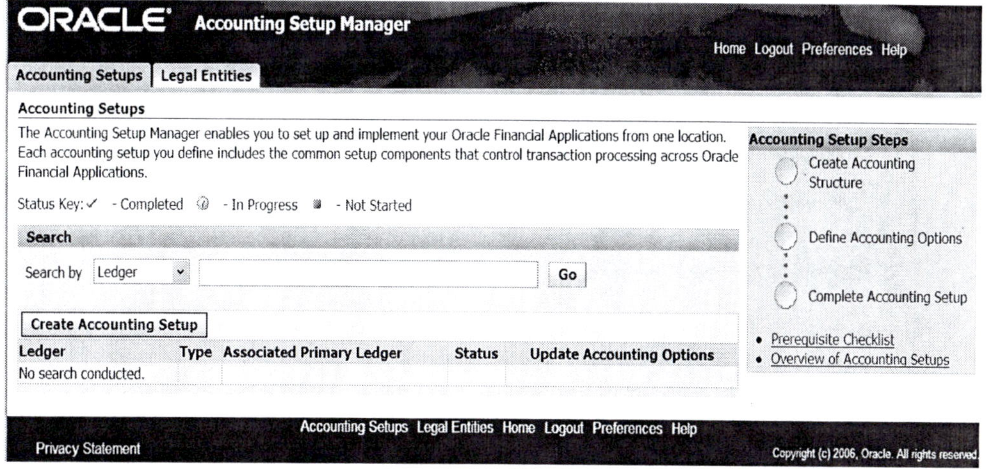

Figure 50 – Accounting Setup Manager Home Page

The Accounting Structure setup defines the Primary and Secondary Ledgers and entails the following steps:

1. Define Legal Entities
2. Assign Legal Entities to Primary Ledger – optional
3. Define Primary Ledger – required
4. Define Secondary Ledger(s) – optional

After the accounting structure has been successfully defined, the next step is to define the accounting options. Many of these are optional but must be marked as completed by the user to ensure that a decision was made to bypass the particular setup. The tool has some intelligence in that the setup steps that are shown are based in part on selections the user has made earlier in the setup process. This speeds setup time and reduces erroneous entries. The screenshot for the accounting options definitions page is shown in Figure 51. The following are accounting option definitions:

- **Ledger Options** – this is the first accounting option definition and must be completed before any additional definitions can be entered. Notice that the form enforces this flow by disabling the update icons for the other option setups. When this option has been completed, the "Ledger Options" wording will change to a link to the ledger associated with these ledger options.

- **Reporting Currencies** (optional) – multiple reporting currencies can be assigned to any ledger
- **Balancing Segments Value Assignments** (optional) – multiple balancing segment values can be assigned to a ledger. The legal entity takes precedence in this case and no balancing segments assigned to a legal entity can be assigned to the ledger.
- **Subledger Accounting Options** (required if subledger accounting method specified) – notice in Figure 51 that the status for the subledger accounting options is already marked as completed. This occurs because the subledger accounting options are inherited from the subledger accounting method associated with the ledger. The user has the opportunity to modify these default values but it is not required.
- **Operating Units** (optional) – Operating Units can also be assigned to the ledger. Remember that the operating unit is associated with the ledger, not with the legal entity. This setup form has a button that links to the HR organization form.
- **Inter/Intracompany Balancing Rules** (optional) – although not shown on Figure 51, this is one of the setups that appear on the form based on whether the user specified that they were using intercompany balancing in the ledger options setup.
- **Sequencing** (optional) – allows the user to define and maintain accounting and reporting sequencing options for both ledgers and reporting currencies.

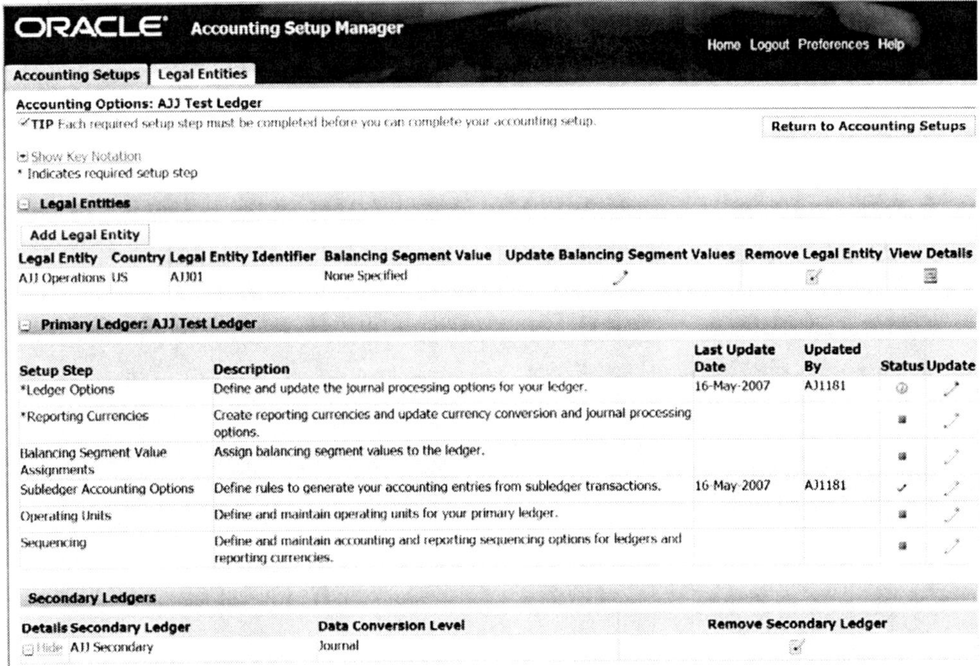

Figure 51 – Accounting Setup Manager Tool

Finally, the accounting setup needs to be completed by following the accounting option setups for all secondary ledgers and creating any necessary mapping from the Primary to the Secondary Ledgers.

Definition Access Set

Another new addition specific only to the General Ledger is the Definition Access Set, which can be used to secure access to definitions and set up components separate from the data. By assigning appropriate privileges, accounting departments retain more flexibility, reduce errors, and maintain greater control of their systems. Through Profile Options, responsibilities or users can be assigned one or more privileges. The privilege options that can be assigned are Use, Modify, and View access. The definitions in Figure 52 can be secured through Definition Access Sets.

Accounting Calendars	Consolidation Definitions	Rate Types
AutoAllocations	Consolidation Sets	Recurring Journals
AutoPost Criteria Sets	Elimination Sets	Revaluations
Budget Formulas	FSG reports and components	Transaction Calendars
Budget Organizations	Mass Allocations	
Chart of Account Mappings	Mass Budgets	

Figure 52 –Definitions that can be secured through Definition Access Sets.

As an example, an organization might assign one responsibility View, Use, and Modify access to Recurring Journals, while another responsibility is authorized only View access to the Recurring Journals.

Journal Copy

Users now have the ability to copy journals using the AutoCopy button on either the Journal form or the Journal Entry form. Users can copy journals with any status and assign a new batch name, period, and effective date for the copied journal. This functionality will improve both efficiency and data integrity.

Alternate Accounts

One potential holdup to period close is disabled account code combinations. Now, new functionality alleviates the need to intervene manually when a transaction has a disabled code combination. When users disable a code combination, they have the option to assign an alternate account to that combination so that any transactions booked to the disabled account will automatically use the alternate account.

Notice in Figure 53, the screenshot represents the form when it is first opened and looks the same as it did in Release 11*i*. To view the alternate accounts users need to use the horizontal scroll bar or tab through the form to the right-hand side (see Figure 54).

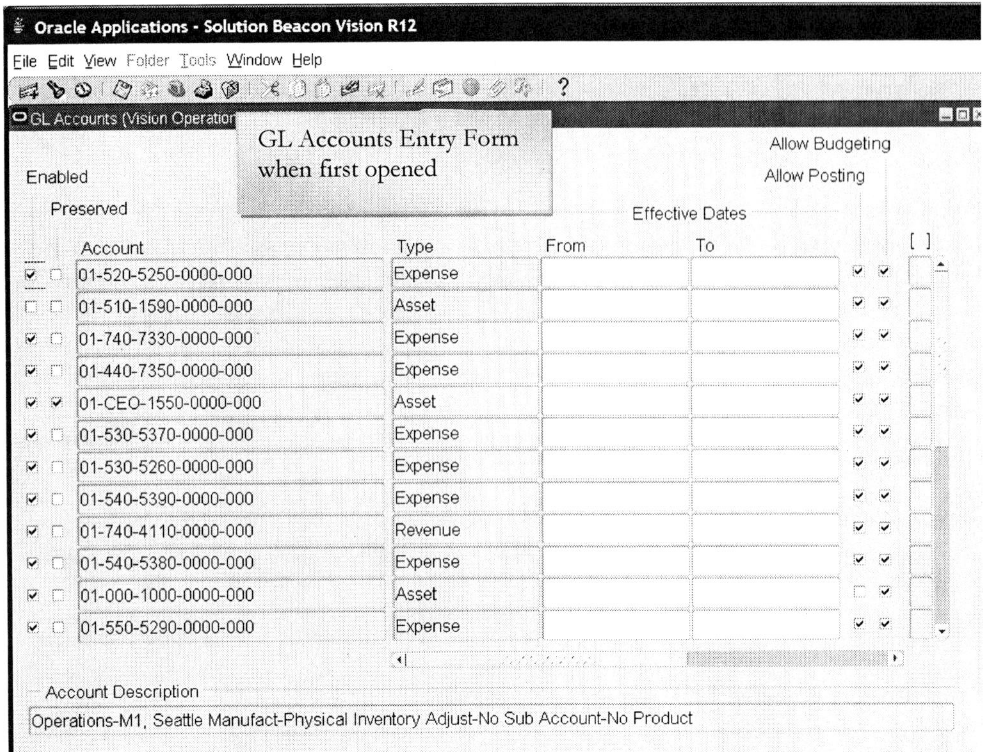

Figure 53 – The GL Accounts Entry Form when initially opened looks the same as in Release 11*i*.

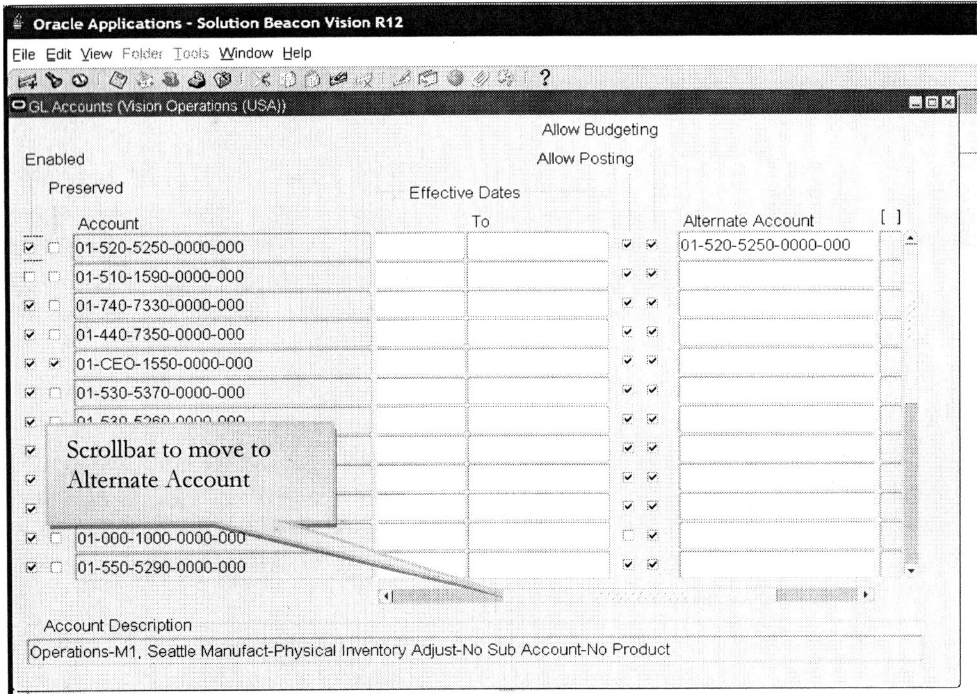

Figure 54 – Use the horizontal scroll bar to access the alternate account field.

Payables

Invoice Lines

Invoice Lines have been added between the Invoice Header and the Invoice Distribution Lines (see Figure 55). Invoice Lines more accurately reflect real-world invoice documents – the actual goods and services listed. This information enhances the flow of information from Purchasing to Payables to Assets. Asset information that is typically entered on a purchase order and tracked through invoice lines are: Item Description, Manufacturer, Model, Serial Number, and Warranty Number. Also, the Asset Book and Asset Category were available for PO/RCV matched distributions but the fields were not exposed in Payables. This disallowed any updates in the Purchasing-Payables-Assets flow. Now, both fields are exposed at the Invoice Line level and the Asset Book is exposed at the Invoice Distribution level. Finally, the invoice line level enables line level approval capability.

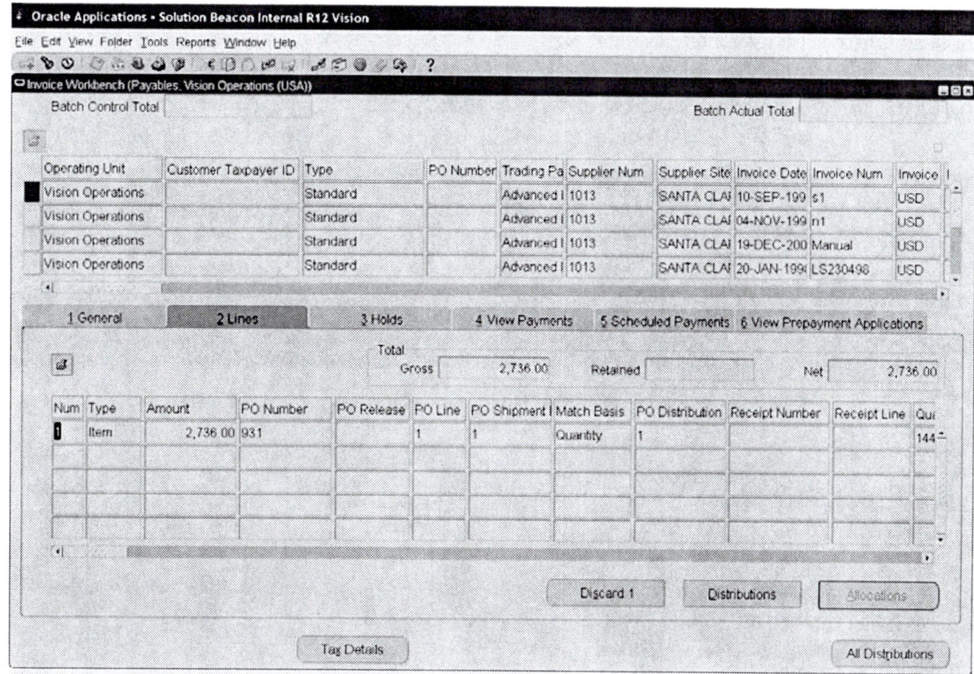

Figure 55 – The redesigned invoice entry form with the new invoice lines tab.

Supplier Maintenance

The Supplier Maintenance form (see Figure 56) takes full advantage of the new user interface. Shortcuts, ease of navigation, and enhanced search functionalities will improve the time and efficiency of supplier creation and maintenance (see Figure 57). The Supplier Maintenance form now has Quick Link notifications from the iSupplier portal detailing the action items for the specific user.

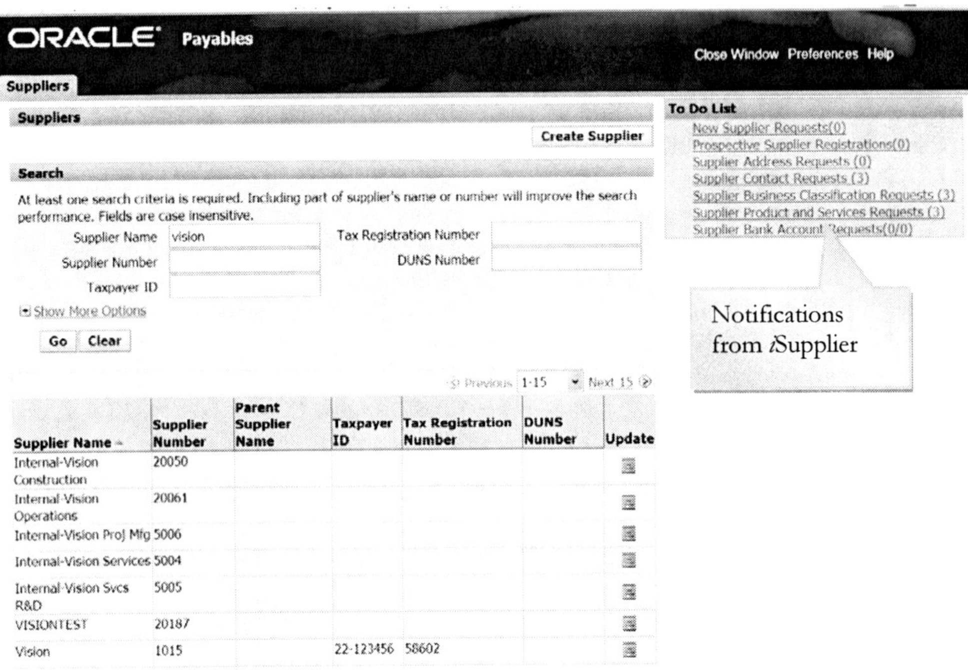

Supplier Name	Supplier Number	Parent Supplier Name	Taxpayer ID	Tax Registration Number	DUNS Number	Update
Internal-Vision Construction	20050					
Internal-Vision Operations	20061					
Internal-Vision Proj Mfg	5006					
Internal-Vision Services	5004					
Internal-Vision Svcs R&D	5005					
VISIONTEST	20187					
Vision	1015		22-123456	58602		

Figure 56 – The new Supplier Maintenance form.

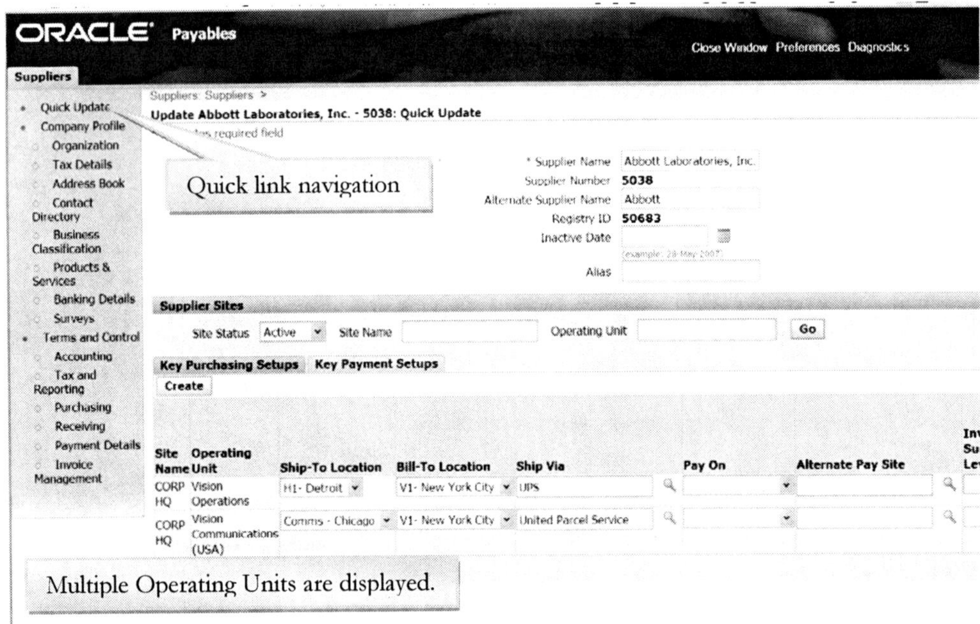

Figure 57 – When updating information, Quick Links speed setup.

Finally, the supplier maintenance form can now also be accessed directly from the Professional Buyer's Work Center.

AR/AP Netting

In Release 11*i*, no relationship existed between AR and AP transactions, even though the customer and supplier might have been the same company. Now, in Release 12, the capability exists to perform invoice netting for trading partners that are both customers and suppliers. The netting process compares the outstanding AR invoices with the outstanding AP Invoices and selects the lower of the two values for the netting amount. It then settles the lower invoice amount and automatically applies that same amount to the higher invoice amount. This functionality provides much needed visibility, reduces the cost of the trading partnership, and improves overall cash flow. Also, data entry is reduced and data processing is more efficient. Figure 58 illustrates an example of the netting functionality. A trading partner with a defined netting agreement has AR invoices totaling $1100 and AP invoices totaling $400. When the netting process is run, a payment is created for $400 settling all of the AP invoices and a $400 receipt is also applied against the AR invoice leaving a balance owed in AR of $700 (see Figure 58).

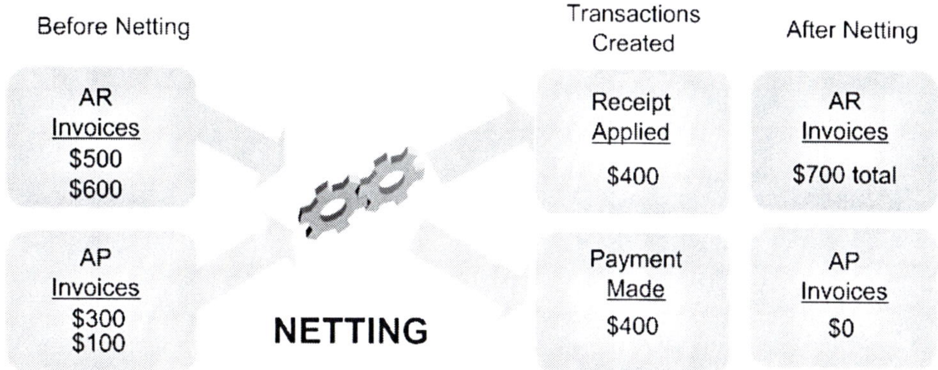

Figure 58 – The netting functionality gives visibility of trading partner activity in both Payables and Receivables

A part of the netting functionality is the netting agreement between the trading partner and the organization that specifies how and under what conditions the netting will occur. The netting process is managed by a user and has a trading partner approval component that reports the automatic transactions that were applied.

Fixed Assets

Automatic Preparation of Mass Additions

Release 12 now supports the automatic preparation of mass additions. Users can use default rules and/or Public APIs to prepare mass addition lines automatically. Required fields such as expense account and asset category are auto-populated. With this enhanced functionality, users will be able to avoid customization and manual intervention.

Automatic Depreciation Rollback

Users no longer are required to rollback depreciation manually when adjusting assets that have already been depreciated. Previously if depreciation had been run before the period was closed and further adjustments were required, the depreciation had to be rolled back manually for the entire Asset book. Adjustments were made and then depreciation was run again – a time-consuming process.

Now, when selected assets are adjusted, the depreciation rollback occurs automatically for just those selected assets and not the entire Asset book. The automatic depreciation rollback is performed when two criteria are met: the period is open and depreciation has been performed in that period. When depreciation is run again or the period is closed, the modified assets will be picked up and depreciated. This new functionality results in more efficient processing of adjustments and enhances the performance of the depreciation process.

Receivables

Revenue Recognition

One area that improved in the Receivables subledger is the enhancements to revenue recognition. Daily revenue recognition capabilities are available that give the user revenue distribution over full as well as partial accounting periods, enable fulfillment of stringent accounting standards, and assure accuracy to the number of days in the accounting period. A wide range of revenue management options are available. They include revenue recognition based on the following criteria:

- Time
    - Ratably over Time
    - Upon Expiration of Contingencies
- Events
    - Payment
    - Customer Acceptance
- Rules
    - Payment Term Thresholds
    - Refund Policy Thresholds
    - Customer Creditworthiness

Line Level Cash Application

Another improvement gives users the option to apply cash at the line level instead of the transactional level. This gives users more control and a more accurate representation of cash flow. The line level cash application functionality can be accessed from the "Apply in Detail" button on the Applications form in Receivables

Both the Receipt and the Transaction are shown at the top of the screen in Figure 59. A tree structure on the left hand side of the screen details the lines, groups, and the freight and charges. Users can choose to show all the transactional lines by clicking on the "Show All Lines" button. Users then select the line and/or lines to which they want to apply the cash. Freight and tax can also be applied within this form. Finally, discounts are automatically applied.

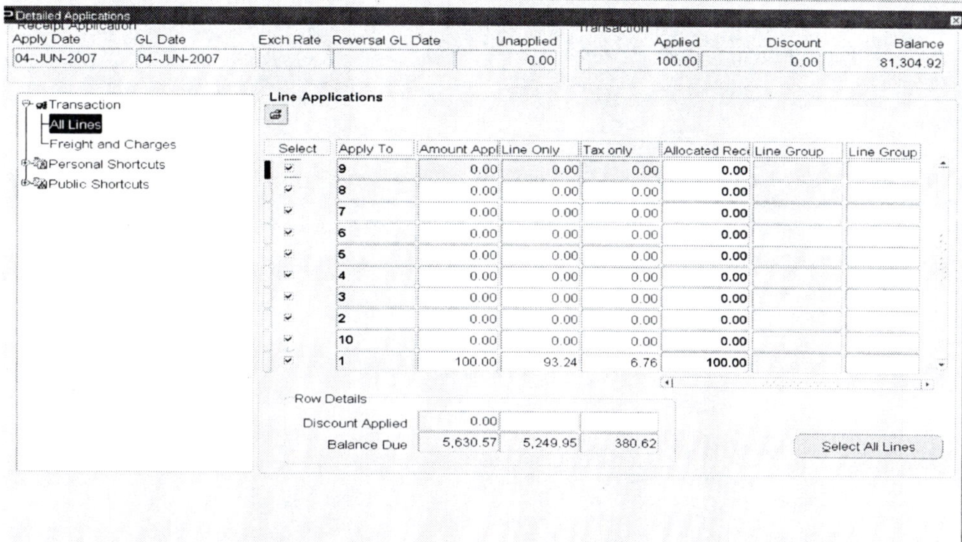

Figure 59 – Specific lines can be selected to apply to the receipt.

DATA REPRESENTATION

Regardless of how reliable the data is in the database, if it is not represented in an understandable way that supports valid business decisions, it is essentially worthless. Release 12 provides several powerful and flexible tools to extract and present data in a variety of ways. These include the Enterprise Performance Foundation, Daily Business Intelligence, and XML Publisher.

Enterprise Performance Foundation

The Enterprise Performance Foundation is the platform for several business reporting tools including the Financial Consolidation Hub, the Financial Services Accounting Hub, the Profitability Manager, the Balanced Scorecard, Enterprise Planning and Budgeting, and Transfer Pricing. These tools can leverage data not only in the General Ledger but can integrate data from third party systems to give companies a complete view of their financial data.

The Financial Consolidation Hub is a new product that integrates data from disparate financial systems to perform statutory and management consolidation. The single user interface shown in Figure 60 enables the user to set up, manage, and interface data from one central location.

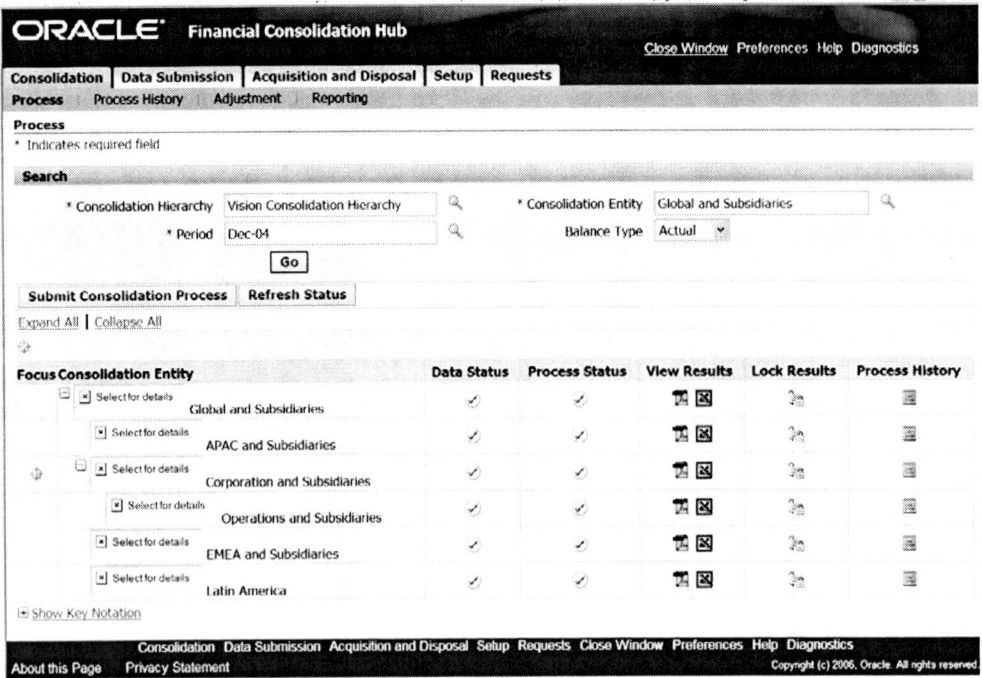

Figure 60 – Users can setup, manage, and interface data from one central location.

The Financial Services Accounting Hub is another new product similar in functionality to the Financial Accounting Hub. It has additional functionality that addresses specific requirements of the financial services industry.

The Oracle Profitability Manager is a resource for the calculation, analysis and reporting of profitability. This open environment accepts data from not only the General Ledger but from external sources such as data warehouses, transactional systems, and spreadsheets. Powerful tools enable you to dynamically maintain business rules, dimensions, and conditions.

Transfer pricing is a mechanism for dividing the net interest income of a financial institution (such as a bank) among its constituent business units (such as the deposit, treasury, and the credit groups). The Oracle Transfer Pricing mechanism uses multiple transfer rates instead of the single rate that traditional approaches advocate. Under the multiple rate approach, assets and liabilities are given transfer rates that reflect their specific maturity and repricing characteristics.

A Global Solution

Hopefully, enterprises implementing or upgrading to Release 12 will quickly see the benefits of "The Global Business Release". In the Financial product family new products and feature enhancements serve to give users shared service center support, greater processing efficiencies, improved accounting capabilities, and robust reporting. Users will see similar enhancements and results in other product families.

The next chapter will discuss Release 12 features in Procurement.

Procurement Product Family

Oracle's goal in enhancing the Procurement Product Family was to migrate from loosely joined individual modules to an integrated procurement suite that focuses on what is being bought, who needs it and where will it be used. Although most of the modules existed in Release 11*i*, Release 12 provides a more tightly integrated web of information between modules.

For procurement departments, Release 12 is a significant upgrade, moving them from standard functionality that required more forms and was less efficient to a feature rich application suite. All of this is long overdue and necessary to operate a sophisticated procurement operation in a global environment.

Oracle Purchasing now consolidates functions across global business units, providing a centralized procurement center that allows local service centers to perform in unison by creating autonomous procurement transactions within the enterprise. Some of the procurement activities include:

- **Global Agreements** - blanket purchase agreements or contract purchase agreements with a supplier that can be shared between business units.
- **Center-Led Procurement Automatic Sourcing** - sourcing rules, sourcing rule assignments and approved supplier lists (ASL) are created in the owning business unit
- **Center-Led Procurement Accounting** - accounts are provided to ensure proper financial reconciliation between the procuring business unit and the receiving business unit using inter-company invoicing. Center-Led Procurement compliments the Shared Services approach and provides a higher level of integrated data.

New Features and Functionality

At first glance, the enhancements for each of the purchasing modules may not appear to be very significant. However, when considered together as part of the integrated procurement suite, the increased functionality is important. The standard features are still present, but the efficiency has been increased by reducing the number of forms and redesigning the user interface.

The Swan Interface not only gives users a new look and feel that is more consistent with most web applications, it also adds efficiency by making it easier to get to the details of a purchasing document. Instead of having to page between forms as in previous releases, users can now click on a tab and go directly to the desired information. The drill down capabilities always existed but now they are seamless and several formats for editing information exist on one page. Overall, the consolidation of forms and the new user interface design provide the ability to get to the integrated information more quickly and with greater accessibility. Compare Figure 61, which shows the new Professional Buyer's Work Center, to Figure 62, which shows the Release 11*i* version of this screen.

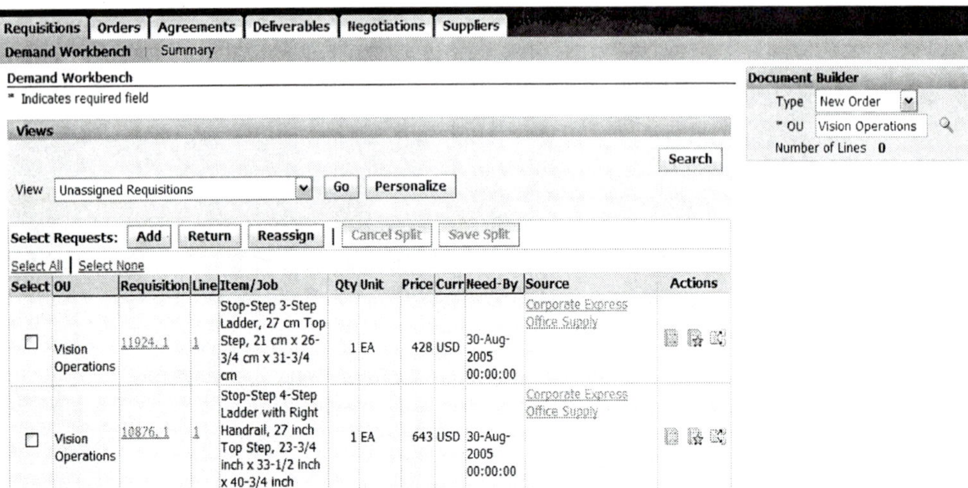

Figure 61 – The new Professional Buyer's Work Center

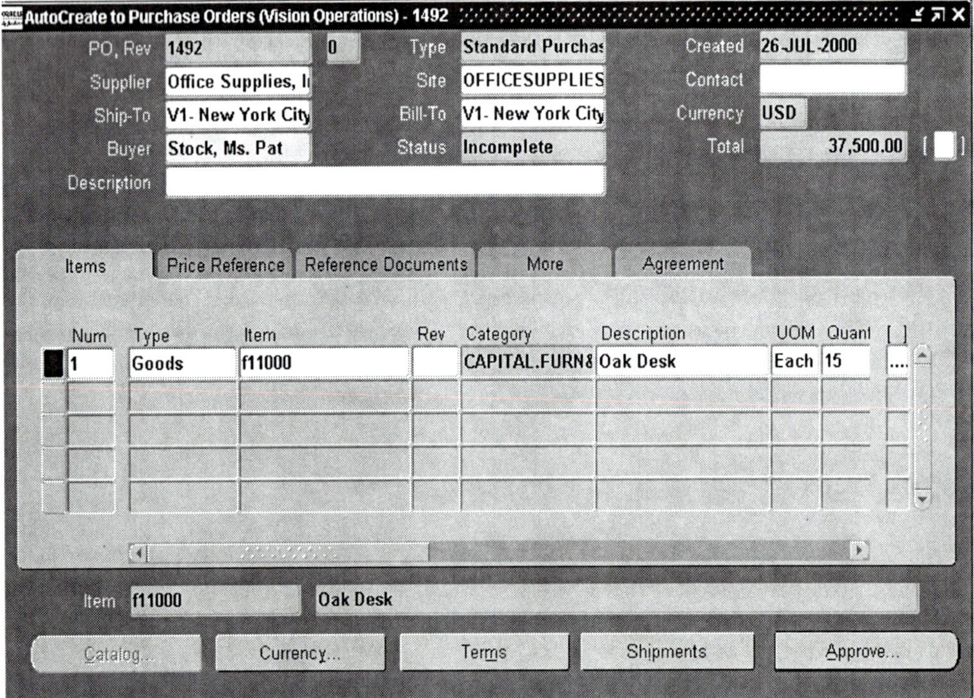

Figure 62 – The Release 11*i* Professional Buyer's Work Center

Professional Buyer's Work Center (PBWC)

Oracle Purchasing Release 12 empowers purchasing agents and speeds up daily purchasing tasks with an enhanced Professional Buyer's Work Center (PBWC). Built on the Swan user interface, the PBWC is a central workbench from which buyers can efficiently perform their daily tasks — such as viewing and acting upon requisition demand, creating and modifying orders and agreements, and accessing Oracle Sourcing to initiate negotiations.

A purchasing agent can see the entire lifecycle of a purchasing document and access information for most of the procurement suite. This is the central point of the integration where the ease of access to information is most apparent. The design of the PBWC supports global functionality and the center-led procurement approach. The three key objectives of the work center are to execute purchase agreements, to view exceptions as they occur and to analyze the performance of procurement and supplier.

The Buyer's Work Center optimizes the standard purchase order creation and management processes. Buyers can edit and view delivery schedules and account distributions across all order lines, thus eliminating the need to drill down on individual lines. For simple purchase orders that do not require staged delivery schedules or multiple account distributions, buyers can quickly enter all necessary information for the order in the header and line sections, without having to navigate to the schedules and distributions sections.

The Professional Buyer's Work Center increases the drill down capabilities between Oracle Sourcing and Oracle Purchasing. Buyers can now easily navigate from purchasing to sourcing documents, and vice-versa, using a single dashboard (Figure 63).

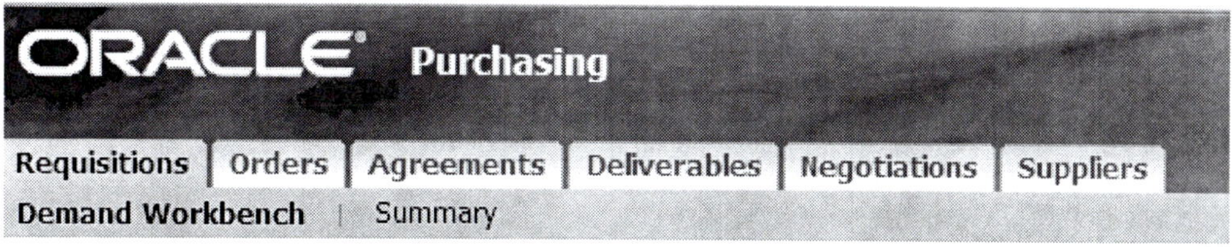

Figure 63 – Tabs on the Professional Buyer's Work Center

The following functionality exists in Buyer's Work Center as tabs within the work center.

Requisitions – Requisitioners can access requisition demand in the Demand Workbench collected from a number of sources: *i*Procurement, MRP, Inventory or any Third Party requisitioning tool. Previously generated requisitions can be viewed under the Summary tab.

Orders – Buyers can create a new standard purchase order, blanket purchase agreement, blanket releases or contract purchase agreement. Existing purchasing documents can be viewed under the Summary tab with updates from the user interface

Agreements – Create, manage and update Blanket Agreements and Contract Purchase Orders using this tab. If Oracle Services Procurement is licensed and implemented, users can create and maintain purchase orders for complex work payments.

Deliverables – Allows a buyer to author contract terms and manage deliverables. It requires Oracle Procurement Contracts to be licensed and implemented.

Negotiations – Enables buyer to create auctions, issue RFIs and RFPs, and also Sourcing RFQs. It requires Oracle Sourcing to be licensed and implemented.

Suppliers – Users can create and maintain supplier information in the Supplier tab while interacting with information entered through the *i*Supplier Portal.

The Professional Buyer's Work Center also increases the drill down capabilities between Oracle Sourcing and Oracle Purchasing. Each of these features is related to other modules in the suite and can be accessed throughout the lifecycle of a procurement contract from the work center.

ORACLE PROCUREMENT MODULES

This section will focus on the new functionality within the modules accessed by Procurement. All the procurement modules have been enhanced and boast the new user interface. The core tables are similar and the underlying data has remained the same, except when the integration required the data to be handled more efficiently. This efficiency is demonstrated by the ability to see more information from one module while operating in another module. An example of this is found in Figure 64 where information from the Enterprise Asset Manager is displayed on the contract screen.

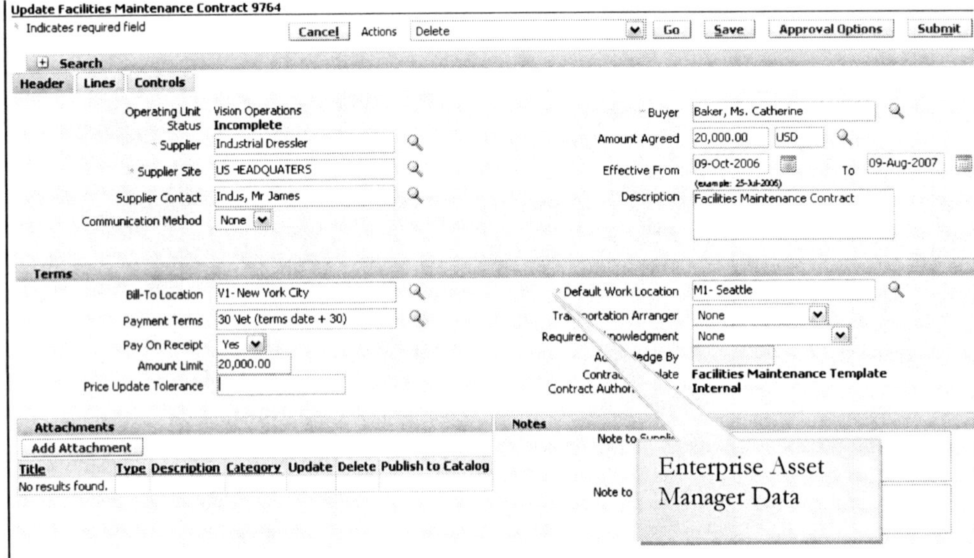

Figure 64 – Notice that you can see information from the Enterprise Asset Manager

The following modules accessed by Procurement will be discussed:

- ***i*Procurement (Schema POR)** – seamless ordering using a web interface based on core data
- **Purchasing (Schema PO)** – streamlined order processing with built-in compliance
- ***i*Supplier Portal (Schema POS)** – a secure supplier portal with improved visibility to purchasing information
- **Supplier Network** – electronic transaction service between parties
- **Sourcing (Schema PON)** – improves strategic sourcing between suppliers and customers

- **Procurement Contracts (Schema PON)** – creates and enforces purchasing contracts
- **Service Procurement (Schema POX)** – control and oversight of services, deliverables and confirmation

*i*Procurement (Schema POR)

This is where a process starts and ends. Oracle *i*Procurement is self-service requisitioning that facilitates and controls employee spending. It is the center point where the execution of procurement processes comes together. This is generally where most requestors start their requesting process, but it is also where the buyers end their process by providing agreements and contracts to the end user for execution. Since *i*Procurement matured in Release 11*i*, the functionality has not changed much and it follows the same requesting process of shopping, adding to the cart, and checking out. The primary changes are underlying and deal with integration that is more efficient.

*i*Procurement now focuses on improved content management, advancements in Requester Driven Procurement and user interface upgrades. Release 12 significantly improves the content management process with features such as online catalog authoring, difference summaries for catalog changes, and a new and improved catalog security model. This release also contains advances in requester driven functionality by allowing requesters to suggest negotiation events when ordering goods, as well as providing tolerance rules to automatically process minor changes without buyer involvement. Finally, numerous user interface upgrades such as multiple search results layouts and multiple favorites lists were integrated to make the ordering process more intuitive and provide end users a more enriched experience (see Figure 65).

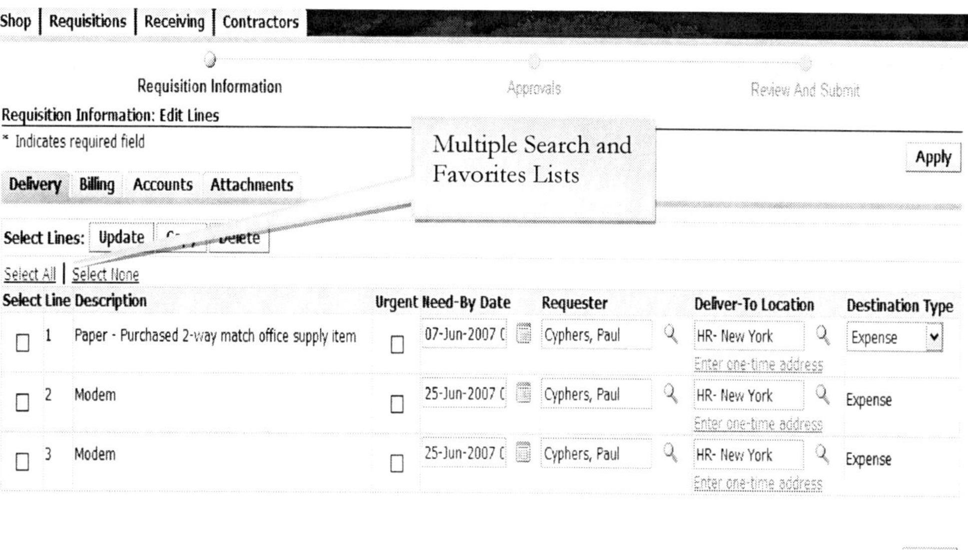

Figure 65 – User upgrades include multiple search result layouts and multiple favorites lists

With Release 12, Oracle *i*Procurement further expands and enhances integration with the Oracle Approvals Management product, giving flexibility to configure business approval processes. Key enhancements include position based hierarchies that allow organizations the flexibility to create reporting structures that remain stable regardless of personnel changes; parallel approvals functionality, giving organizations the option to speed up the approvals process by routing a requisition to multiple approvers simultaneously; and support for FYI Notifications that inform individuals of purchases and decisions. FYI Notifications do not require a response or impede the procurement process.

Purchasing (Schema PO)

Oracle Purchasing allows buyers to streamline purchase order processing while strengthening policy compliance through agreements and contracts. It is the key component of the integrated suite and dramatically cuts procurement cost. Buyers can now easily navigate from purchasing to sourcing documents, and vice-versa, using the Professional Buyer's Work Center.

Also, some of the enhancements to core purchasing include support for Unified Process Manufacturing/Discrete Inventory Material Status Control and Dual Unit of Measure Control. With Release 12, Oracle merged the Process Inventory and Inventory applications into a single version of Oracle Inventory. This single application supports process manufacturing characteristics such as dual units of measure, grade, lot controlled inventory, and the use of material status. This convergence removes the need for integration between Process Inventory and Purchasing. Oracle Process Quality for receiving inspection was enhanced specifically to support the procurement suite.

Oracle Purchasing leverages Multi-Org Access Control (MOAC) capabilities to enable more streamlined operations of Shared Services or Center-Led Procurement Service Centers. Using a single responsibility, users can manage demand (i.e., requisitions), conduct sourcing events, enter into agreements, and issue purchase orders on behalf of any of the operating units that they serve. Similarly, receiving clerks can now easily inquire about, plan for, and receive expected shipments against purchase orders or requisitions or RMAs originating in multiple operating units without changing responsibilities.

Another key enhancement is the support for contractors. Because more companies are outsourcing part or all of their procurement processes in an effort to reduce costs and improve efficiencies, contingent workers can create requisitions, conduct negotiations, and confirm work. Work confirmation allows the requestor to confirm that work done on a contract has been completed, much as a receipt confirms delivery of a product.

Requisition Management

As previously mentioned, PBWC delivers a streamlined user interface to review and act upon requisitions. The demand workbench replaces the AutoCreate functionality in previous versions. Buyers can aggregate demand from different organizations and consolidate it in a single document in or across organizations (see Figure 66). The requisition could be used to create a Standard Purchase Order, a Blanket Release, or a solicitation (Auction/RFx) for bids (requires Oracle Sourcing).

Figure 66 – Demand Workbench replaces AutoCreate functionality

Buyers can search for requisitions using pre-configured views or advanced search criteria. Also, buyers can create their own views, specifying custom search criteria and columns to display. Buyers can also view details of the requisitions by clicking the requisition links. Buyers can return requisitions to requesters to solicit additional information, reassign requisitions to other buyers, split requisition lines in order to source from multiple suppliers and replace off-catalog requests with items available in the catalog. There are also "Actions Icons" like update, split and reject that allow the buyer to execute directly from the workbench. All of these features either did not exist or existed in multiple areas requiring a purchasing agent to navigate among many forms. Oracle Advanced Procurement Suite offers exciting possibilities for today's purchasing agents.

Purchase Order Creation and Maintenance

The Orders tab of PBWC optimizes the standard purchase order creation and management processes. This feature allows buyers to edit and view delivery schedules and account distributions across all order lines, eliminating the need to drill down on individual lines using the different forms. For simple purchase orders that do not require staged delivery schedules or multiple account distributions, buyers can quickly enter all necessary information for the orders in the header and line sections, without having to navigate to the schedules and distributions sections. An additional feature is that users can now define tolerances for auto-approval of document revisions.

Purchase Agreement Creation and Maintenance

The work center provides a dedicated user interface for creating and maintaining agreements, along with targeting the strategic buyer responsible for agreement maintenance and compliance. Oracle Purchasing extends the integration with Oracle Advanced Pricing to allow procurement professionals to model complex pricing rules for items listed on global blanket agreements. Requisitions and orders sourced to these agreements can now leverage dynamic pricing formulas and/or modifiers defined in Oracle Advanced Pricing, in addition to the agreement line price and price breaks. Oracle also allows finer control of how blanket agreements are enabled for automatic document sourcing. Buyers can now choose to enable them only in specific inventory organizations. Thus, buyers can negotiate a blanket agreement to meet requisition demand for a set of inventory organizations and enable AutoSourcing.

A new Unified Catalog in Purchasing Release 12 enhances the catalog management process (see Figure 67). This provides online authoring capability for *i*Procurement catalog administrators. From the Demand Workbench, buyers can access the catalog to find negotiated alternatives to non-catalog requests. While creating orders and agreements, buyers can use the catalog to add items quickly, thereby accelerating the requisition creation process.

Content management is now a collaborative process between the buying and supplying organizations. This creates a need for suppliers to be able to view, create and maintain their content on behalf of the buying organization. Buyers can now view the Oracle *i*Procurement catalog while adding lines to the negotiation. From the negotiation creation flow, buyers can navigate and browse the *i*Procurement catalog, select the appropriate items, and automatically add them to the negotiation.

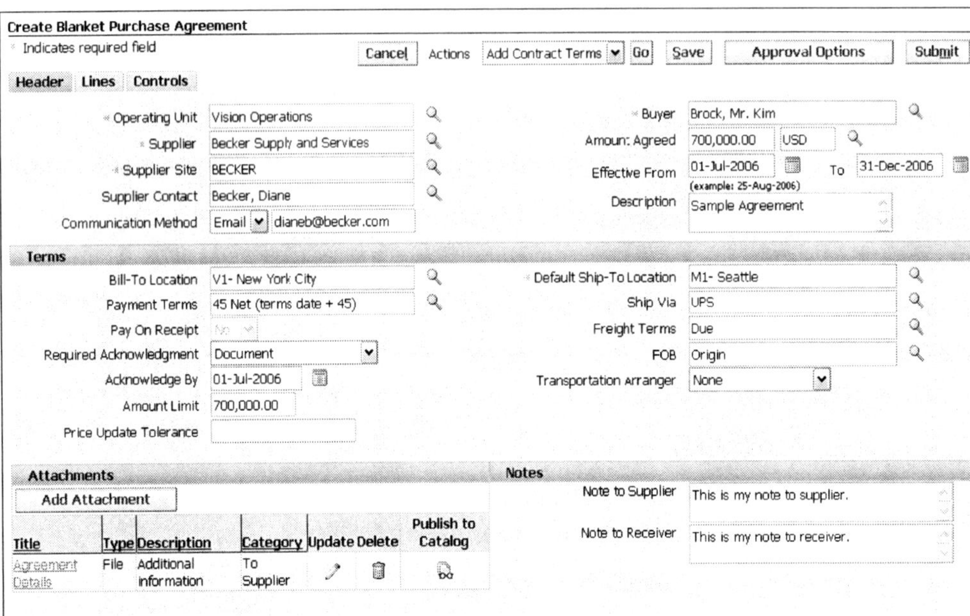

Figure 67 – Unified Catalog enhances the catalog management process

Contract Creation and Maintenance

Creating and maintaining contracts while monitoring deliverables and compliance is part of the PBWC. The contract workbench (see Figure 68) provides contract administrators easy access to all of their contracts. Administrators can use the workbench as a launch pad. The workbench provides relevant information for all contract activities that can be personalized by the administrator to improve their productivity. The workbench supports complex goods and services procurement by providing visibility to information. Simple and advanced search capabilities provide a buyer with a rich set of attributes enabling ad hoc queries or reporting on all enterprise procurement contracts.

Contracts

Search Contract Number Go Advanced Search

Logged In As pcyphers

Notifications

Below is a list of your most important notifications. Select the subject to respond or select "Full List" to see all your notifications.

Full List

From	Subject	Sent	Due
There are no notifications in this view.			

Shortcuts

- View Bookmarks
- Create Contract
- Analyze Contract Clauses

Recent Contracts

Full List

Contract Number	Contract Name	Operating Unit	Document Type	Status	Last Updated By	Last Update Date	Update
No Contracts found.							

Expiring Contracts

Full List

Contract Number	Contract Name	Operating Unit	Contract Type	Effective Date	Expiration Date
No Contracts found.					

Contract Deliverables

Manage Deliverables

Indicates deliverable is overdue × Indicates responsible party failed to perform the deliverable

Deliverable Name	Deliverable Type	Document Type	Contract Number	Party Name	Contact	Due Date	Status	Alert
No deliverables found.								

Figure 68 – The Contract Workbench

Previously Oracle Procurement Contracts enabled buying organizations to authenticate a user's identity by requiring users to re-enter usernames and passwords when signing contracts electronically. A new alternative is to validate a user's unique digital certificates, normally issued by a Certification Authority. This new signature process can be enabled in the existing workflow approval process. Signed documents are kept in an evidence store in case of future disputes. Oracle Procurement Contracts supports digital certificate authentication of electronic signatures. With increases in outsourcing, support for this type of operation has become a necessity.

Release 12 now supports the procurement processes in an effort to reduce costs and improve efficiencies for contractors. An example of this could be chargeable subcontracting of assemblies from an OEM to one or more manufacturing partners. In this practice, the OEM ships and makes a provisional sale of component materials used to build the assemblies at the manufacturing partner. When the assemblies are completed and returned to the OEM, the partner bills the OEM for the gross price of the assembly (Figure 69). In order to provide support for this business practice, the "Pay on Receipt Auto-invoice" concurrent program has been enhanced to create separate invoices for these items.

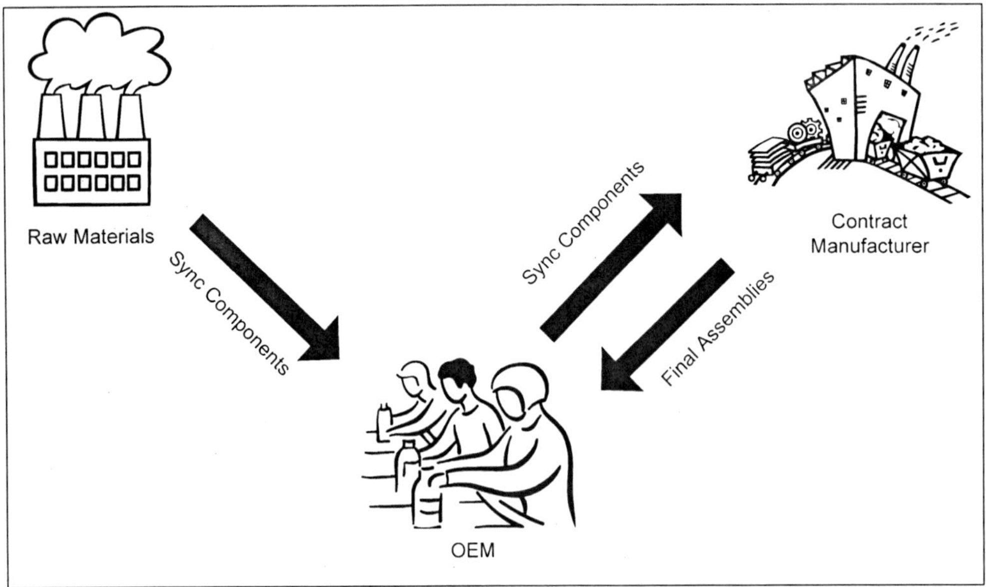

Figure 69 – Chargeable Subcontracting

Chargeable Subcontracting is the term that describes the process where Original Equipment Manufacturers (OEMs) sometimes ship critical components to their contract manufacturers at the same time they place orders for complete assemblies. These "sync" components are meant to arrive at the contractor's facility right before assembly of the ordered item begins. Non-sync items, which are generally non-critical components, are usually shipped in volume quantities to the contract manufacturer. Both types of components are sold to the contract manufacturer, but any realized or unrealized gain is not recognized by the OEM for "sync" components. While ASCP will provide the planning support for these components, Release 12 offers comprehensive support across the E-Business Suite for managing the underlying transactions. Replenishment Purchase Orders and Sales Orders are associated with Chargeable Subcontracting.

E-Business Tax / Tax Capability

Oracle E-Business Tax includes new functionality for tax management that supports complex taxes in purchasing using a global system architecture that is configurable and scalable for adding specific tax content. As the single point solution for managing transaction-based tax, this functionality will provide tax services to the procurement transactions by allowing better control of the process through increased visibility, ease of configurability, and usage. Oracle E-Business Tax significantly enhances the current tax code/tax group based tax computation capabilities within the Procure-to-Pay business flow by creating greater efficiencies through automated processing.

Supplier Modules

Oracle has enhanced the end-to-end supplier process through improved multi-organization configurations that support the entry and maintenance of suppliers more efficiently, and enhanced control of access to supplier information. This includes an improved layout for accessing all aspects of a supplier's setup, providing a clear distinction between the supplier's company details and the terms and controls used to manage the relationship. Supplier and supplier site level setup parameters are now available on a single page and setup preferences are across fewer sub-tabs, allowing quicker access to information.

Also, a new "Quick Update" screen gives each administrator access to an initial summary page that can be personalized to suit their needs. In the Supplier Maintenance screen, purchasing and payables setup are split to provide long overdue segregation of duties between the two modules (see Figure 70). Security controls are incorporated into the screen so that companies can limit access to specific purchasing and payables setup tabs within the supplier setup. This feature assists companies with Master Data Management or to comply with the separation of duties elements of different regulations such as Sarbanes-Oxley.

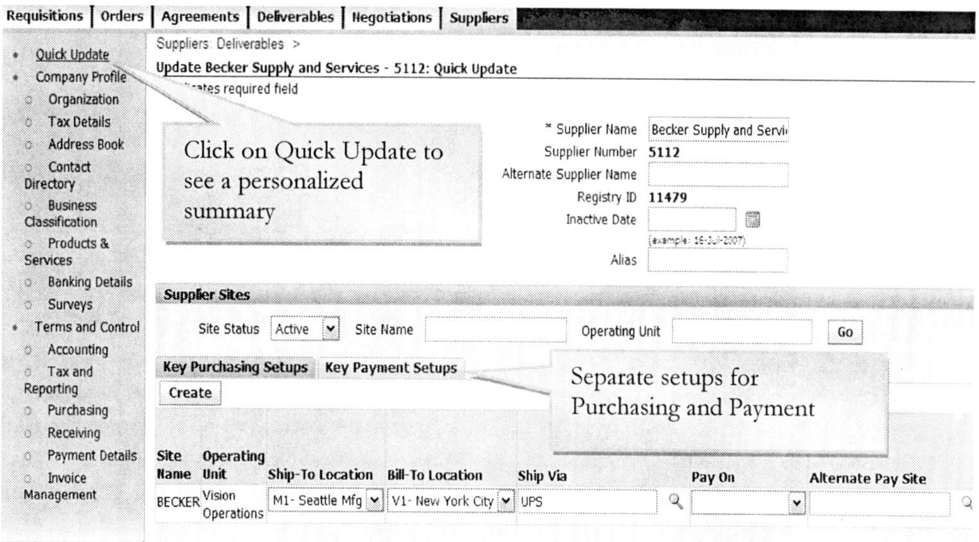

Figure 70 – The new Quick Update page

Internal users can use the "New Supplier Request" screen (see Figure 71) to enter requests and qualification details for new suppliers. An approval hierarchy allows deploying organizations to ensure that once the qualification details have been gathered, the relevant stakeholders within the business are involved in the review process for the requested supplier. Following approval, a new supplier record will be set up automatically using the supplier's qualification details.

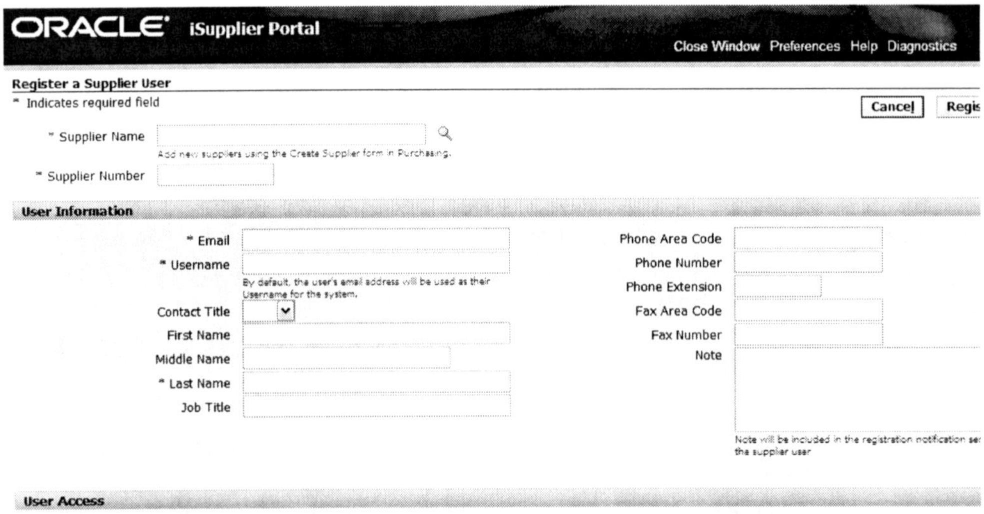

Figure 71 – The new Supplier Request screen

In Release 12, suppliers are now represented in the Trading Community Architecture (TCA). TCA is a flexible architecture that allows users to model entities in their trading community and represents complex relationships among those entities. It is the core data model for trading partners. By representing suppliers as part of the trading community, users have access to many of the features provided by TCA. Data Librarian tools assist with activities focused on improving data consistency, eliminating duplicates and modeling relationships. Although this functionality is a step in the right direction, it is still limited and does not provide full integration.

iSupplier (Schema POS)

Oracle iSupplier is the external internet-based module that gathers all supplier communication through a secure supplier portal. New functionality supports the procurement and management of complex work. Significant enhancements have been made to the supplier change order process and supplier on-boarding, in addition to many usability improvements for external and internal users.

For those companies that have enabled supplier access to their profile information through the portal, the Supplier Profile Management tools are integrated into the new screens, affording administrators a single view of a supplier's setup and any updates provided by the supplier to the buying organization. The current change order functionality allows suppliers to acknowledge orders and initiate change requests one purchase order at a time. This functionality has been extended to enable suppliers to acknowledge or process changes across multiple orders simultaneously.

Tracking the formal approval of each new supplier request is traditionally a manual process that requires coordination across multiple departments as credit checks are carried out, customer references called, quality standards reviewed and production facilities inspected. Oracle iSupplier Portal leverages the Approval Management Engine allowing companies to generate customized approval flows for processing supplier requests and registrations.

Release 12 introduces the Supplier Managed User Maintenance feature. Buying organizations can hand over the task of supplier user account administration to nominated administrators at each supplier (see Figure 72). The Supplier User Administrators can create or obsolete supplier user accounts and alter the security access rights for each user within their company. This benefits both organizations. Suppliers can directly control which of their users have access and what activities they can perform. In this release, supplier contact records and supplier user accounts are harmonized so that any changes need only be made to a single record. The Supplier Profile Management tools have been significantly enhanced for both supplier users and buyer administrators. For suppliers, the enhancements enable them to access and update additional profile details such as their tax information and payment preferences.

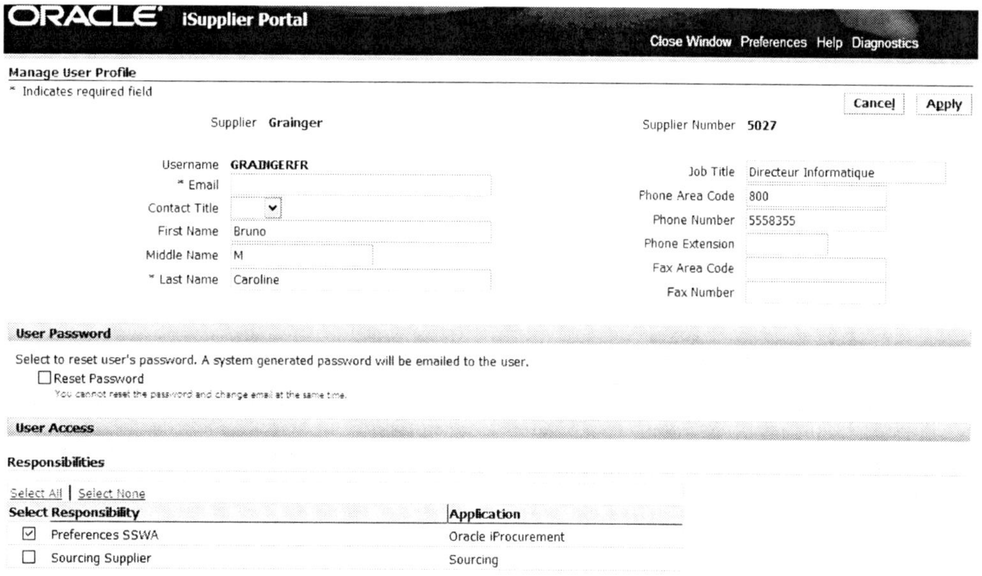

Figure 72 – Using the Manage User Profile screen, the supplier can do user account administration

Increasingly, content management has become a collaborative process between buying and supplying organizations through Supplier Self-Service Catalog Authoring. Many enterprises now outsource the content authoring responsibilities to suppliers or third parties. Therefore, suppliers must be able to view, create and maintain their content for the buying organization. Release 12 provides suppliers the capability to author their own content online, either via bulk file upload or on-line authoring. Content provided by the supplier is subject to the buyer's approval before it is made available to the requesters in *i*Procurement.

PO Status Tracking allows suppliers to track the status of their purchase orders throughout the order lifecycle. The redesigned purchase order page gives suppliers real-time order status and the ability to drill down to see the details of the associated ASN/ASBN, receipts, invoices and payments. Receipt Inquiry is also redesigned to provide suppliers with a streamlined process to view receipt information and the details of the associated purchase orders, shipments and invoices. The receipt details page includes on-time performance information and values for quantity/amounts received, ordered, returned and rejected.

Now suppliers can submit an invoice if a purchase order was not obtained up front or is a non-PO invoice. In this case, the invoice request first goes through an approval process. Along the approval process, users can add accounting information that is used when an approved request becomes an invoice. Suppliers can also submit an invoice request that provides a correct invoice when the accuracy or verification of the services or goods may be in question. Collaboration and approval processes route the invoice request to the employees in the company that can resolve these issues.

Another feature is the ability to view complex contract payments. Long term-contracts may require complex payment arrangements such as milestone payments, progress payments, advances, retainage and recoupment. The payment schedule will include the contractual deliverables for the project and the associated progress payments for completing the deliverables on time. Oracle *i*Supplier Portal streamlines the work confirmation and payment authorization process. Once the Supplier submits an online work confirmation, the request is automatically routed for approval to those who are qualified to confirm the work. In addition to supplier-initiated work confirmations, work confirmations can also be initiated by internal users within the buying organization. To ensure accurate and timely payments, once the work confirmation is approved, an invoice can be generated.

By integrating with Oracle Daily Business Intelligence, *i*Supplier Portal allows a buying organization to view the Supplier Scorecard by monitoring the performance of suppliers and sharing the supplier's quantitative performance measures (see Figure 73). Buyers and suppliers can examine and track the results to provide feedback for continuous improvement, which is a key procurement priority. This provides relevant and reliable supplier performance information and a view from aggregated data to granular details on Key Performance Indicators (KPIs). Also, this new feature enables the buyers to focus their efforts on managing and selectively scoring performance of the most strategic suppliers.

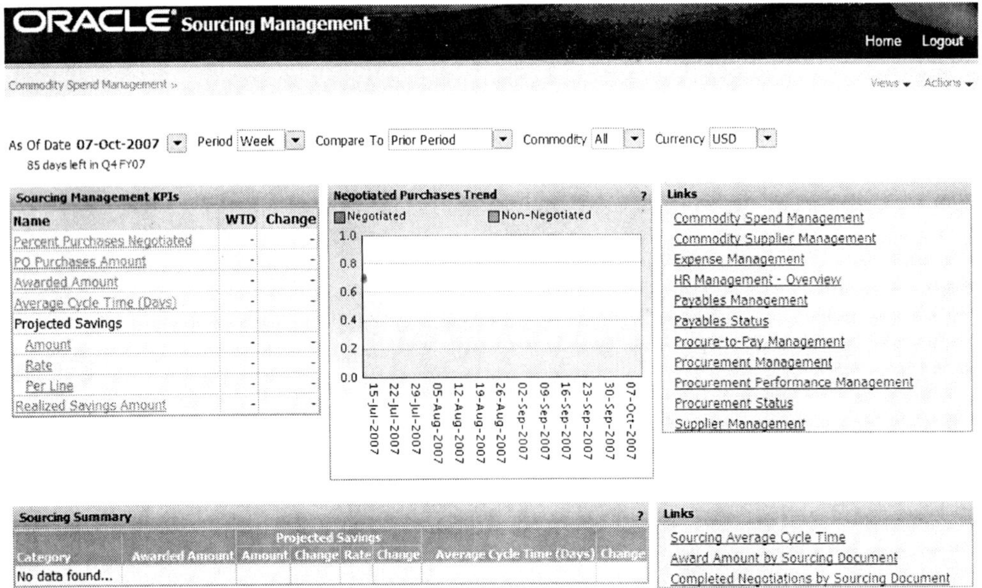

Figure 73 – A buying organization can view the Supplier Scorecard

Supplier Network

Oracle Supplier Network allows Oracle Purchasing customers to leverage pre-defined connectivity to quickly enable electronic messaging with suppliers. The Oracle Supplier Network (OSN) enables suppliers to integrate transactions such as sending and receiving XML documents, including Purchase Orders and Invoices. The hosted network service eliminates the costly IT effort involved in building and maintaining direct connections with specific suppliers, since each trading party only has to maintain a single connection with the

OSN. This enables companies to use fewer resources to drive machine-to-machine messaging down to a larger base of their repetitive suppliers.

Sourcing (Schema PON)

Oracle Sourcing is the enterprise application that improves the effectiveness and efficiency of strategic sourcing. Sourcing enables buyers to source more of the organization's spend at lower total cost. Sourcing creates immediate savings through rapid deployment, and ensures long-term savings with consistent execution and contract compliance. Oracle Sourcing provides a platform for online collaboration between the buying organization and the contractors for negotiation of contracts for complex services. Complex contract payment arrangements that are typical of these contracts include advances, retainage, and progress payments. These can now be included in the RFQs or Auctions for negotiation between two parties.

Once the RFQ is published (see Figure 74), the buying organization can make changes to the proposed contract payments through the existing RFQ amendment process, if needed. Suppliers can review the proposed complex contract payment terms online and submit their quotes accordingly. If permitted by the buying organization, suppliers can propose a different payment schedule, add payment milestones, request more advances, or change the retainage and financing terms as part of their quotes. When the contract is awarded, the agreed terms along with the payment schedule are transferred along with other contract terms to Purchasing for signature, execution and payment.

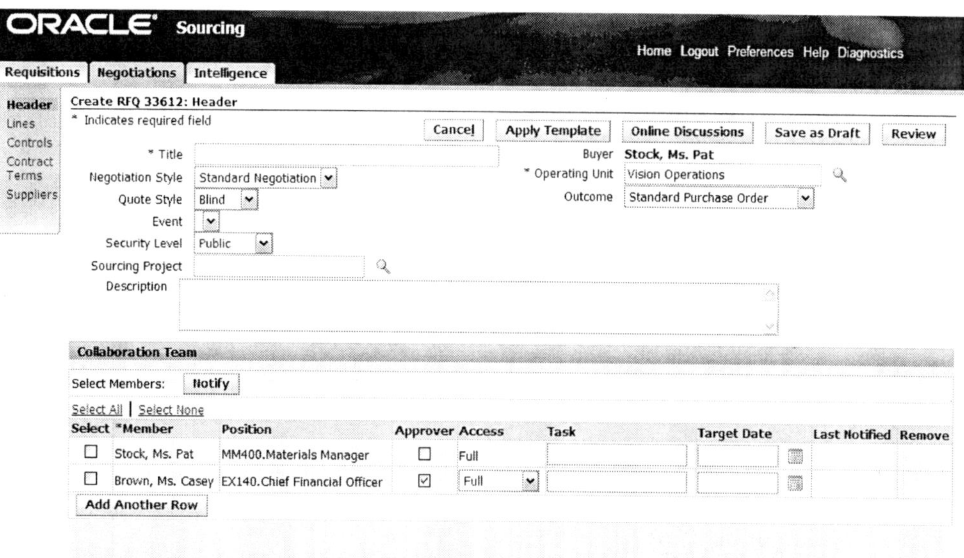

Figure 74 – Buyers can create and update RFQs with Oracle Sourcing.

Over the last few releases, Oracle Sourcing has evolved to support increasingly complex electronic negotiation sourcing practices. The introduction of advanced features (e.g., multi-attribute scoring, transformation bidding, etc.) has made the product extremely powerful. However, this rich functionality has come at the cost of some unnecessary user interface complexity for those events where the advanced features are not required.

Sourcing also expands support for RFXs/Auctions, allowing thousands of line items on a single negotiation. In prior releases, Sourcing supported large RFXs/Auctions with only hundreds of line items. Buyers can create large negotiations using the spreadsheet upload feature, or by re-negotiating an existing catalog with thousands of lines. The award approval process in Sourcing uses the Approvals Management Engine (AME) as the approval engine. In prior releases, AME could only be set up to use an employee-supervisor hierarchy for Sourcing award approvals. With Release 12, companies can also use position-based hierarchy rules to determine the approvers for negotiation award approval. Position-based hierarchies allow organizations the flexibility to create reporting structures that remain stable regardless of organizational changes.

The new Sourcing Dashboard enables procurement managers to monitor the performance of their sourcing efforts using Daily Business Intelligence. The dashboard contains key performance indicators (KPI) such as the percent of total purchases that are negotiated, total projected savings from sourcing activities, realized savings from previously negotiated contracts, and the average sourcing cycle time by commodity. Buyers can obtain additional information about a sourcing KPI by drilling down to the report that shows supporting information.

Sourcing integrates with Procurement to provide buyers with a Supplier Scorecard based on quantitative measures of supplier performance. Buyers can view relevant and reliable supplier performance information when determining which suppliers to invite to sourcing events, and while analyzing supplier bids. Buyers get a complete view, from aggregated data to granular details, on Key Performance Indicators (KPIs) .

Sourcing Optimization

Sourcing Optimization is a new module that allows the buyer to create scenarios that can be automatically optimized to determine the best award, while adhering to policies and goals defined for the scenario. This results in better and faster award decisions. When allocating business to suppliers, buyers often must strive to meet multiple purchasing goals and business policies.

Procurement Contracts (Schema PON)

Procurement Contracts creates and enforces better purchasing contracts. Procurement Contracts allows you to take control of your contract lifecycle, from authoring and negotiation through implementation, enforcement, evaluation and closeout. Procurement professionals can quickly author contracts that comply with corporate standards, and monitor compliance to make sure that negotiated savings are achieved. With Procurement Contracts you can standardize contract processes, reduce time-to-contract, and enforce contract compliance.

Using Contract Expert, companies can define their business rules that govern the contract clauses to be included in a purchasing or sourcing document. Contract Expert is a rules-based contract creation configurator that assists purchasing professionals in authoring complex contracts. During authoring, Contract Expert takes users through a contract creation questionnaire and automatically adds needed clauses based on previously defined policy rules.

In addition to user answers, clause selection rules can also be based on the business terms and other values contained in the purchasing or sourcing document, such as purchasing category, payment term and agreed contract amount. Contract Expert allows users to author standards-compliant contracts with minimal legal department supervision. Buyers or contract administrators can choose to remove the clauses brought in by Contract Expert or select alternates during negotiation.

While Procurement Contracts provides all the necessary tools for authoring contracts that conform to your corporate standards, it is often convenient during negotiation and redlining to edit the contract offline using Microsoft Word synchronization. Procurement Contracts supports importing a Microsoft Word document and synchronizing the changes to a structured contract stored in the system. Modifications to the original contract can be reviewed before changes are accepted. This two-way integration with Microsoft Word streamlines the contract collaboration process involving the buyer, the contract administrator, the legal department and the supplier.

To improve future contract negotiations, or to comply with regulatory requirements, contract administrators or legal may need to periodically review and revise their contract standards clauses. Analyzing the contract language used in existing contracts is a critical step in effectively updating existing standards. Users can now search for all contracts where certain clauses are used, or have been modified. The search can be filtered by various criteria such as contracts with a specific supplier, contracts above a certain amount, contracts for one or all operating units, or contracts authored using a specific template. Information on the number of times a certain clause has been used or modified is also part of the results set.

Services Procurement (Schema POX)

Services Procurement enables complete control and oversight for services spending while further streamlining all aspects of the acquisition process for complex services. Services Procurement allows for the negotiation service contracts with an emphasis on the terms related to contract financing and progress payment arrangements. Work progress can be tracked against the agreed schedule in the contract. This module also processes payment requests.

Complex service contracts are characterized by their high dollar value and long lead times. These complex services include consulting, advertising, construction, research and development, and professional services. These services require complex negotiated contracts that often include complex payment arrangements. These arrangements can include progress payments based on cost, stage of completion or performance milestones, advances and recoupment of advances, and retainage and retainage release.

Release 12 supports complex services by allowing buyers to author, negotiate, execute and monitor contracts for complex services with one or more of these payment arrangements built into the contract. Suppliers can review the proposed complex contract payment terms online and submit their quotes accordingly. If permitted by the buying organization, suppliers can propose a different payment schedule, add payment milestones, request for additional advances, or change the retainage and financing terms as part of their quotes. When the contract is awarded, the agreed terms along with the payment schedule are transferred along with other contract terms to Purchasing for signature, execution and payment.

These complex contract payments can include progress payments based on cost, stage of completion or performance milestones, advances and recoupment of advances along with retainage and retainage release. In order to provide working capital to smaller contractors, buying organizations may often pay advances to these contractors right after contract signing, before any work or product delivery has been performed.

With this release, buying organizations can negotiate and finalize the terms of such advances, and ensure compliance to those terms. In order to track progress and release payments between the time the contract is signed and the final deliverable is completed; it is typical of the buying and selling parties to agree on a progress payment schedule. Buyers can negotiate with their contractors and incorporate a detailed progress payment schedule as part of the contract. The schedule consists of "pay items" which specify the work component, the associated dollar amount and due date for completion. The solution provides for maximum flexibility in defining these pay items based on the way progress needs to be measured.

Retainage represents funds withheld from payment to ensure that the supplier finishes work as agreed. The buying organization releases these funds only after verifying that the contractor has fulfilled all contractual obligations. Retainage is also called "retention" or "contractual withholds". Contract administrators can negotiate retainage terms with the supplier and capture these as a part of the contract. These terms include:

- **Retainage Rate** - Determines the percentage of the amount requested that will be withheld before releasing payments to the supplier.
- **Maximum Retainage Amount -** Puts a cap on the total amount that can be withheld from payments released to the supplier.

At the end of the project or when the agreed criteria are met, the withheld amount can be released upon receipt of a retainage release request from the supplier.

Managing the execution of complex services contracts presents unique challenges to the buying organization and the contractor due to their high-dollar values and long lead-times. One of the challenges is to accurately track and monitor progress as required by the contract before releasing progress payments. Oracle provides a streamlined process for contractors to report progress in the form of work confirmation requests, which can then be electronically routed for approval. Organizations can leverage the flexibility of the Approvals Management Engine to configure their business approval processes for Work Confirmation Requests. The solution allows online negotiation on the amount of work eligible for payment through multiple rounds of resubmissions of the work confirmation request until both parties agree and the request is approved.

The *i*Supplier Portal streamlines the process for managing these complex service contracts between the buying and supplying organizations. The portal provides contractors with the ability to check on the status of their contracts in real-time. Using the portal, they can look up progress status, billing/payment status, advance and retainage balances associated with their contracts. The portal extends process automation beyond the enterprise by allowing contractors to enter contract related transactions online. Such transactions include:

- Acknowledge or sign the contract before starting work
- Change requests including changes to the progress payment schedule
- Request to confirm work
- Request to release advance payments
- Request to release progress payments

*i*Supplier Portal extends process automation beyond the enterprise eliminating inefficiencies linked to paper-based processes.

PROCUREMENT SETUPS

In this new Release 12, the existing Oracle Purchasing setup forms use the new user interface. Several setup functions have also been enhanced, without losing any of the underlying functionality, so that purchasing modules are upgradeable without reconfiguration. Figure 75 shows the significant enhanced setup steps that use the new interface.

Define Approval Groups	Assign Approval Groups
Define Job and Category Association	Define Buyers
Define Purchasing options	Define Receiving options
Define Line Types	Define Document Types
Control Purchasing Periods	Setup Expense Account Rules
Define Hazard Classes	Define UN Numbers
Define Quality Inspection Codes	Material Status Control

Figure 75 – Forms that were replaced in Release 12.

DOCUMENT PUBLISHING ENHANCEMENTS

Oracle now allows buyers to control the application to meet the needs of the purchasing process and documents. These enhancements include the ability to:

- Apply and display names to document types
- Create styles for documents, especially for complex documents
- Display the document name based on style definition
- Limit line types for document types and styles
- Display corresponding attributes
- Display type in printed documents

Through reusable document styles, deploying organizations can turn on or off various Oracle Purchasing features, thereby simplifying the user interface. When a purchasing document is created using a document style, disabled features are hidden to simplify the user interface. For example, organizations can create a document style for a specific commodity, such as temporary labor. This document style optimizes field labels and association with categories and commodities. This simplifies purchase order entry by hiding regions/attributes that are only relevant for that commodity.

Also, document styles provide the ability to name purchasing documents appropriately to align more closely with the naming conventions of the deploying organization's business. In other words, the same purchasing document type (e.g., Standard Purchase Order) can assume different names based on the style applied. These names are exposed throughout the Work Center and to the supplier. Format for such documents were limited to a single layout template as configured in the Document Types Setup. Buying organizations can easily publish documents on demand using any predefined layout template. To generate a document using a certain layout, organizations simply provide the layout name as a runtime parameter while submitting the "PO Output" concurrent program.

SUMMARY

As part of the Global Business Release, Oracle has introduced a new user interface and numerous enhancements for the Procurement Suite, along with enhanced integration of the modules to provide more comprehensive support of the Procure-to-Pay process. Additional enhancements have also been added to the applications without losing any of the underlying functionality that made the purchasing modules upgradeable without reconfiguration. It is this functionality, missing in past releases, that has turned a set of modules into an integrated suite that supports the central global approach while providing functionality across multiple applications and operating units.

Coupled with this are greater efficiencies through automated processes, not only within a module, but also between modules. The key concept is that a many of the Procure-to-Pay processes can now be automated and human intervention should only be at the beginning of the process, when exceptions occur and when monitoring takes place. This allows better control of the decision-making process through increased global visibility. Also with the underlying functionality available to deploy a more robust accounting approach, procurement can now be configured differently. The new user interface also leverages MOAC, making it easier for procurement staff and system administrators to perform setups and document creation in multiple operating units in the context of a single application responsibility.

The next chapter discusses some of the new features and enhancements in the Supply Chain Products.

Supply Chain Management Products

The purpose of Supply Chain Management is to optimize revenue, minimize cost and give customers what they want, when they want it. The E-Business Suite Release 12 includes some noteworthy enhancements to Supply Chain Management, including changes to inventory convergence, secondary unit of measure pricing, Cost of Goods Sold (COGS) deferral, parallel pick releases, line level scheduling, integration of release rules with warehouse management, asset tracking, lot, genealogy and serial number controls, material workbench, and demand plans.

Inventory Convergence

E-Business Suite Release 12 has brought together Discrete (Core) and Oracle Process Manufacturing (OPM) inventories to provide an exchange in the two methodologies and bring more supply chain visibility to the enterprise (see Figures 76 and 77). Functionally there is an exchange in that OPM can now leverage features that weren't available until now, and vice versa. Technically, the inventories have converged in that they both use the `MTL-SYSTEM_ITEMS` table now.

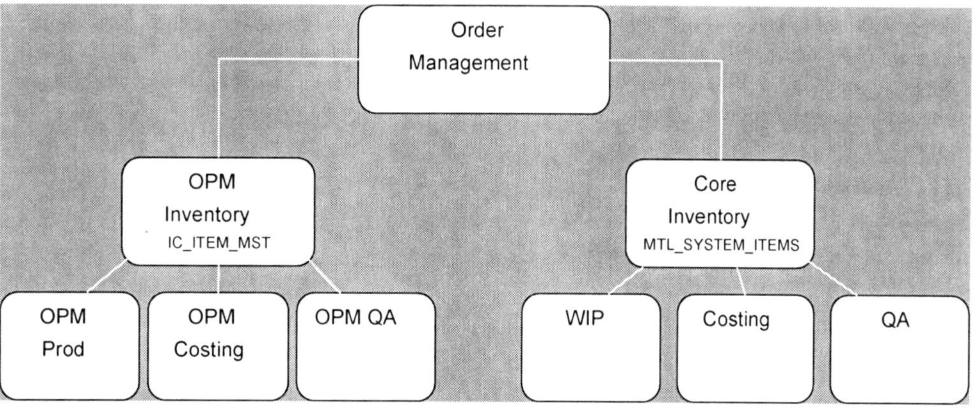

Figure 76 - Inventory Structure prior to E-Business Suite Release 12

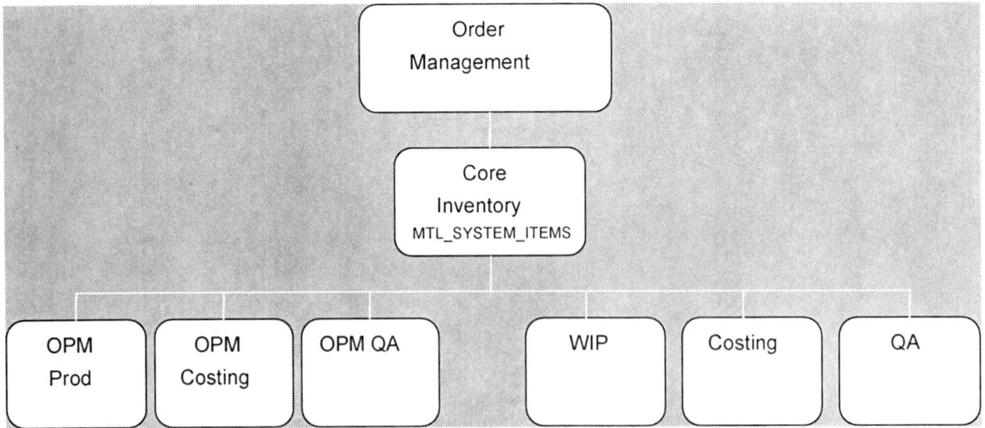

Figure 77 - E-Business Suite Release 12 Inventory Structure

Impact on Oracle Process Manufacturing (OPM)

Can't you just hear it now from the OPM'ers – "we had our own thing going on – we were happy with our own separate inventory – why paste us in with all those discrete inventory folks?" This is an excellent question from the OPM side of the room – and the answer may not be so obvious, but the Order Management and Enterprise Planning departments will enjoy increased visibility into on-hand quantities and a more complete view of the entire supply chain.

But before the OPM'ers storm out of the room, let's pause to think what integration with the E-Business Suite might mean. How about vendor-managed and consigned inventory? Maybe some consideration should be given to the benefits of reservations, kanban, min/max replenishment and physical inventory and cycle counting – is anyone's interest piqued yet? No? Well, the last point of interest might be the integration with Oracle Warehouse Management, which allows OPM'ers to leverage complex picking rules, license plates, putaway rules and task management.

Impact on Discrete Manufacturing

While the OPM'ers mull that over, let's turn our attention to the Discrete Manufacturing folks – what's in it for them? They are in store for dual unit of measure control for any item, advanced lot control, material status and enhanced inventory allocation rules, increased item search functionality and enhanced picking rules. While some of these features are more to support the OPM functionality, having on-hand quantities across the entire enterprise consolidated into one inventory is a useful feature for all parties! Add to that the fact that Order Management can now provide pricing on either unit of measure, and that transaction quantities, onhand balances, availability and reservations are carried in both units. Well, that's what we call visibility into the supply chain. How often does Order Management get a new feature that does not require a new form with countless fields on it? The added item search feature accomplishes that very thing (see Figure 78).

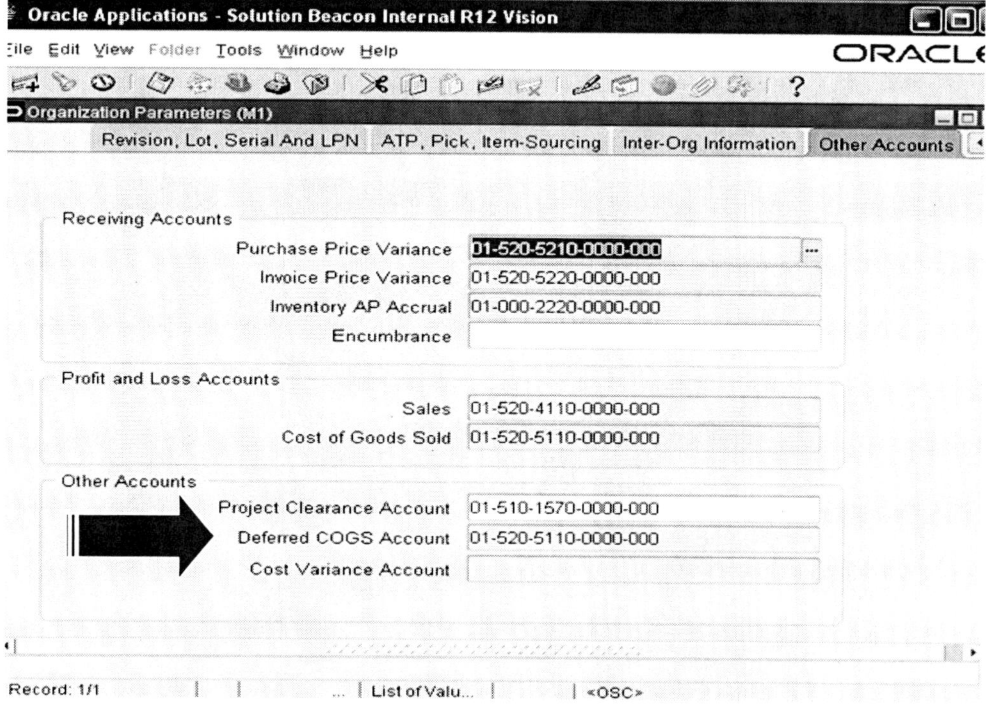

Figure 78 - Order Management gets a new item search capability

SECONDARY UNIT OF MEASURE PRICING

One of the benefits of inventory convergence is that there is a secondary unit of measure (UOM) available across the entire inventory, and upstream applications such as Order Management can integrate with this new feature. Order Management now provides the ability to price the secondary UOM. This has been a requirement for Process users, but Discrete users can now avail themselves of this feature should their product(s) lend themselves to being tracked in multiple units of measure.

COST OF GOODS SOLD (COGS) DEFERRAL

In business school, there is a foundational accounting case called "McDonald's Farm" about a farmer who grows crops. There are different revenue recognition scenarios whereby you are asked to expand on the accounting implications of each (i.e., revenues are recognized when the crops were harvested, or when they were taken to the grain silo, etc.) A lesson learned from that exercise is that revenue recognition is not always an easy proposition. The Matching Principle is a generally accepted accounting principle that goes hand in hand with revenue recognition and it is foundational for generation of income statements. Matching between the Accounts Receivable and Inventory subledgers is a difficult job to say the least, because there are a myriad of variables that can and will come up during the manufacturing, distribution and shipping processes.

Oracle has delivered the ability to specify a COGS deferral account (Figure 79). With this enhancement, the value of goods shipped from inventory can be put in a Deferred COGS account and as revenue is recognized, a matching percentage of the value of goods shipped from inventory will be moved from the Deferred COGS account to the COGS account, thus providing synchronization for matching purposes. The COGS deferral account can be "customized" to meet the business needs using the subledger accounting rules. There are even options to allow for customer acceptance.

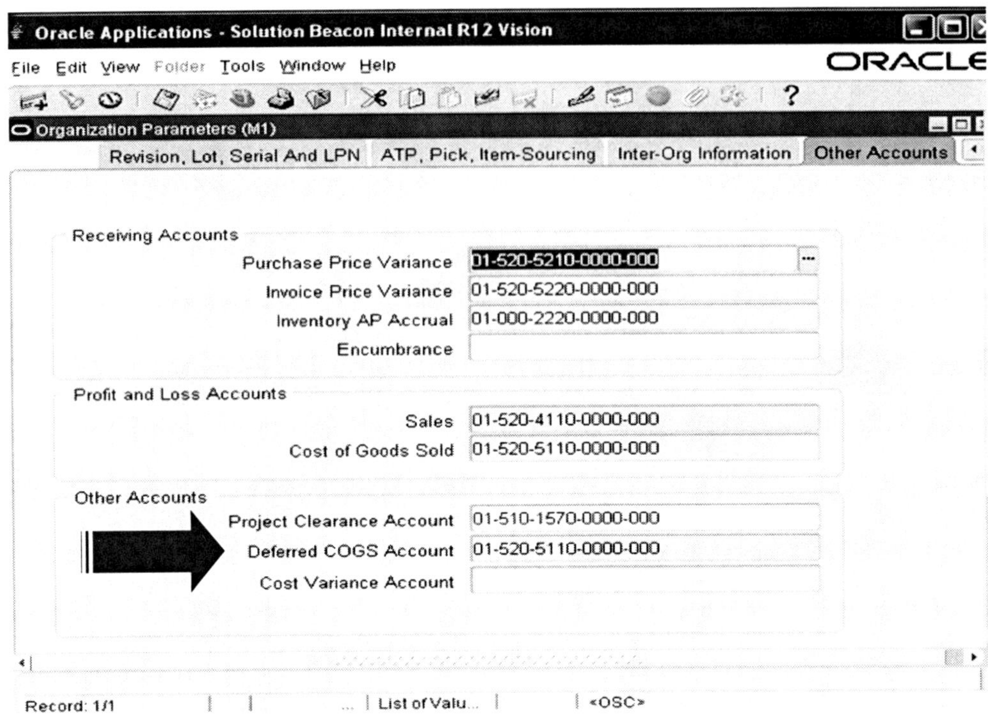

Figure 79 - A Deferred COGS Account can now be specified in E-Business Suite Release 12

PARALLEL PICK RELEASES

How can something be incompatible with itself? Well, it happens with Order Management, up until E-Business Suite Release 12, the "Pick Release" concurrent program was incompatible with itself, meaning that Oracle would only allow one execution of the pick release concurrent program to be run at any given time. Large manufacturing companies felt the brunt of this constraint in that deliveries were not being created as optimally as desired. Release 12 has removed this bottleneck and now allows multiple pick release processes to run concurrently at any given time.

LINE LEVEL SCHEDULING

New parameters have been added to the "Schedule Orders" concurrent program that allow scheduling at the line level of all lines that have yet to be scheduled or those lines that failed manual scheduling. The new parameters are Ordered Date Lo/Hi, Warehouse, Demand Class, Planning Priority, Shipment Priority, Line Type, Request Date Lo/Hi, Ship-To Location, Schedule Ship Date Lo/Hi, Schedule Arrival Date Lo/Hi, Booked, Scheduling Mode, Apply – Warehouse, Apply – Schedule Date, First Order By and Second Order By.

This flexibility will help companies better match their demand with their supply, especially when supply is not consistently available for all lines when an order is scheduled. If desired, a Warehouse or Schedule Date can also be specified at the time of scheduling or rescheduling.

Integration of Release Rules with Warehouse Management

Pick Release Rules can now contain cross dock criteria, task priorities and allocation methods, which can serve as integration defaults for work orders created for Oracle Warehouse Management System (WMS). These new elements allow work orders to be created at the same time product is being picked out of inventory. These work orders can then further instruct WMS on what to do with the picked inventory. This should provide efficiencies from both a time and effort perspective.

Asset Tracking Attributed in Inventory Transactions

As parts become more miniaturized, the ability to track these smaller sized parts can present challenges; however, the smaller size doesn't necessarily imply lower costs. Smaller, higher cost parts can cross asset dollar thresholds and if those parts are misplaced then both the balance sheet and the income statement are at higher levels of risk. To support parts movement within the warehouse, inventory transaction types in Release 12 can now require asset tracking locations to be entered as part of miscellaneous transactions. This will help track assets as they move from inventory and/or the warehouse to points beyond.

Improved Lot, Genealogy and Serial Number Controls

In today's environment where companies operate in a minefield of regulatory governance and where quality mistakes are tried in the court of public opinion, the ability to trace a product to its end assembly could be essential. Enter product genealogies. Genealogies link the final assembly to lots and/or serialized components manufactured or procured from suppliers so that if recalls should occur or some quality audit notices an unacceptable level of defects, then it is easier to reconstruct root cause of the problem.

To this end, Oracle Inventory has consolidated the lot and genealogy inquiries to provide a comprehensive view into product composition. Also, Discrete Manufacturing users can tie their WIP issue transactions to component lot and/or serial numbers to a parent assembly. If this parent relationship is used, users can determine product composition from the consolidated inquiries rather than being forced to change responsibilities over to WIP and examine the discrete transactions there. Also, E-Business Suite Release 12 Inventory will maintain the integrity of the genealogy in that only lots issued to a work order can be returned when a component return is performed for a lot-controlled item.

Material Workbench

Having better information on the inventory levels within a warehouse or across an organization can allow managers to make quick decisions about demand fulfillment across both of these spectrums. To this end, E-Business Suite Release 12 now provides three new material buckets - "on-hand," "receiving" and "inbound". These material buckets allow users to drill down into the individual transactions, including purchase orders, advanced shipping notices and internal sales orders. This can all be accomplished from one consolidated view on the Material Workbench.

Demand Plans

Internal sales orders can now be included in demand plans on an organizational basis and for those companies that have high number and/or high dollar amounts of sales orders. This enhancement will allow for a more comprehensive picture of demand. This should result in the construction of better forecasts and more accurate planning

Summary

Neither time nor space allow us to mention everything Oracle has engineered for Supply Chain – but hopefully, the enhancements that we've described give you a taste for why this product family has improved in Release 12.

Next, the new features and functionalities for the products that compose Customer Relationship Management will be explored.

Customer Relationship Management (CRM) Products

Customer Relationship Management (CRM) includes products which encompass the people, process and technology capabilities that enable companies to organize and manage their internal and external customer relationships. It entails implementing relevant IT systems and tools to automate and consolidate customer information. An effective CRM strategy is measured by how well it improves a company's bottom line and how much it increases customer and employee satisfaction.

From measuring marketing campaigns to automatically dispatching field technicians to remote locations, Oracle has more than 50 CRM-specific applications within Release 12 that help companies address every phase of the CRM cycle. This chapter will describe three sets of products: Service Execution, e-Commerce Orders and Oracle Content Management.

Service Execution

In Release 12, Oracle enhanced the Customer Service applications, specifically the Customer Support, Case Management and Field Service applications, to help companies manage touch points with a global customer base. Service Execution applications focus on driving revenue and customer loyalty by enabling delivery and service management capabilities.

Service Execution is composed of four modules: Field Service, Depot Repair, Spares Management, and Installed Base. Figure 80 shows the components of the Service Execution product family. The Field Service Core, Spares Management, and Depot Repair modules will be discussed in more detail.

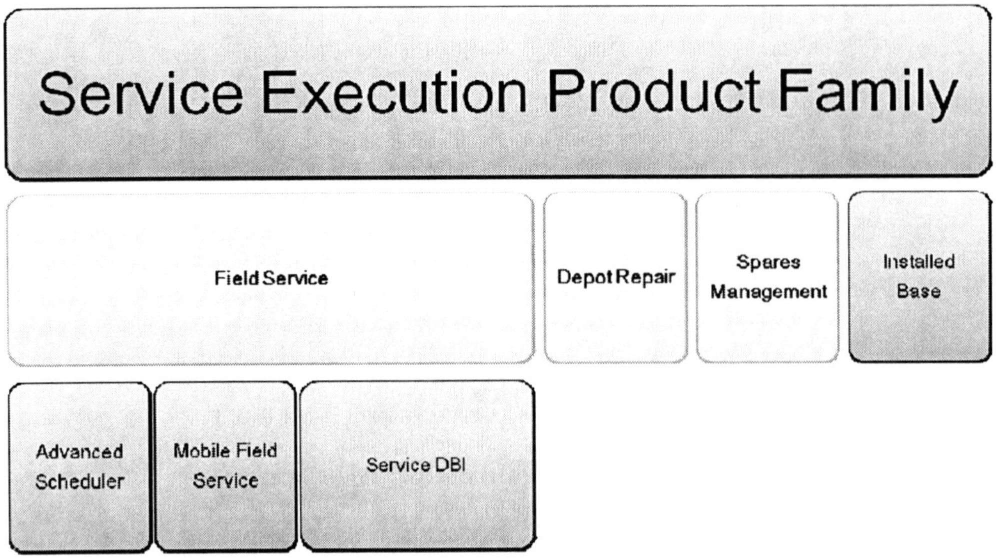

Service Execution Product Family

Field Service

Depot Repair

Spares Management

Installed Base

Advanced Scheduler

Mobile Field Service

Service DBI

Figure 80 – The Service Execution Product Family

Field Service Core

Using Oracle Field Service, companies can dispatch field technicians to service calls in remote locations. Field Service improves customer satisfaction by more accurately predicting a service delivery window for customers. Release 12 made improvements in four important areas in the Field Service Core to achieve the goals of increased customer satisfaction and improved application usability. New or improved functionality includes a Field Service Support dashboard, E-records and E-signatures that comply with 21 CFR Part 11, a Service Request data purge, and location time zone support.

Field Service Support Dashboard

The Field Service Support Dashboard (see Figure 81) is an example of how Release 12 seeks to improve usability. Notice that a Field Service Representative can now access and perform actions on multiple transactions in one form. The new dashboard also allows users to personalize the dashboard views to support their individual job roles. Expanded search capabilities give users quick access to the data they need. The portal integrates with other Service modules such as Install Base and Knowledge Base so that users do not have to navigate away from the dashboard to access these other modules. Finally, using Quick Links, users can create service requests, access spare parts information, and receive and return parts.

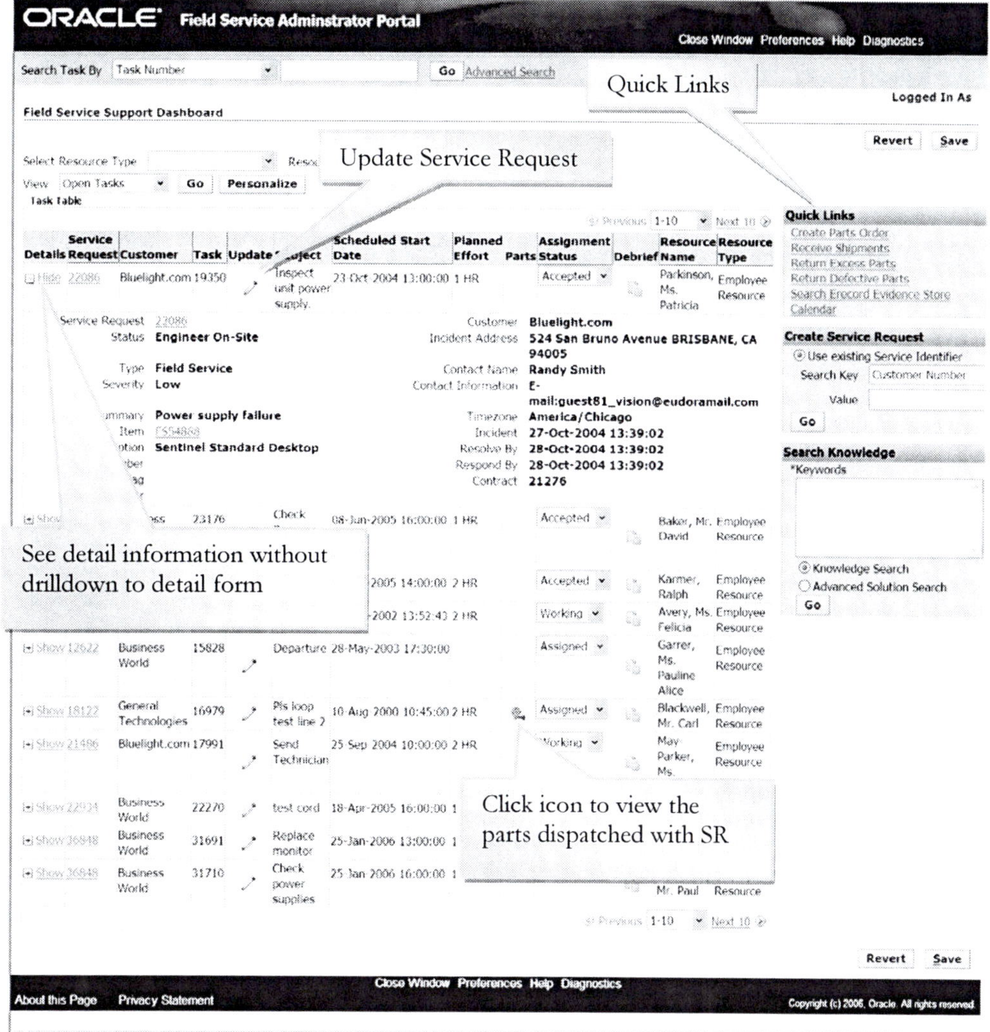

Figure 81 - The Field Service Support Dashboard

E-Records and E-Approvals

In Release 12, the Administrator and Technician Portals provide support for electronic records and approvals. This entails creating e-Records and capturing the approver ID and password. The key application transactions recorded are Task Debrief and Closure.

The regulatory standard, 21 CFR Part 11, deals with the FDA guidelines on electronic records and electronic signatures in the United States. It defines the criteria under which electronic records and signatures are considered trustworthy, reliable and equivalent to paper records. According to 21 CFR Part 11, the software application's role in the data management process is to guarantee and substantiate that manufactured product data is electronically captured, manipulated, extracted, and coded during the manufacturing of the product. All subject data and definitional objects (metadata) must have a complete audit trail. This new feature is supported in other Release 12 modules as well, including Inventory and Work in Process. Refer to www.fda.gov/ora/compliance_ref/part11 for a complete definition of 21 CFR Part 11.

To view transactions that have E-records and E-signatures, users can navigate by clicking on the quick link called Search E-record Evidence Store from the Field Service Support Dashboard. Figure 82 shows the E-record detail page. Notice that users can click on the links across the top of the form to jump quickly to different sections of the form. The E-signature can be seen in the Signature Details section. This E-document conforms to the standards set forth in 21 CFR Part 11 and would hold as much weight legally as a paper document.

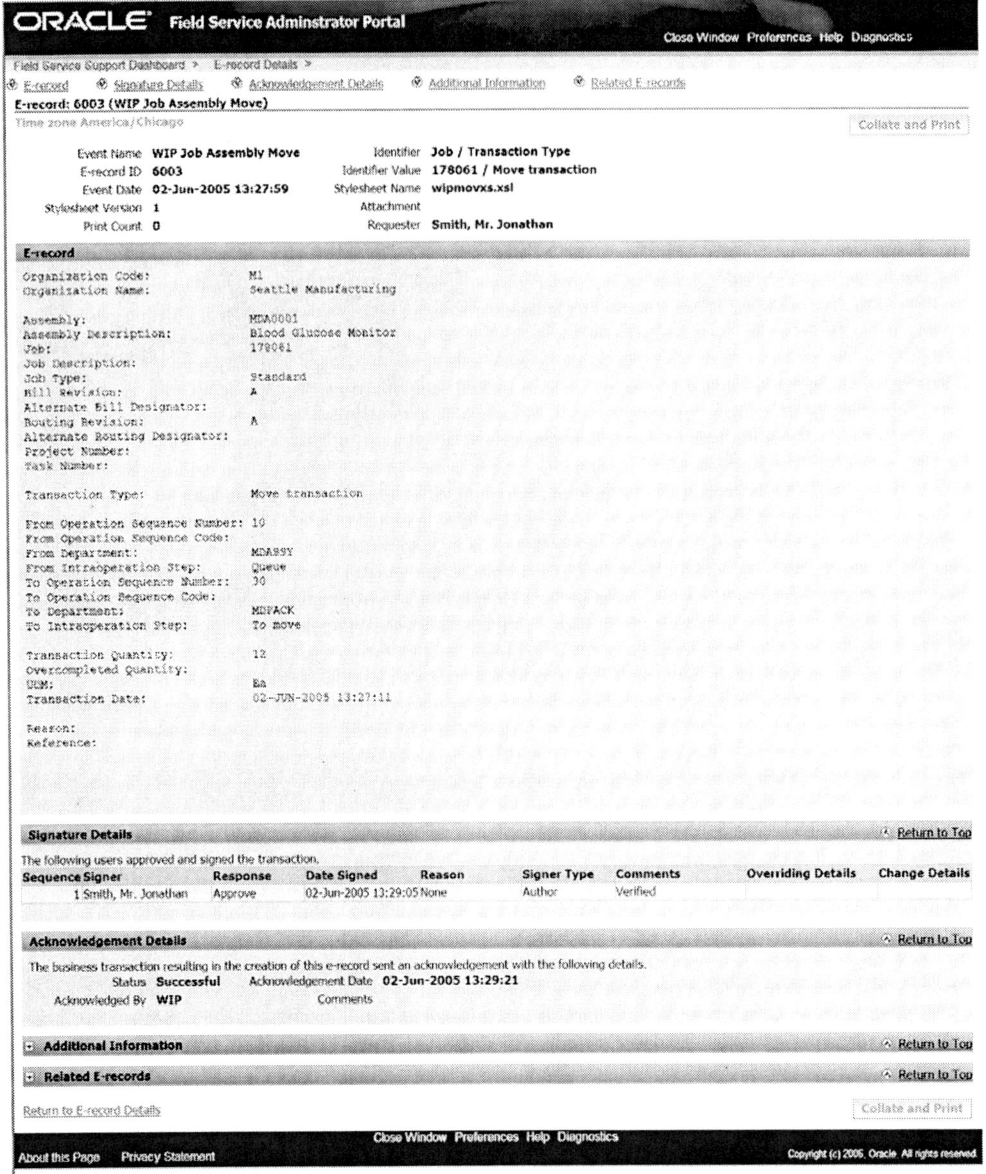

Figure 82 – An E-record with an E-signature

Setup

Follow these setup steps to enable E-records and E-signatures for your company:

- Set the Profile Options "EDR: E-records" to Yes and "EDR: E-Signatures" to Yes.

- Using the ERES Administrator responsibility, navigate to Administration Task > Setup (see Figure 83). Search for Transaction Name: "ERES Debrief Report Event". Set the transaction variable name "E-record Required" to Yes. Set the transaction variable name "E-signature Required" to Yes.
- The ERES workflow business event subscription should be "Enabled" and should be in "Synchronous mode".
- The Approval Management Engine should have one rule defined.

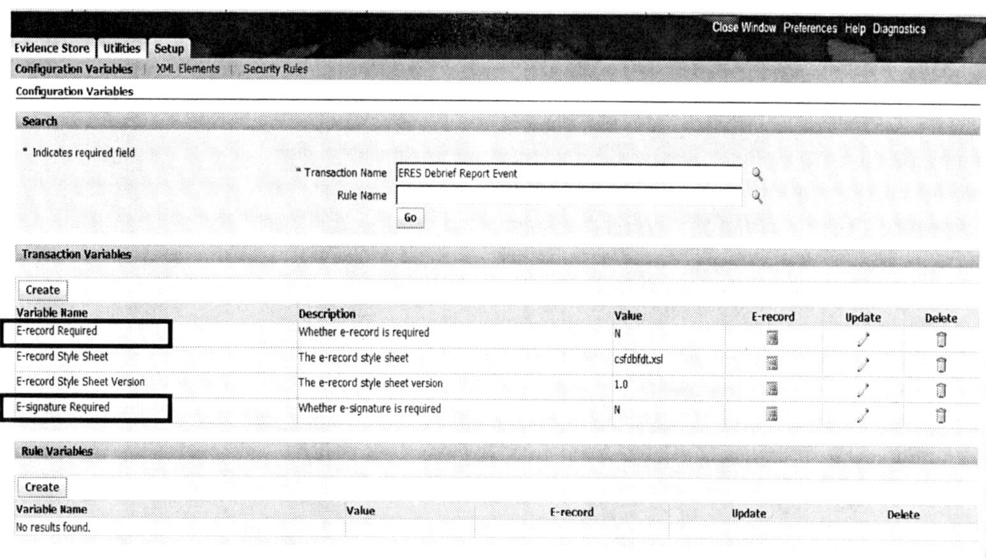

Figure 83 – One of the steps to enable E-records and E-signatures is to enable transaction variables

Service Requests Data Purge

With the "Service Request Data Purge" concurrent program, users can delete single or multiple service requests or cases. CRM System Administrators can manage system performance and downtime by controlling the size of the service request/case data. This feature also helps companies meet regulatory requirements related to the retention of customer or citizen information.

The purge program can be accessed from the Service responsibility and imposes certain restrictions. For example, a service request cannot be purged if it has open Depot Repair orders or open Field Service Tasks. To respect enabled security, the program will only purge service requests the user has permission to update under their current responsibility. Two service request types cannot be purged: Complex Maintenance Repair and Overhaul, and Enterprise Asset Maintenance. Finally, the program will not purge service requests with unsubmitted charge lines. Note: The purge program does not delete e-mails processed by the Oracle E-Mail Center. Users must run the Oracle E-mail purge program to accomplish this task.

If the service request is eligible for purging, all the information related to that service request will be deleted. All of the additional attribute types, including user-defined extensible attributes and Descriptive Flexfields, will be deleted. All service request tasks and notes, attachments, audits, messages, contact points, and charge lines will be deleted. Links from other service requests to the purged service request and links from knowledge base solutions to the purged service request will also be purged. Also, all information regarding the request in the Universal Work Queue will be purged.

The purge program records the purge information in a concurrent log file. If the "Maintain Audit" parameter is selected (see Figure 84), all of the detailed log information will be written to the `CS_INCIDENTS_PURGE_AUDIT_B` table. A SQL query must be written to retrieve data from table.

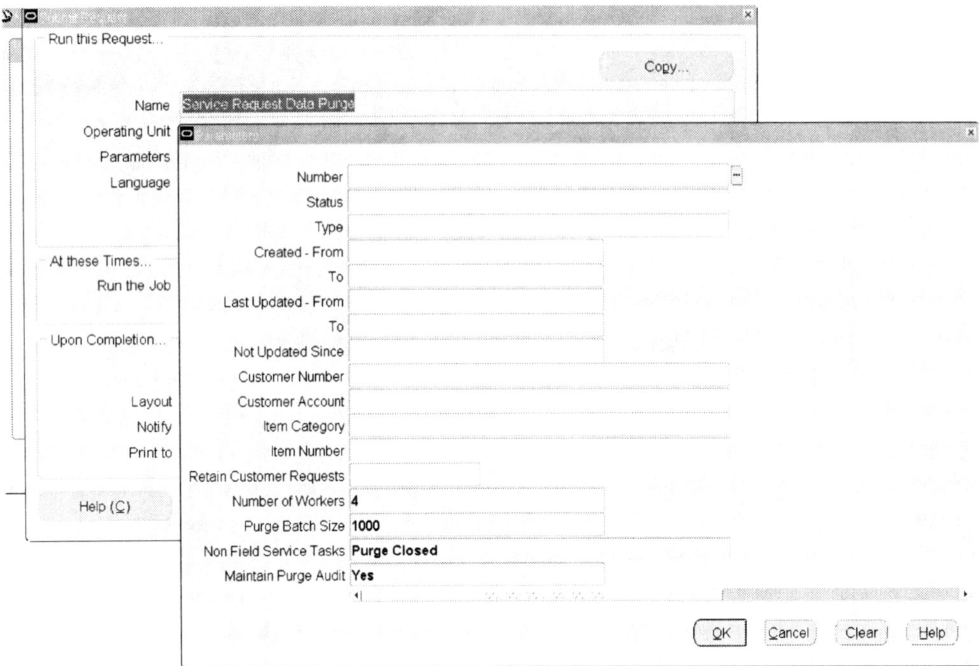

Figure 84 – Set the parameter, Maintain Purge Audit to Yes to retain information from purged service requests

Time Zone Support

In Release 12, all Field Service and related products provide, where appropriate, full support for Customer/Incident and Technician Time Zones. With this new capability, call center agents, dispatchers, managers and administrators can communicate with customers and field technicians in their local time zones. When multiple time zones are enabled, agents can view the dates and times in their own time zone. They can also indicate their own individual preference by setting a system profile at the user level. Agents will also be able to view the resolution and response times in the time zones of the incident address and the primary contact on the service request.

When creating a service request, agents will be able to specify the time zone whether they are entering an Agent Time Zone or Corporate Time Zone (see Figure 85).

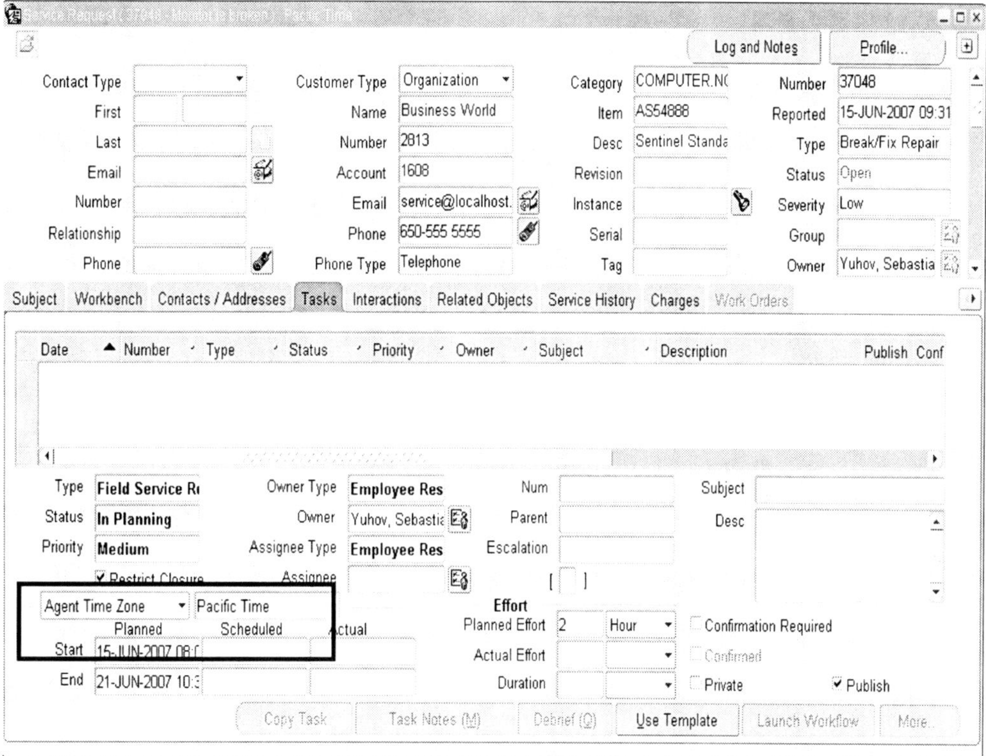

Figure 85 – When creating a service requests, users can specify time zone.

In the Oracle Forms Folder tool, users can display the time zone dependent fields they want on the Service Request tab of the Contact Center window and the Workbench tab of the Service Request window. Figure 86 shows the Workbench tab:

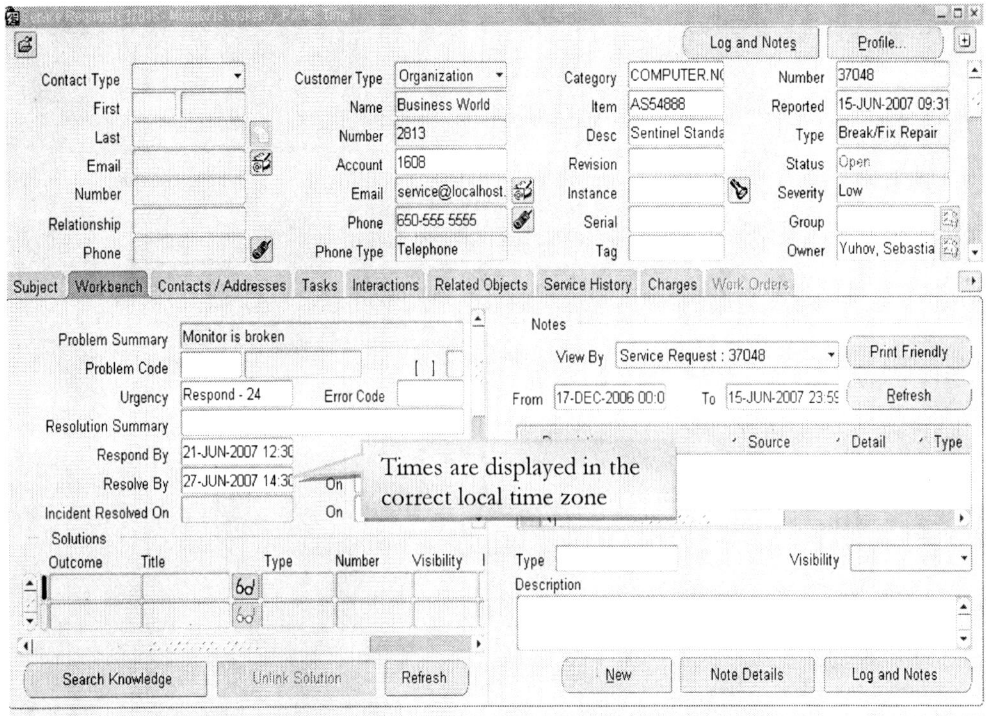

Figure 86– Time Zone Support

Setup

Multiple time zones can be enabled using the following Profile Options (see Figure 87):

- **Enable Timezone Conversions** - Setting this system Profile Option to "Yes" enables multiple time zone support for your application
- **Server Timezone -** This Profile Option specifies the server time zone and can be set only at the Site level.
- **Client Timezone -** This Profile Option specifies the agent time zone and can be set at all levels. Because this system profile can be set at the user level, agents can be instructed to set it themselves for the time zone they prefer.
- **Service Default value for Service Request -** This system Profile Option specifies the default time zone the application uses to display task dates

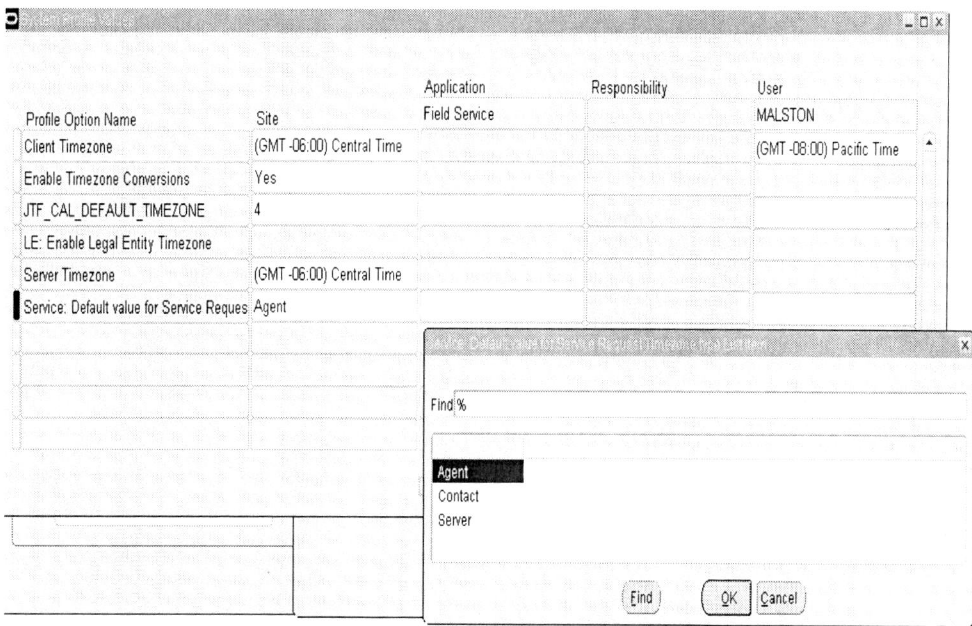

Figure 87 - Local Time Zone Profile Options

Spares Management

Moving on from the Field Service Core, Spares Management provides logistics and planning features that directly address the selection and delivery of spare parts to field locations. This application also fosters spares planning by giving technicians full access to multi-echelon stocking levels that are tied back to replenishment and fulfillment. Full use of this application helps to reduce inventory cost because it allows inventory management at a more granular level. Two new functional areas are external repair execution and warehouse replenishment planning.

External Repair Execution

New functionality in Release 12 provides the ability to manage and track defective parts throughout the entire vendor repair cycle. Vendor repair as well as internal repair are initiated from the new Spares Warehouse Replenishment Planning (WRP) module. The repair execution process takes repair planning recommendations from WRP and automatically creates the documents necessary to execute external repairs. Repair Suppliers in the field service supply chain can be both internal and external. External Repair Execution (ERE) provides automated functionality to execute a repair at an external repair supplier and replenish the field service warehouse with repaired parts based on need.

The external repair suppliers are defined using Sourcing Rules and linked to the warehouse being planned in WRP in Assignment Sets for replenishments. Users should create a Sourcing Rule for organizations where external repair suppliers should be used for the replenishment of the warehouse being planned (see Figure 88).

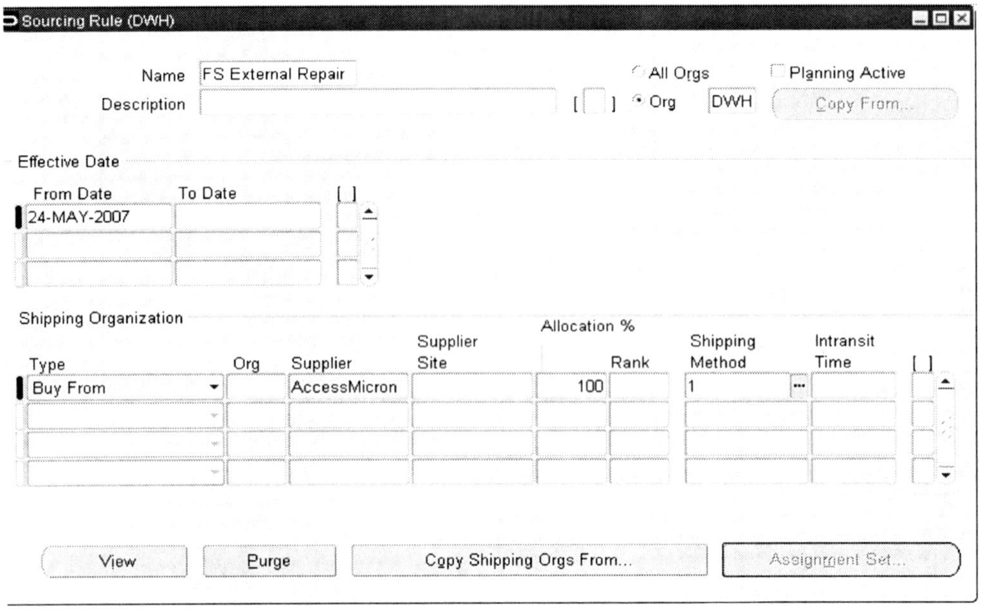

Figure 88 – Create a sourcing rule to support External Repair Execution

With this capability, buyers and planners can see the repair purchase order status and all transactions relating to the repair purchase order. Currently, most Field Service Planners rely on purchasing for this information. They are not able to see when the repaired item can be included in the on hand inventory supply.

Warehouse Replenishment Planning

Planning warehouse inventories in a field service supply chain experience requires a different approach compared to warehouses that support a manufacturing supply chain. Some of the more significant differences are higher volume of defective returns, higher volume of repair operation activities, redeployment of excess inventory, inventory plans driven by product component failure rates forecasts, and supersession of parts impacts.

The process for creating warehouse replenishment plans consists of running three concurrent programs. First, the "Usage for Recommendation" concurrent program updates usage history so forecasts calculations are based on the latest usage information. Next, the "Process Supercede Items" concurrent program collects the latest supersession information. The third concurrent program is "Create Warehouse Replenishment Data". This program is the planning engine that creates or regenerates plans for one or all warehouses.

The new Warehouse Replenishment Plan form, with time phased planning and a horizontal view is available with Release 12. After creating warehouse replenishment plans, users enter search criteria to retrieve plans and recommendations of interest. Figure 89 shows this new interface.

ORACLE

Diagnostics Preferences Help Close Window

Find Warehouse Replenishment Plans

Specify parameters and values to filter the data that is displayed in your results set.

Show table data when all conditions are met.

Show table data when any condition is met.

Organization is Dallas Manufacturing

Item is

Recommendation Type is Planned Orders Inside of Lead Time

Inventory Class is

Go Clear Add Another Inventory Class Add

Item	Description	Inventory Class	Planner	Recommendation Type	Date	Excess	Repair	New Buy	Excess Value	Repair Value	New Buy Value	Details
No search conducted.												

Diagnostics Preferences Help Close Window

About this Page Privacy Statement

Copyright (c) 2006, Oracle All rights reserved

Figure 89 – Use the Find Warehouse Replenished Plans screen to search for a specific plan

After retrieving plans that meet the search criteria, view the search results table to identify the specific plan. From the Warehouse Replenishment Plan form, a Field Service Planner can regenerate named plans, view dates horizontally (past, current, and future), create a forecast based on population and failure rate of parts, create a forecast of repairable returned parts, manually adjust or replace a forecast, determine projected planned orders by source type, and determine projected on-hand and available inventory balances.

Depot Repair

Depot Repair streamlines the entire in-house repair process, from the creation of the Return Material Authorization (RMA) to billing and shipment of the repaired product back to the customer. Technicians use a workbench to initiate RMAs and other repair activities, while customers are able to minimize down time with exchanges and loaners while products are serviced. Some of the improvements in the Depot Repair module include changes to repair flow processing, high volume processing, logistics, and repair management.

Repair Flow Processing

In earlier releases of Depot Repair, only repair statuses existed to categorize repair order progress. There were four seeded repair statuses - Draft, Open, Hold, Closed - and they were not extensible. This concept has been extended to allow statuses to be defined within states. The current states correspond to the earlier statuses. Users can now define many lower-level statuses within the new states that have workflow capabilities. In Figure 90, new statuses "In Process" and "Complete" have been defined.

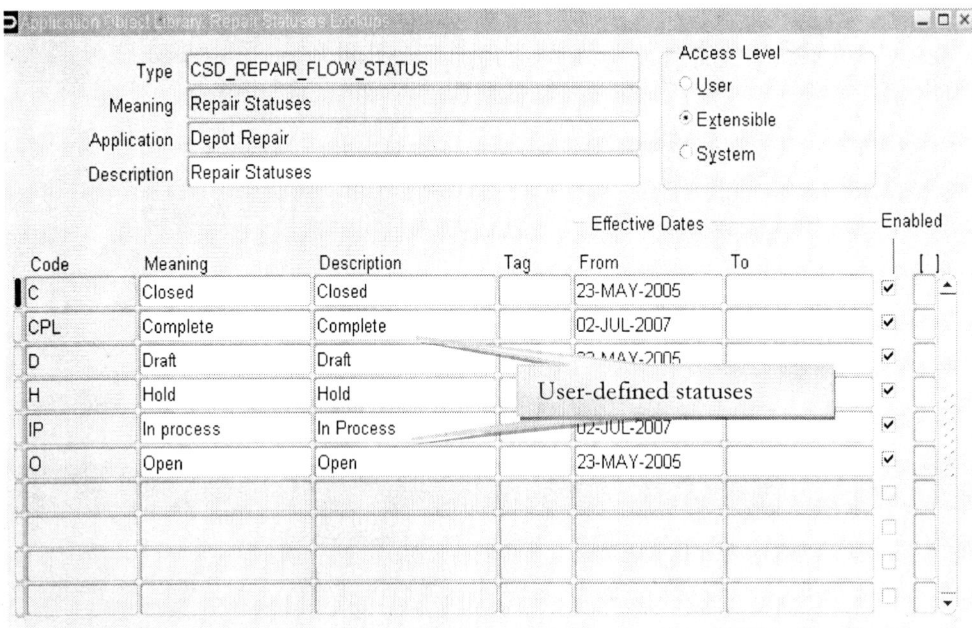

Type CSD_REPAIR_FLOW_STATUS
Meaning Repair Statuses
Application Depot Repair
Description Repair Statuses
Access Level: User / Extensible / System

Code	Meaning	Description	Tag	Effective Dates From	To	Enabled
C	Closed	Closed		23-MAY-2005		✓
CPL	Complete	Complete		02-JUL-2007		✓
D	Draft	Draft				✓
H	Hold	Hold				✓
IP	In process	In Process		02-JUL-2007		✓
O	Open	Open		23-MAY-2005		✓

Figure 90 – Release 12 supports user-defined statuses

Once the new statuses are defined, they are then assign to one of the seeded states – Draft, Open, Hold, and Closed (see Figure 91) through the Repair Order Status Set-Up form. Each status associated with a state inherits the limitations that are associated with that state. Statuses associated with the Hold or Closed states restrict users as to what operations they can perform. Notice that more than one status can be assigned to a state.

Repair Order Status Set Up

Status	Description	External Display Status	State	Seeded Flag
Closed	Closed		Closed	✓
Hold	Hold		Hold	✓
In process	In Process		Open	
Open	Open		Open	✓
Complete	Complete		Open	

Save Close

Figure 91 – Statuses can be assigned to one or more states

In addition, users can create custom repair status transitions. A Repair Order Status Transition is the definition of two repair order statuses, the Current Status and the Next Status. For each repair type, a Start Status and one or more Repair Status transitions must be defined. These transitions determine the only allowable status transitions for the given repair type. Figure 92 shows the setup of repair transitions for the Advance Exchange repair type. Notice that Workflows can also be associated with transitions.

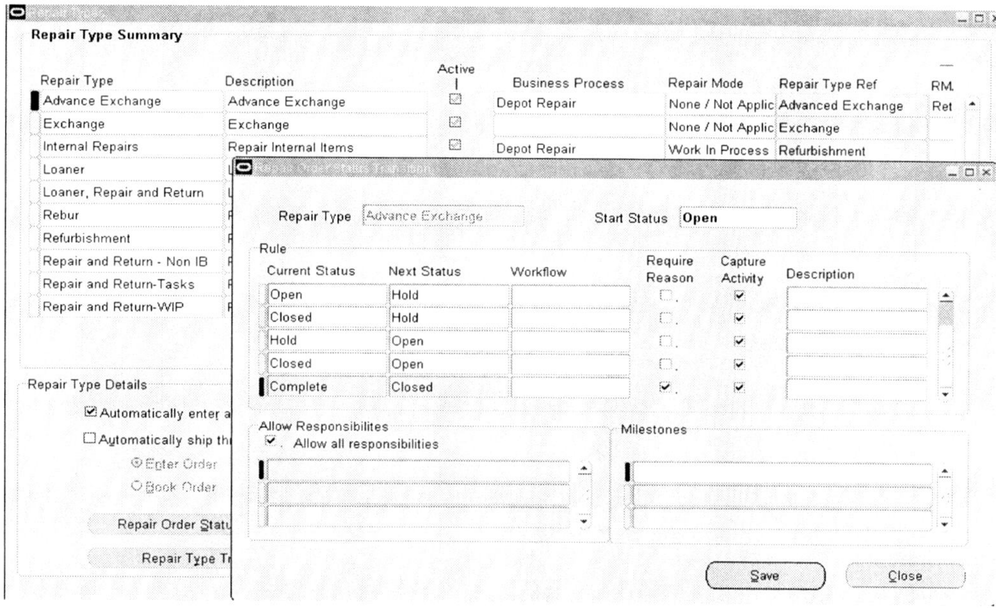

Figure 92 – Defining custom repair status transitions

Users can also change from one repair type to another during the course of a repair. In this situation, when a repair order status has been defined as associated to other repair types, and one repair order has the appropriate common status, the repair type of the repair order can be updated to any of the other repair types. For example, a user defines a status of "In Repair" for the repair type "Repair and Return" and for "Loaner, Repair and Return". The repair type of a repair order, whose repair type is currently "Repair and Return" and whose status is "In Repair", can be updated to "Loaner, Repair and Return". Note: Repair Type Transitions do not add, delete, nor default any logistic lines. After a repair type transition is performed on a repair order, users must perform manual adjustments to logistic lines, if the organization processes require this.

High Volume Processing

High volume repair is an enhancement to the standard repair and return process. It automates and facilitates the creation of work orders, procuring and issuing materials, and assigning resources with minimal input and decision-making from a repair technician. User interfaces now exist that focus on the repair technician role, as opposed to the customer service and material handler roles.

This new user interface enables a repair technician to perform various functions from one form as shown in Figure 93.

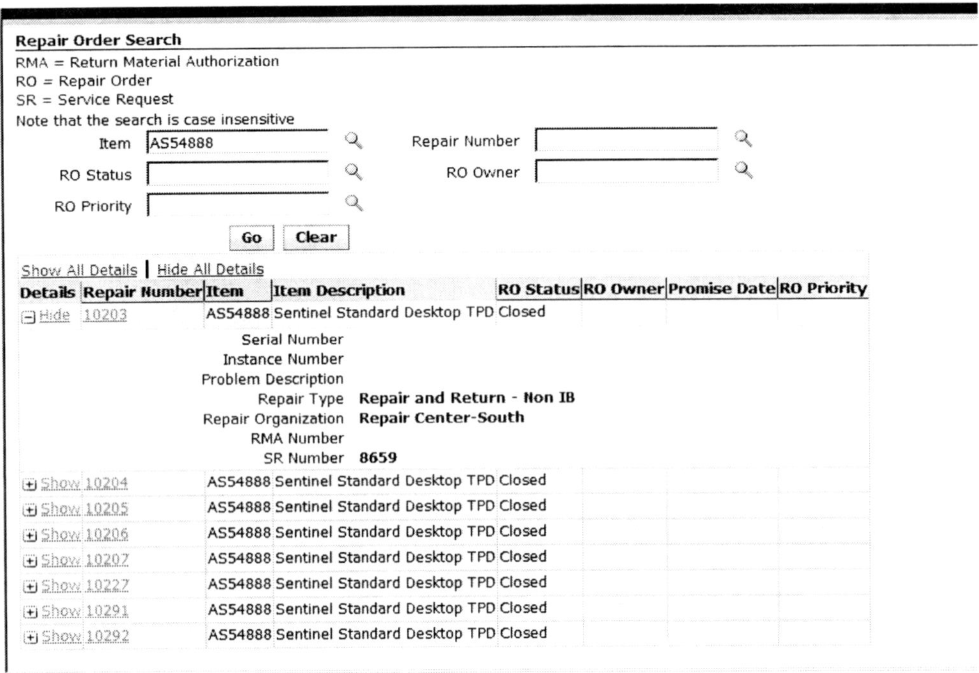

Figure 93 – The Repair Order Search screen

Repair technicians can drill down by clicking on the associated Repair Number link. From the detail screen (see Figure 94), users can query for recommended services, generate jobs, and update statuses with one click of a button.

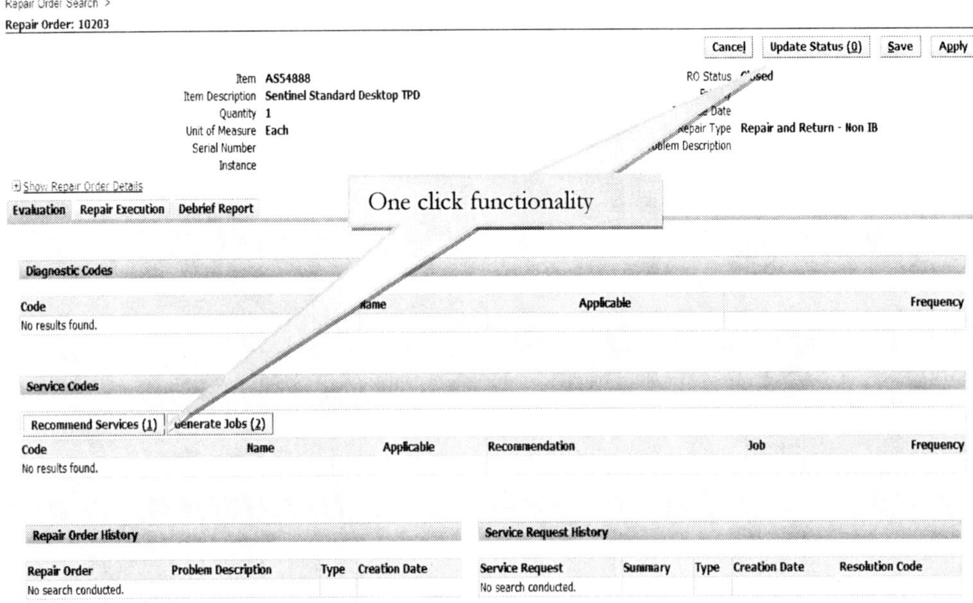

Figure 94 – Access functionality with one click of the button

This is another example of how Oracle is striving to increase usability. This functionality is available only for "Repair and Return" Repair Types. If Service Codes are used, the system can make recommendations. Depot Repair provides users with statistics of the most common materials and resources used in previous repair orders for the same item.

Enhanced Logistics

Release 12 has a couple of areas that have been enhanced in the logistics area. Additional line-level logistics capabilities enable greater functionality and flexibility for a given repair order. Also, improved bulk receiving capabilities enable quantities of serialized items to be received quickly.

Line-level Logistics

With the enhanced line-level capabilities, users now have more visibility to help manage at the Depot Repair Order level rather than when the order becomes a sales order. Line-level warehouse and subinventory selection, detailed line-level status with display of the order, and shipping status are all available. Figures 95 and 96 show the data that is now displayed on the logistics tab of the Repair Orders form.

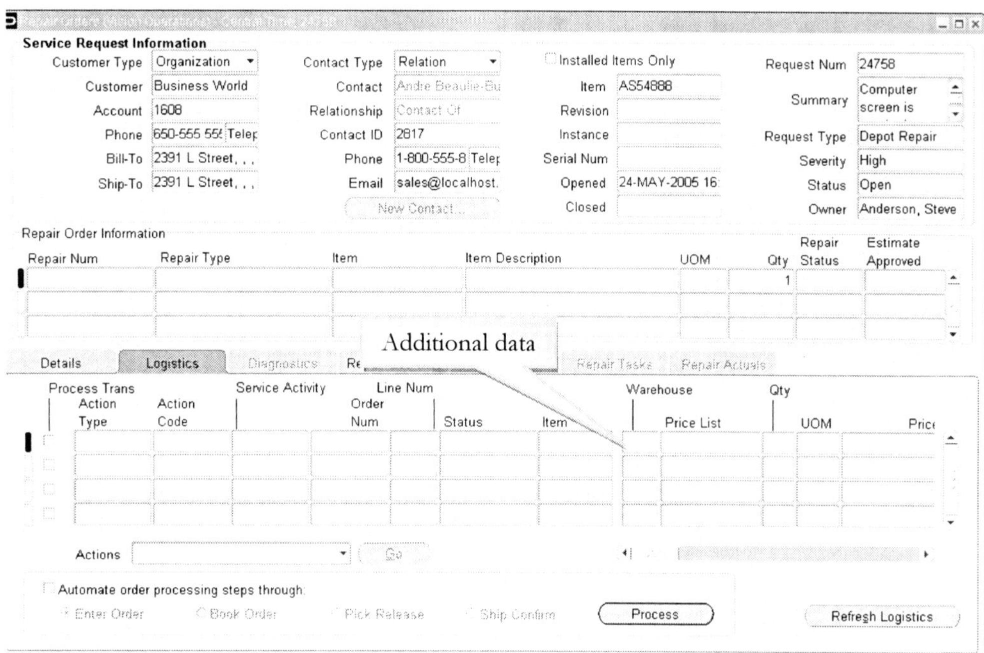

Figure 95 – Additional line-level logistics provides greater visibility

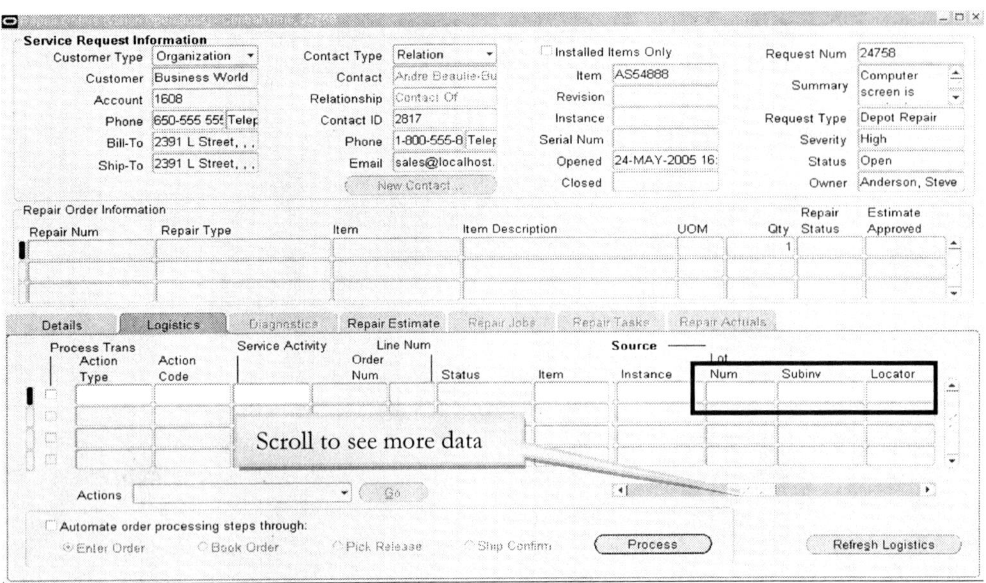

Figure 96 – The Lot Num displays the item Lot Number, for lot controlled items. Subinv displays the subinventory into which the item is received for Return lines and subinventory from which the item is shipped for Ship lines. Locator: displays the Locator information if the item is Locator controlled.

Bulk Receiving

With improved bulk receiving users can generate the service requests, repair orders and RMAs, and receive items into inventory with minimal button clicks. The general principle behind bulk receiving is to enable users to record the information required to process repair order items as easily as possible when they arrive in the depot without an RMA. Generally, the bulk receiving function will be used to create a batch of items per customer per shipment.

In order to perform batch receiving, execute the following steps in the Bulk Receiving form shown in Figure 97:

Enter either the customer account number or a service contract number – Depot Repair derives the account number.

For each item, enter as much of the following data as possible

- Item Name
- Serial Number, for serialized items
- Quantity (required)
- UOM (if the UOM is not entered, the primary UOM of the item is derived)

Click Process to process the batch

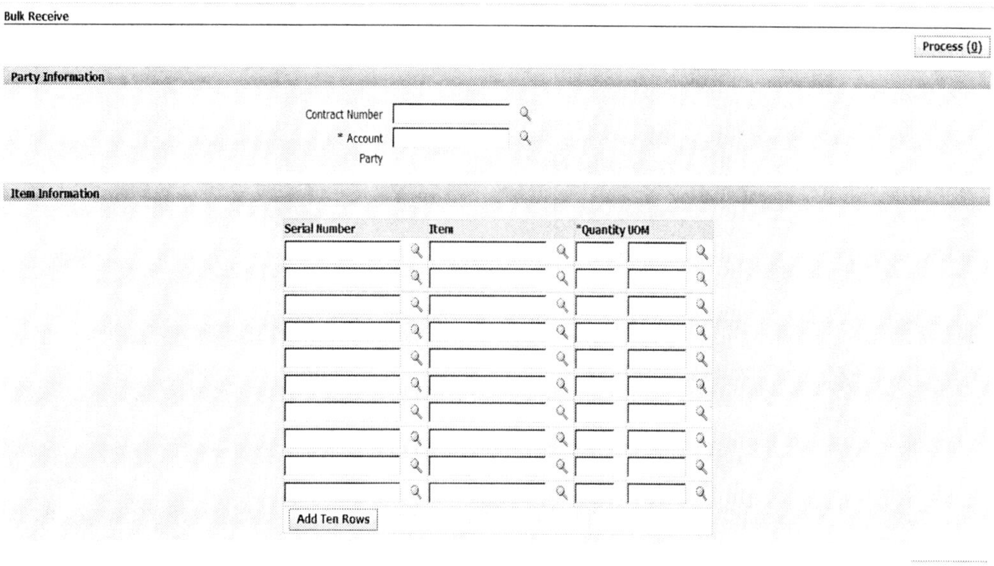

Bulk Receive

Process (0)

Party Information

Contract Number
* Account
Party

Item Information

Serial Number	Item	*Quantity	UOM

Add Ten Rows

Figure 97 – The Bulk Receiving form

When the process button is pressed, the "Depot Repair Bulk Receive Item" concurrent program is submitted to create the following objects for each batch of items: one service request, a repair order and an RMA for each item. The concurrent request will also attempt to auto-receive the items. When an item is auto-received, its status in the return line in the Logistics tab of the Depot Repair Workbench is set to "Received".

Enhanced Repair Management

In Task mode, enhancements include the ability for quality results input for a task-based repair. Work done to completed repairs complies with electronic record and signature regulatory requirements. Task mode provides an alternate repair process that is intended to manage simple repair work that does not require extensive tracking or management processes. After task completion, the technician uses the "Debrief Report" in Oracle Depot Repair to log the material, labor, and expense transactions. Users can assign Oracle Quality collection plans to tasks through setups in the Oracle Quality module. Depot Repair provides E-records and E-signature (ERES) functionality in Task mode via the Debrief screen for each Task. In WIP mode, the ability for repair job resource assignment from Depot Workbench is now available. In the Repair Execution tab, you can add materials and resources to jobs. Figure 98 highlights the Repair Execution tab on the Repair Order.

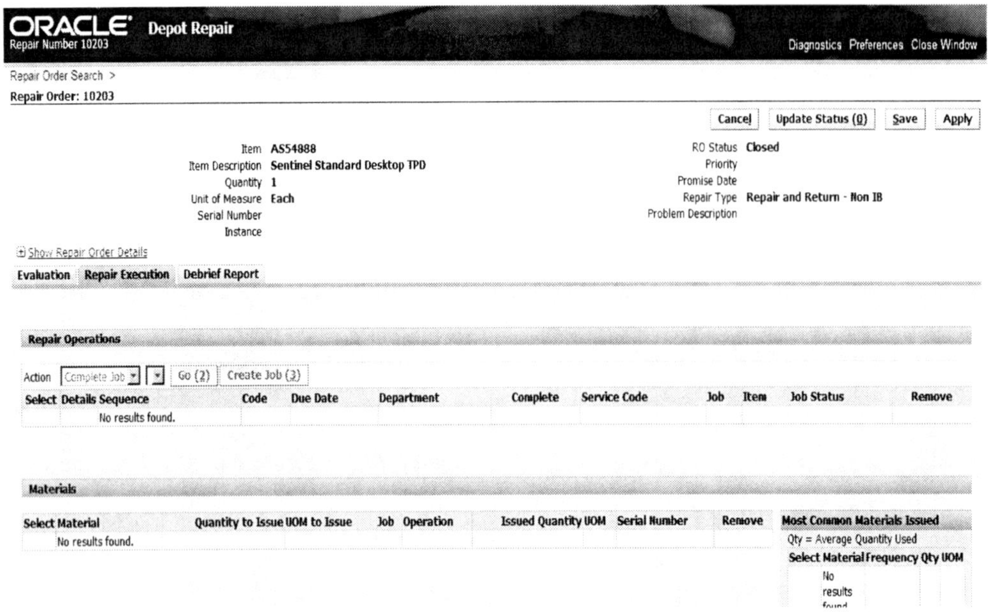

Figure 98 – The Repair Execution tab on the Repair Order form

Summary

Many benefits to an enterprise can be derived from implementing Release 12 Service Execution. With the improved Field Service Core, better response time and call tracking means offering customers better customer service. This improves the probability of selling aftermarket services to an existing customer base. Enhanced logistics reduces the time it takes in the repair and return cycle by allowing more of the transactions to take place and be recorded by the person actually performing the repair. Faster processing time means a more streamlined and efficient process for initiating billing. Similarly, improved bulk receiving and high volume processing enable organizations to shorten the cycle of realizing revenue. Decreased service delivery costs can be realized by understanding where the optimal location for delivering service parts to meet field service demands has a direct impact on decreasing and organizations delivery costs. External Repair Execution allows companies to manage external vendors' repairs to facilitate replenishment of warehouses. Finally, reducing trunk inventory is always a challenge in a Field Service Organization where most of the time the high value inventory is out of the spare parts loop. Spares Management helps manage this inventory and contributes to better inventory planning.

E-Commerce Orders

Using the internet as a sales channel has become an absolute necessity for enterprises hoping to compete in today's global marketplace. e-Commerce is a general industry term that emphasizes the complete integration of the global internet into a "go-to market strategy and operational basis" for processing customer sales orders. Figure 99 shows the complete integration of Oracle modules in the e-Commerce environment. iStore is seamlessly integrated with Oracle's CRM and ERP applications, providing everything necessary to sell products and services in a secure and user-friendly environment. iStore is a business-to-business (B2B) or business-to-consumer (B2C) end user module used to create sales orders, access quotes and provide a web based sales channel for end users. It integrates with both marketing campaigns and the field service quotation process. Field Sales is a web based remote sales representative tool used to generate quotes, and is linked to quotes and marketing campaigns. Telesales is an "inside sales desk" used to coordinate all sales related activities and provide a 360 degree customer profile.

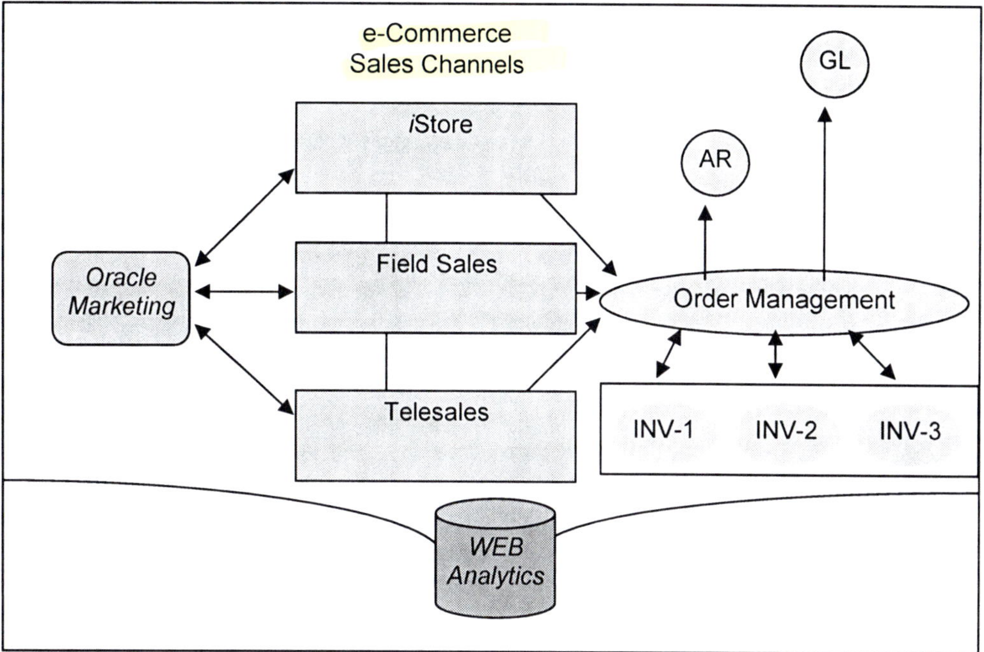

Figure 99 - Major Integration Points for e-Commerce Orders

*i*Store

Oracle's *i*Store is an electronic commerce application that enables companies to build, manage, and personalize powerful, global and scalable internet storefronts into a total sales management strategy. This includes integration with field sales, quoting and marketing applications into one seamless "internet sales strategy".

The major functional attributes of *i*Store include:

- An electronic commerce application that companies can use to build, manage, and personalize powerful and scaleable global internet storefronts
- Complete order and inventory management capabilities
- Support for the sales process, from lead generation to post-sales support
- Integration with Oracle Marketing to effectively target and personalize offers to the most profitable customers and more quickly translate store visits into actual orders

*i*Store's key features include sales assistance, the ability to publish quotes to specialty stores, and the ability to provide terms and conditions based on the items in each shopping cart. Sales representatives can download, change and upload quotes. They can also upload leads. *i*Store includes customer event tracking, deep link functionality, on-line return enhancements and web analytics. Unlike basic "web stores", *i*Store has advanced cart features that allow customers to ask for live sales assistance, apply promotion codes and check for product availability. The opportunity to cross-sell and up-sell is tied to a compelling and easy to use user interface. Among the most important aspects of any e-Commerce application is the user experience. The designers of Release 12 made several improvements aimed at improving the user experience, including a focus on the check out experience. Oracle incorporated an express single page check out so experienced users within B2B can use *i*Store to quickly place orders for multiple products. Checkout processes are brief and efficient, which decreases cart abandonment. The B2C checkout uses a single page. *i*Store even allows users to specify the "end-customer", which makes it possible to do drop-shipments. Also, Oracle incorporated a "check out train" for the B2C environment so that inexperienced casual users can follow a simple flow chart process to complete the checkout. Users can even skip steps, since they can see all the steps that they might take.

Both the B2B and B2C environments benefit from improvements in statement addresses, contracts integration and the use of credit card verification (CVV) procedures. Finally, checkout enhancements include a single order review page. The new order review page displays complete order information, including end customer information and additional information, if enabled. The user can change shipping, billing, end customer and additional information before placing an order. The order header information is organized in two columns and displays additional information and end customer information with the shipping and billing information. Users can click the navigation link at the bottom of the page to go back to the order summary page. Order tracker improvements to the order detail review page follow the same model used for the order review page. Searches are quick, intuitive and accurate. Oracle has also improved customer returns processing. These improvements make the customer experience increasingly positive.

Release 12 has also insured more reliability in account creation by incorporating self-service account creation, which ensures that typical errors like account duplication and accidental deletion do not occur. Users can also create their own usernames and passwords instead of being given a username-password pair that they have to modify.

With these improvements at their fingertips, customers will be inclined to transact online more often, which means they benefit from all aspects of e-Commerce, including 24/7 availability, zero error order capture, and access to post-purchase services.

Integration with Procurement

An important Release 12 improvement is *i*Store's integration with a customer's procurement system. Integration with third party procurement systems means that customers can use a "punch out" from their internet procurement system. They shop on *i*Store while still logged into their own procurement environment. From there the customer can have the check out cart automatically populate their procurement requisitions. This feature eliminates the need to maintain remote catalog exchanges while substantially increasing the volume and purchases of each storefront visit.

Integration with Oracle Quoting

The integration of *i*Store with Oracle Quoting allows quote sharing, published quotes, terms and conditions and customer assistance. Quoting is the sales application provides capabilities to automate and manage the information exchange and negotiation in the pre-sales quoting process. Quoting integrates quote creation straight into the *i*Store sales process. It helps increase the speed and efficiency of the sales process by reducing redundant data entries and approval workflows to insure business requirements compliance throughout the entire order to cash cycle. The application accomplishes this by:

- Integrating with the sales opportunity to provide a seamless information transfer of lead to opportunity to quote to cash
- Providing a robust set of product selection, configuration and pricing options to match valid products/services to customer needs
- Providing a complete approval workflow to ensure that every quote receives the correct scrutiny and compliance to business requirements and objectives
- Integrating with Order Management to provide a direct connection to the downstream order-to-cash process

Integration with Sales Assistance and Sales Contracts

The integration of *i*Store and the Sales Assistance application begins when a customer requests help from the shopping cart or checkout pages. For this integration to occur, Sales Assistance must be integrated with Quoting. Also, a negotiation flow must be integrated with Sales Contracts.

By insuring the transactional compliance of quotes and orders to agreed upon terms and conditions, data and information is appropriately shared and incorrect orders do not affect transactional operations downstream. Remote sales representatives can create quotes and publish them to prospects via *i*Store, which encourages up selling and cross-selling opportunities. In addition, quotes can automatically adhere to terms and conditions associated with *i*Store by means of sales contracts.

Summary

Oracle's e-Commerce solution provides a seamless and efficient way to coordinate product maintenance and to market strategies in one environment. This increase in the speed of new product introduction provides complete analytics for campaign effectiveness. Enabling campaign tracking and analytics insures we can constantly improve our market and sales strategies based on past experience. Finally, accurate and timely information – what sells, when does it sell, and to whom – is a key component to a successful sales environment. It permits businesses to target limited resources to the most effective use of limited resources.

ORACLE CONTENT MANAGEMENT (SCHEMA IBC)

The Applications have traditionally focused on dealing with structured databases that use predefined tables made up of fields, rows and columns. However, enterprises use more than just structured data to do business. Enterprises have information embedded in web pages, documents, spreadsheets, images and e-mail archives. Managing all this "unstructured" data has proven difficult and expensive, particularly because this type of "content" has grown exponentially over the past several years. Firms now need applications that can help organize, control, track and secure this information.

In Release 12, Oracle added to a module called Oracle Content Management (OCM) that is incorporated into the Oracle iStore, Marketing and Proposals modules. OCM provides a tool to organize "content" such as product documentation, problem resolutions, and training documents into a structured format that can be used from a centralized repository to provide online help and product support.

Key benefits include the ability to search and browse an entire knowledge base using multiple criteria and search attributes. Users can search multiple structured repositories using a single "unified" search command. Oracle Content Management supports multiple languages by translating content and sharing it with multinational sites. Also, users can download documentation and use it in third party applications. Since the data is contained in a centralized repository, security profiles can be used to limit access to certain information.

Implementing Oracle Content Manager

To implement Oracle Content Manager (OCM) successfully, Oracle strongly recommends executing these tasks in this order:

Set Profile Options

The Applications System Administrator enables data security by setting the Profile Option "IBC: Use Access Control" to Yes at the Site Level (see Figure 100).

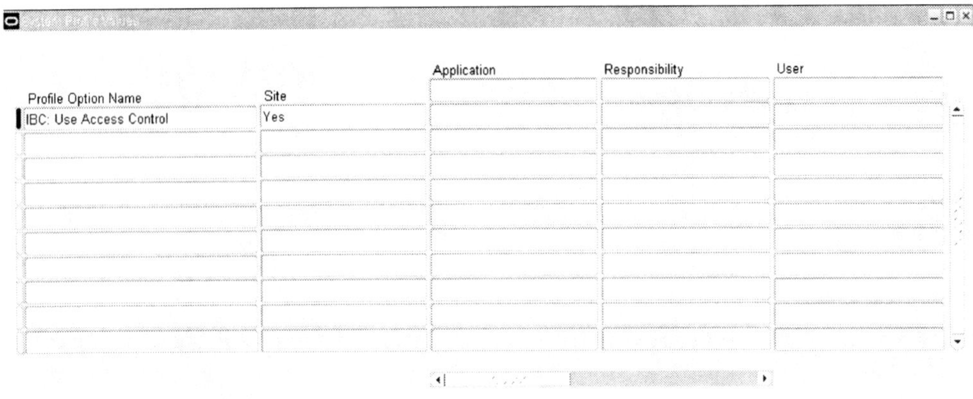

Figure 100 – Set IBC: Use Access Control to Yes

Set up OCM Users

To use OCM, at least one user must be granted the Content Super User responsibility. This defines the user as an administrator with all the privileges in the OCM application. It is the Content Super User's job to create and assign access control on folders for users. To do so, organizations need to categorize users according to the functions they will perform in OCM. Users can be administrators, content item creators, approvers, or translators.

Once assigned the correct responsibilities, verify that the user was created successfully by launching the OCM User Interface (see Figure 101) by using the Content Super User responsibility and navigating to the Content tab.

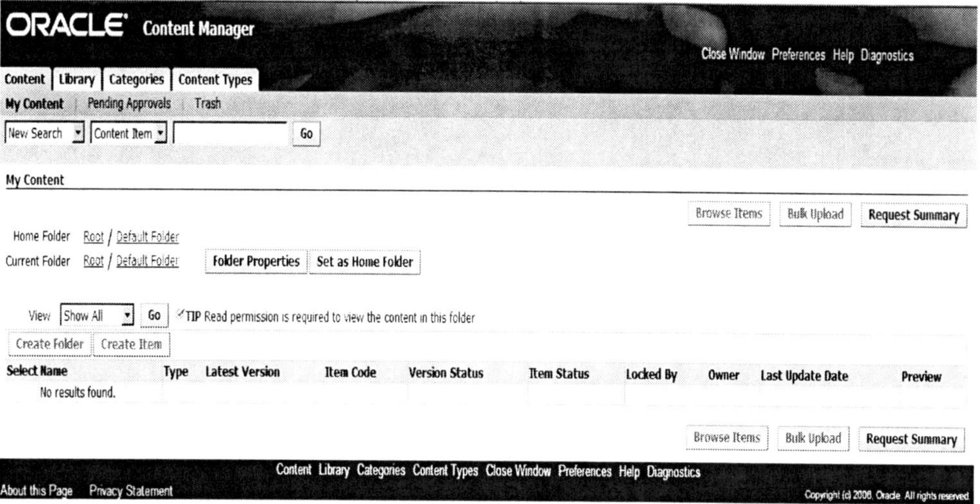

Figure 101 – After setting up an administrator, launch Content Manager to make sure it was setup correctly.

Set up Environments for Translations

The "Update Translations"' feature shown in Figure 102 can be used to select content items for translation. To be able to translate and view translations, the UTF8 character set must be used on all three tiers (database server, middle tier application server and browser client). UTF8 is an encoding of the Unicode character set that includes all the characters in all modern languages. In effect, UTF8 supports all languages. The universal nature of UTF8 allows Oracle Applications to be run from one database instance using a combination of supported languages.

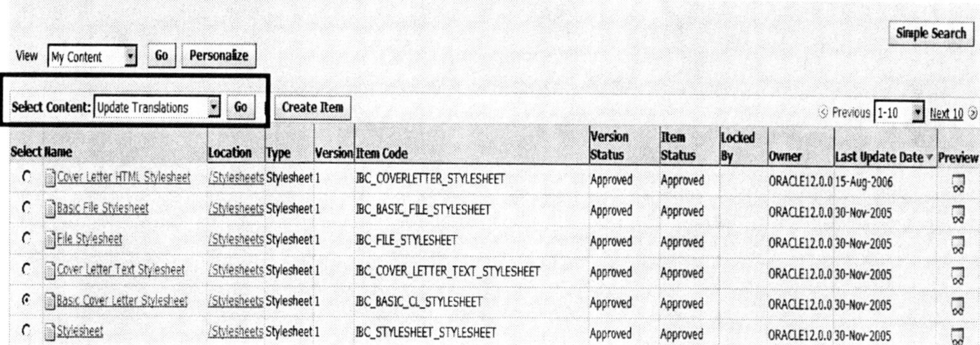

Figure 102 – Select "Update Translations" to view and update content items that are selected for translation.

Assign Folder Permissions

The Content Super User must grant folder permissions to all OCM users. No privilege is automatically granted, even to the Content Super User. Folder Access Control involves assigning a user, responsibility, group (resource groups that have been defined as JTF Resource Groups) or global level permission to access a folder. Access control is a combination of permissions and exclusions.

Initially, only the Content Super User can access the Root folder, which provides a list of all folders. Click on the Root link and Folder Properties to assign access to users (see Figure 103).

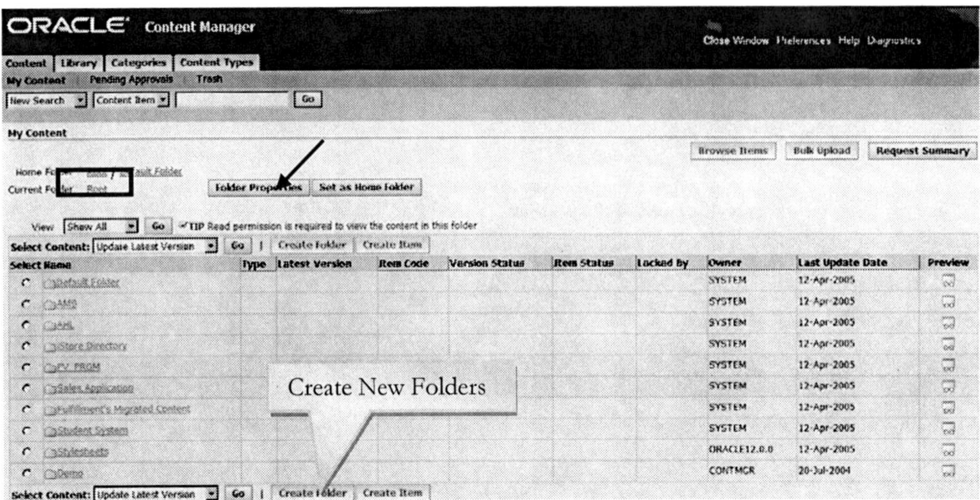

Figure 103 – The Content Super User assigns access to users

While creating a folder, users can select the option to inherit parent access control, which means the permissions and exclusions are disabled. This is the default selection. The subfolder inherits all the permissions from the parent folder. If the parent folder access control is modified, the subfolders also reflect the changes. The parent access control can be overridden and doing so enables the Permissions and Exclusions regions (see Figure 104).

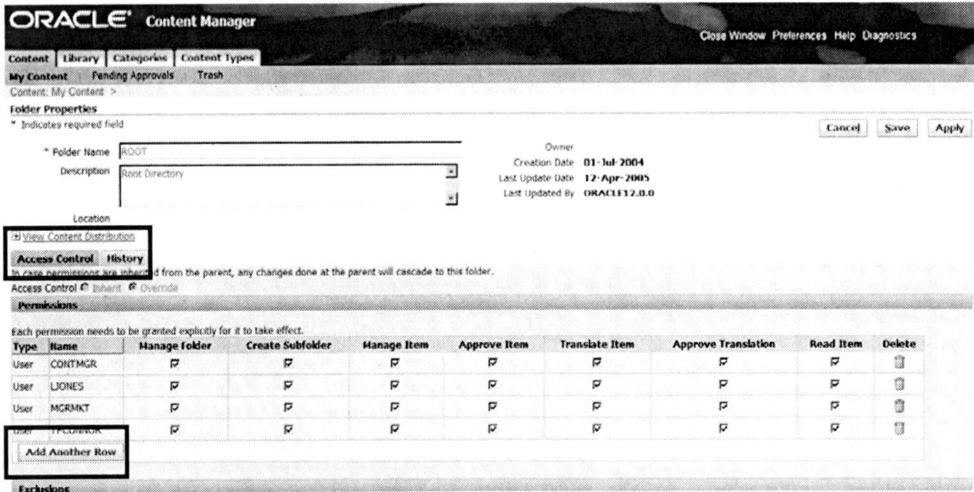

Figure 104 – After clicking on "Folder Properties", the Content Super User sets up access control.

In the "Type" field, select User, Responsibility, Group or Global from the list, then enter the username in the "Name" field, and then click on the functions this user should be able to perform. Exclusions can be set up to exclude certain users from doing certain functions (see Figure 105).

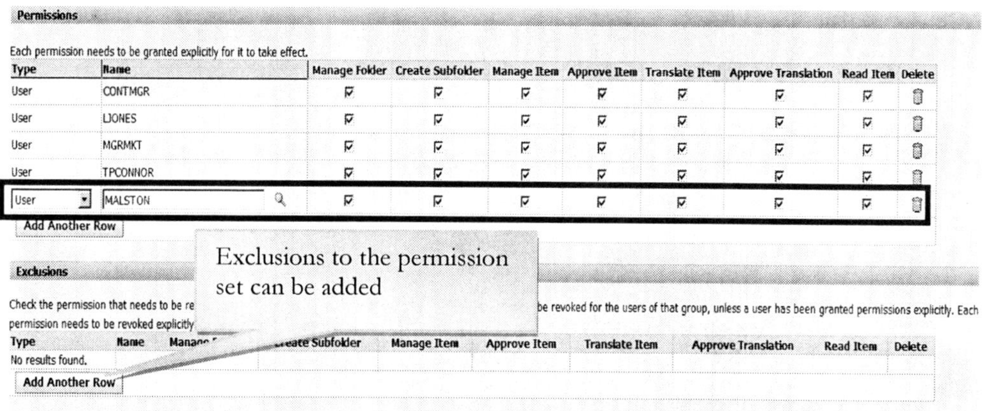

Figure 105 – Now each user can be granted access permissions.

Users can view items that are assigned in the "My Content" folder (see Figure 106). Click on the Content Name link to view the specific Content detail

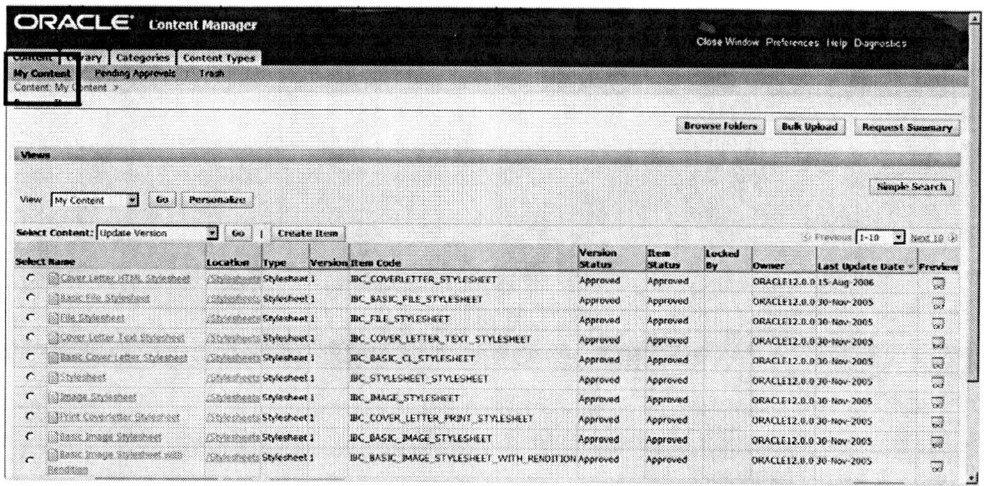

Figure 106 – View assigned items in the My Content folder.

Users can preview content with any of the stylesheets associated with this content type. In Figure 107 choosing the "Product Information Summary" stylesheet and clicking the preview icon displays the Desktop LX2400 Content.

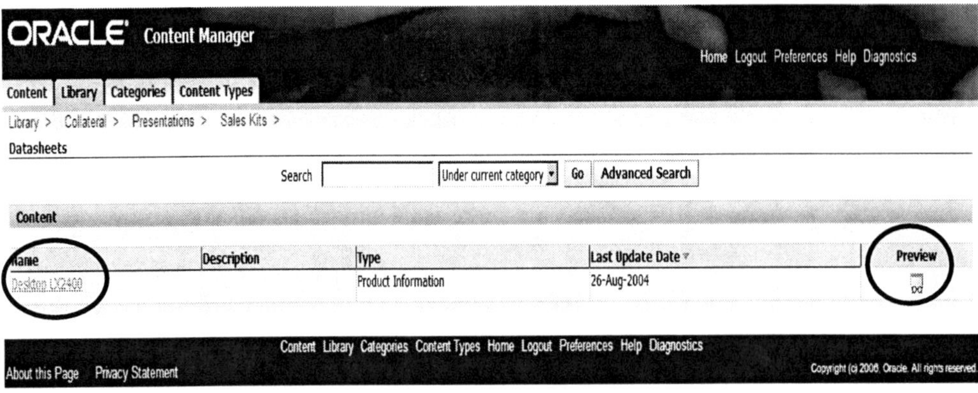

Figure 107 – View individual content items

Figure 108 shows Content Details for the Desktop LX2400. The attributes for this content item are Overview, Highlights, and Specification:

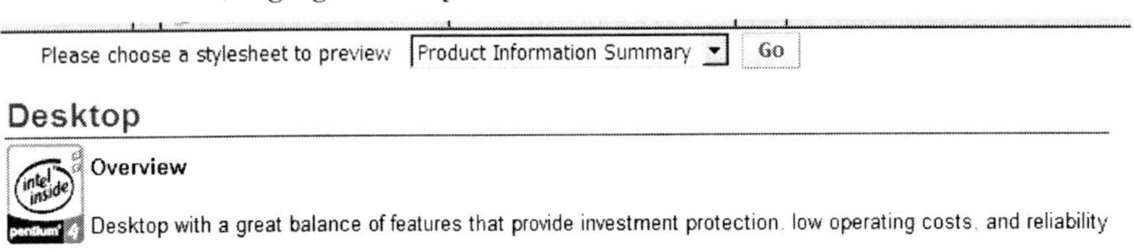

Figure 108 – The Desktop LX2400 item content

Users can view item content details by clicking on the Content Name link (see Figure 109 and 110).

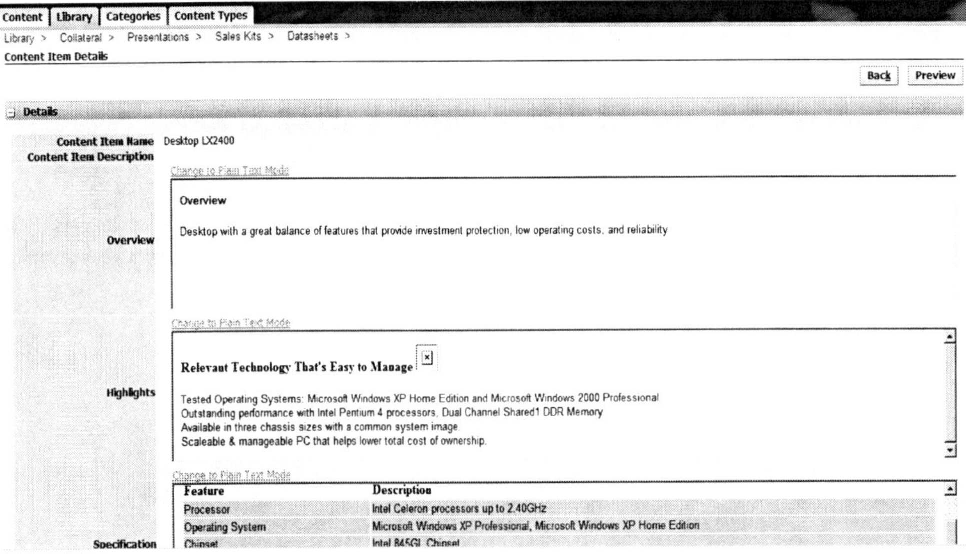

Figure 109 – Content Item Details

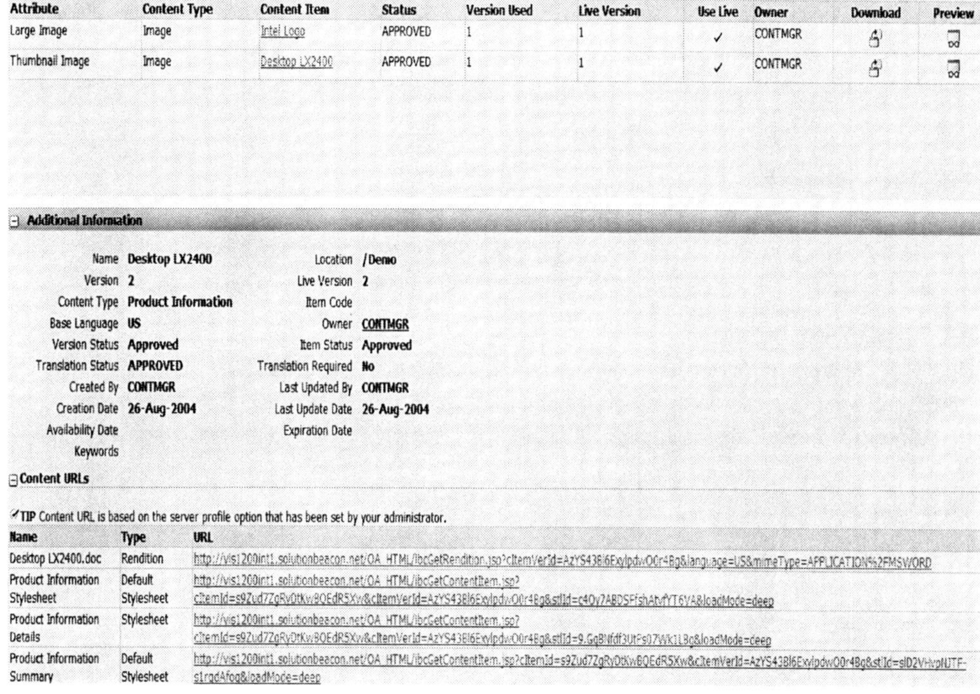

Figure 110 – Click on the links to see more detail

Associations are linked to CRM objects. In Figure 111, a proposal is linked:

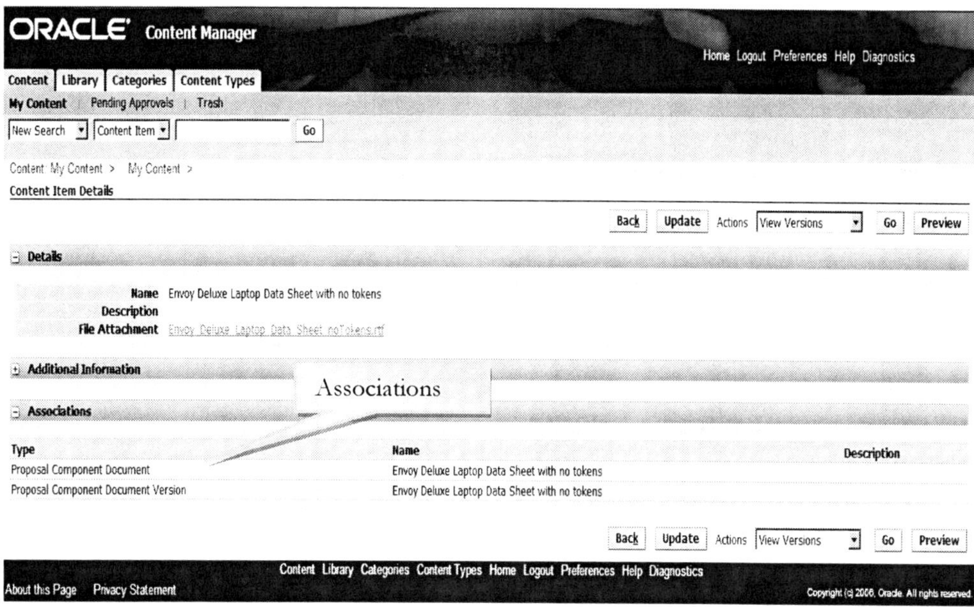

Figure 111 – A proposal is linked

Set Session Timeouts

OCM is built on two frameworks - the OA framework and the JTT framework. The session timeout in the OA framework must always be *greater than* the session timeout in the JTT framework.

JTT Framework

The JTT session timeout is configured at the JTT Administrative Console. Log into Oracle Applications and navigate to Settings > System > Sessions. Enter a value in the `Expires if idle for (mins)` field. The default value is 30 minutes.

OA Framework

The OA session timeout is driven by the `Session.timeout` parameter in the `zone.properties` file of the Apache configuration. The default value is 60 minutes. Set this value to a number that is greater than the JTT Framework session timeout value.

Set Up Inter-media Index Searches

A user with the Oracle Content Manager responsibility should schedule the concurrent program "Content Manager: Text Index Optimizing operation for Attribute Bundle" to run periodically to maintain Oracle text indexes to optimize searches (see Figure 112).

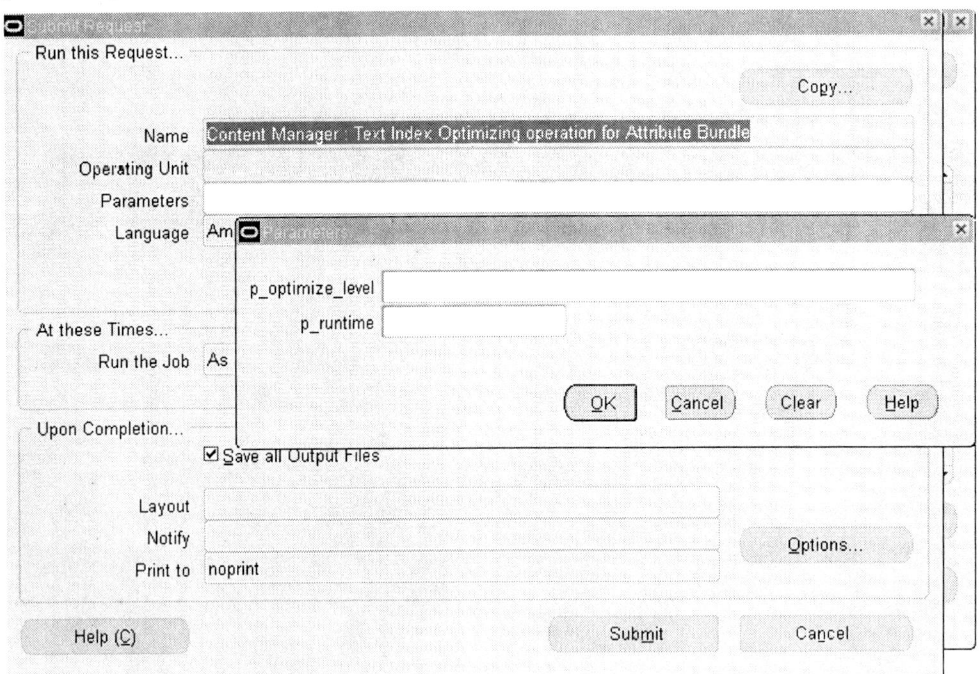

Figure 112 – Run the concurrent program "Content Manager: Text Index Optimizing operation for Attribute Bundle" periodically to main indexes.

Set up Workflow for Document Approvals

OCM uses Oracle Workflow to send notifications that alert users of content items that require approval, items that have been approved, or items that require translation. Users can view their "Pending Approvals" from the Content tab (see Figure 113).

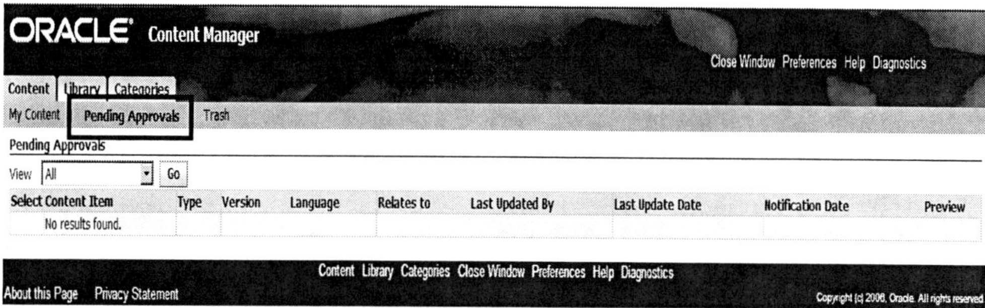

Figure 113 – Pending Approvals

Administering Content Management

Once all the setup details are complete, users can create new folders, grant permissions on those folders, create items, view status, define new content, create and manage content types, and map stylesheets to content types. Users can move a folder and change the folder hierarchy under which the folder belongs. Users can also move content to a different folder location and search within content attributes.

With Release 12, Content Management also supports more options with its bulk upload feature, which enables users to map file extensions to content types. To run a bulk upload, click on the Bulk Upload button (see Figure 114).

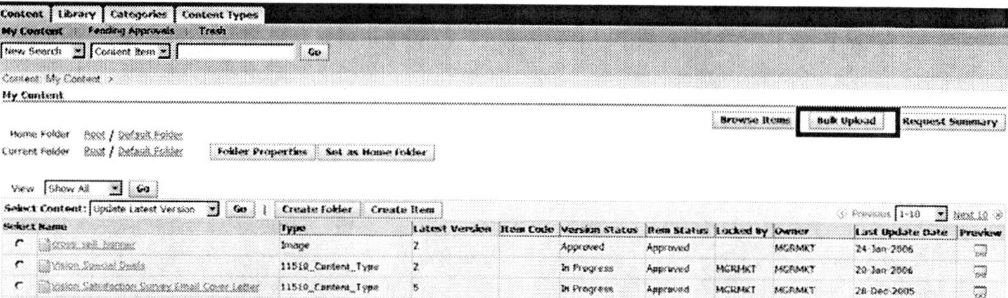

Figure 114 - Click on the Bulk Upload button

Users first enter the general parameters, continue to the next form, and then map file extensions to content types. When all file extensions have been mapped, click on the Submit button to submit the concurrent program "Content Manager: Bulkupload Process". See Figures 115, 116, and 117 for the complete flow.

Figure 115 – Enter the parameters

Figure 116 - Map file extensions to content types.

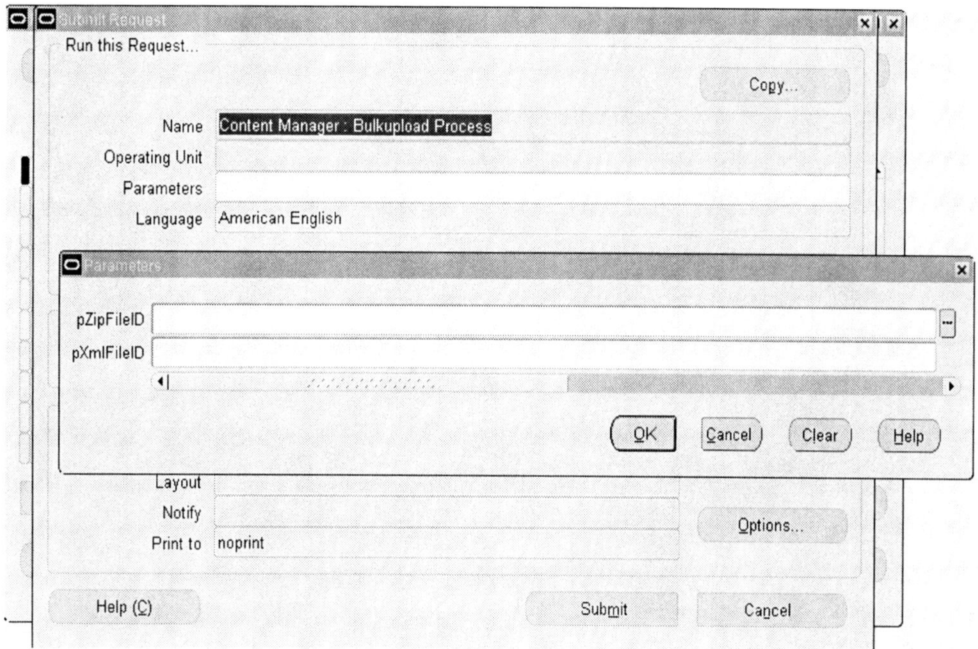

Figure 117 – Concurrent program for the Content Manager Bulk Upload

Summary

For CRM users, content management can allow service technicians to diagnose symptoms and propose potential solutions for service calls before dispatching field service resources on unnecessary service calls. Just as MetaLink allows Oracle's customers to log problem descriptions, upload files and search through and download documentation for answers to problems that have already been resolved by others, content management can allow the same type of support for service requests. Content management can capture critical data upfront via an option that requires customers to answer key questions online before contacting an agent, and allowing the customer to search for the answer before logging a service request.

The ability to provide a centralized repository of searchable data, whether stored in a database or in some other form, will surely expand the horizons of what CRM users can do to meet their customer's needs.

Our next chapter will describe the benefits of Oracle Projects, the final product family that we are reviewing for Release 12.

Projects Product Family

Release 12 Oracle Projects provides a powerful new single-source user interface that enables enterprise visibility of projects or groups of projects. Since Oracle Projects inception a decade ago, the application has grown into a product family with functionality to meet the needs of most organizations. With improved analysis and reporting, project information can now be shared across the entire organization using a single collaborative framework. Figure 118 shows the Oracle Projects Suite Architecture, which includes Portfolio Analysis, Project Resource Management, Daily Business Intelligence, Project Costing, Project Billing, Project Collaboration and Project Management. *Oracle Project Foundation itself provides the shared functionality across the Oracle Enterprise Project Management solution with the intent of packaging all of those common elements of Oracle Projects into one place.*

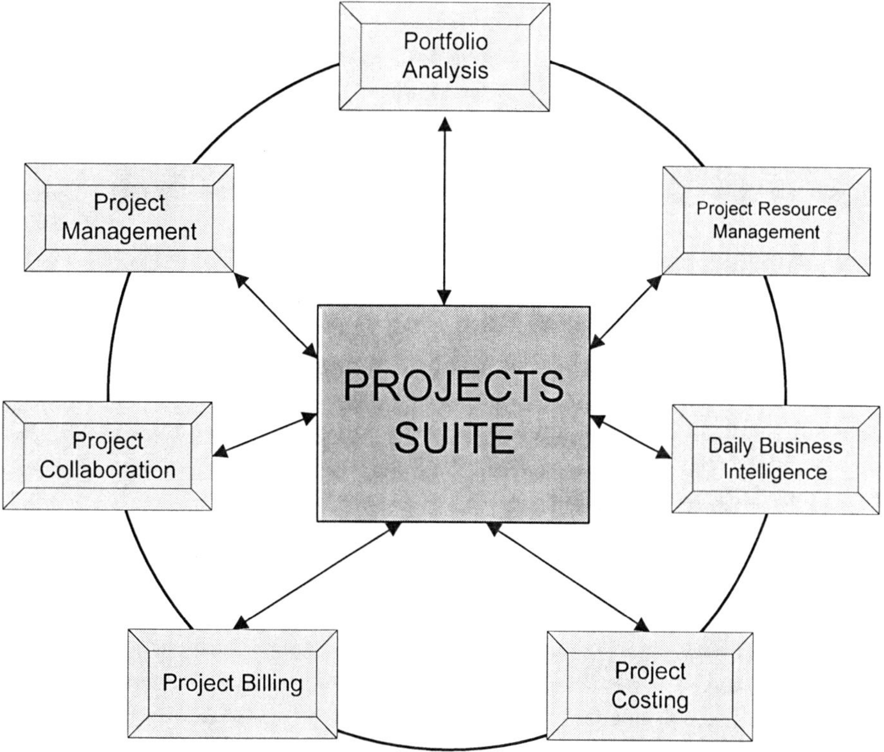

Figure 118 - Oracle Projects Suite Architecture

Prior to E-Business Suite Release 12, access to project information was limited to Projects or to specific source applications such as Purchasing, Payables or Fixed Assets. Users could not view the project information status without developing custom objects and data sets against standard Project Status Inquiry (PSI). To provide more flexible access to project data at the task and subtask levels, customers often chose third party enterprise tools. Tools such as Discoverer, Business Objects, Cognos and the like allowed more reporting visibility but with limited capabilities unless extensions or customizations were integrated into the solution. Ultimately, businesses had to cross-reference the expenditure tables in Oracle to generate detailed reconciliation reports, and/or define custom columns within PSI to retrieve Inception to Date and Year to Date for both Capital Expenditures and Operating Expenditures.

Now, however, visibility has been enhanced within Projects itself. This chapter will discuss some improvements and additions key to the Release 12 Projects Suite. As a note of reference, certain improved functionality within Oracle Projects Suite was previously released as part of Oracle Projects, Family Pack M (PA.M) . Though we refer to enhancements to Release 12, it is important to know that PA.M had already provided a large majority of the improvements. Release 12 just made it better. You should contact your Oracle Sales Representative with any questions regarding licensing fees or whether you may already have a license for any of the functionality seen here. Also, review your business objectives clearly and plan accordingly for both the implementation time and cost associated with the deployment.

PROJECT PORTFOLIO ANALYSIS

With Release 12, Projects offers a set of solutions to help deliver global projects by integrating, managing and providing important insight into enterprise project information. Project Portfolio Analysis facilitates better global visibility, as well as strategic evaluation of current and future project objectives. It helps organizations evaluate, analyze, prioritize and select the right projects by making information available about financial goals and strategic goals. Decisions are based on an accurate understanding of budget changes, strategy changes, acquisitions, and mergers. With the Project Portfolio Analysis tool, the user can define organizational investment criteria for projects, analyze current and proposed projects, and define and compare multiple what-if scenarios with groups of projects, thus automating the decision process for changing project portfolios.

Projects now can be selected into a portfolio aligned with organizational objectives based on the portfolio's budget. Projects can be evaluated based on portfolio, total project and portfolio costs, and strategic objectives. Like other Release 12 modules, such as E-Business Tax, Projects includes the ability to create "what-if" scenarios to evaluate the true effect of a proposed business change before actually changing a production environment. These scenarios can help identify risky projects and fund only those that make sense or meet organizational goals. Various portfolio scenarios can be compared and only those that provide financial value to the business can be funded.

Other features of Project Portfolio Analysis give users the keys to use the portfolio model successfully. First, robust portfolio management functionality allows users to create portfolios to group and manage projects, build scenarios, and balance those scenarios in a portfolio plan based on specific investment mixes. Users are also able to manage planning cycles by gathering and analyzing proposals in order to make decisions based on those portfolios.

Project Portfolios can be assessed by scoring or ranking the projects in a portfolio using Release 12 Business Intelligence that includes standard Key Performance Areas (KPA) and graphical representations for portfolio comparison. The tool also calculates Net Present Value (NPV), Return on Investment (ROI), and Internal Rate of Return (IRR) based on financial plan information. Workflows are also automated for both planning and approvals, and are triggered by events such as budget changes. With workflows, project information and recommend scenarios can be collected; plan approvals can be required; and planning cycle status notifications can be sent. Finally, users can create advanced filters based on selected metrics to prioritize projects to make decisions that are more informed.

The Project Portfolio Planning Process

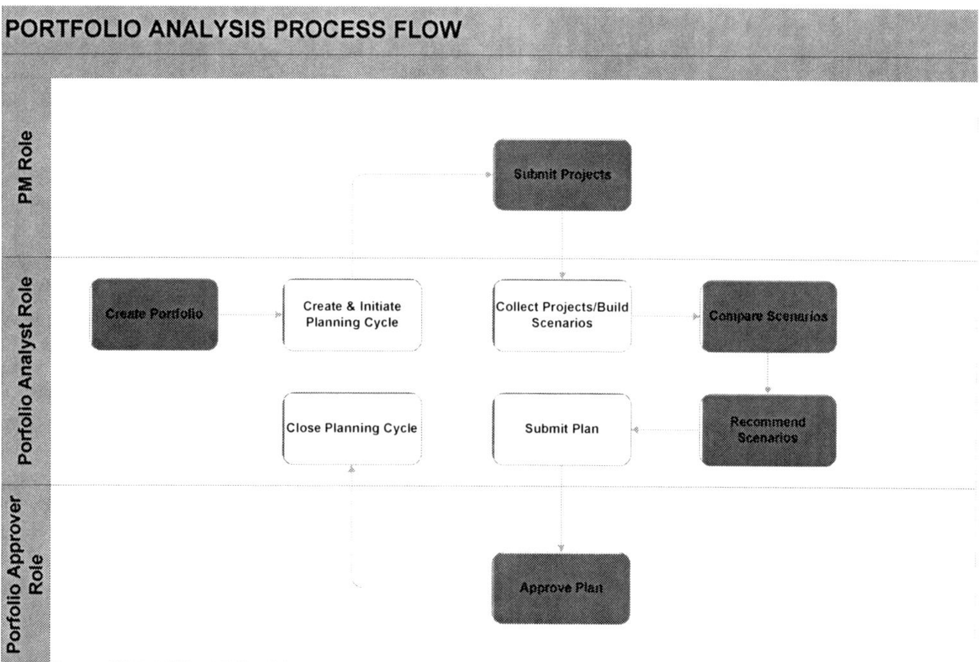

Figure 119 - Portfolio Analysis Process Flow

Figure 119 illustrates the Portfolio Analysis Process Flow. When a portfolio is created, portfolio information is entered to help track what projects are part of the specific portfolio. In creating and initiating the planning cycle, strategic targets, funding, and investment mix criteria are set. After the planning process, the cycle is initiated by collecting projects into what-if scenarios.

When projects are submitted to the planning cycle, project managers are notified that the current planning cycle is available to receive projects into an initial scenario. The project managers must validate that their projects meet the criteria of the planning cycle. Once projects have been collected into an initial scenario, more projects can be added, and then the initial scenario can be used to build more scenarios.

Portfolios are managed by comparing and ranking the projects, and comparing the scenarios with each other. This allows users to identify those projects and scenarios that are better suited to the organization's strategic and financial goals. A portfolio plan can be submitted to the portfolio approver, who can, after careful review, approve or reject the portfolio plan.

The portfolio analyst closes the planning cycle after all cycle activities are completed. Once closed, users can view the historical version of the portfolio plans and review the scenarios and projects.

Enabling Project Portfolio Analysis

Several steps must be complete in order to enable the Project Portfolio Analysis.

- The Profile Option "PJP: Licensed to Use Project Portfolio Analysis" must be set to "Yes" at the site level.

Other Profile Options that are required for enabling full functionality of Project Portfolio Analysis are:

- "PJP: Portfolio Selection Class Category"
- "PJP: Portfolio Organization Hierarchy"
- "PJP: Nominate Risk from Investment Criteria"
- "PJP: Default Discount Rate"
- "PJP: Financial Plan Type for Project Benefit, set at Site Level"
- "PJP: Financial Plan Type for Project Cost, set at Site Level"
- Portfolio Analysis Calendars must be configured in the General Ledger
- Financial Plan Types for Cost and Benefit, Portfolio Type Classes and Additional Investment Classes must be defined by the System Administrator responsibility

Creating Your Own Portfolio

The Project Portfolio Analysis responsibility (see Figure 120) will be visible in the navigator menu once the product is licensed. Once in the Project Portfolio Analysis module, users will only be able to view their portfolios, including those projects that have been added to their portfolios (see Figure 121).

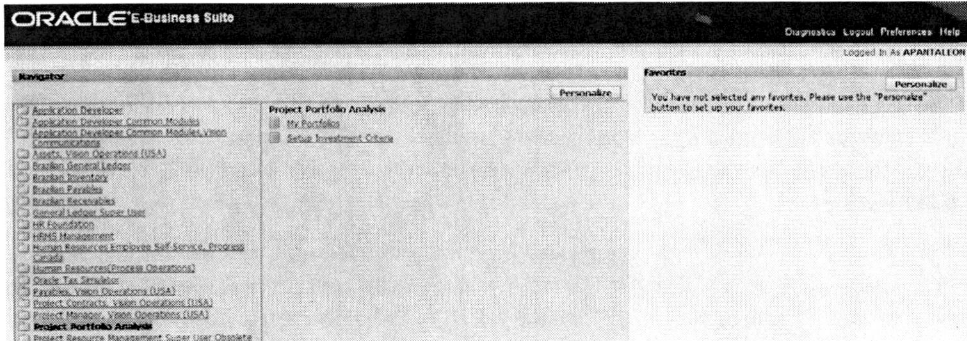

Figure 120 - The Project Portfolio Analysis menu

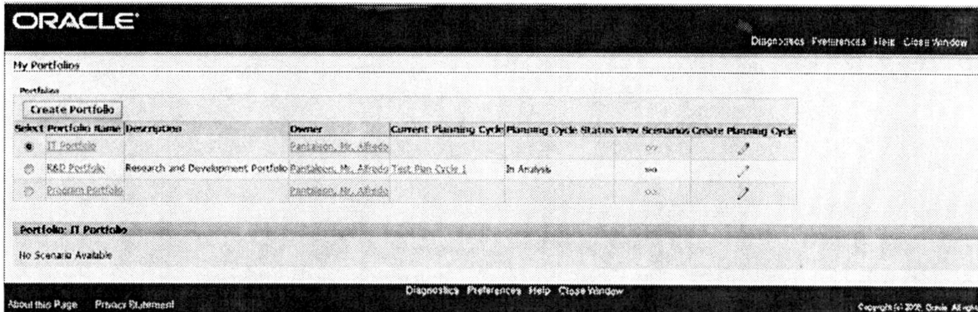

Figure 121 – The My Portfolios home page

From the My Portfolio home page, users can create, as well as manage, portfolios. Users click on the pencil icon to create a planning cycle (see Figure 122).

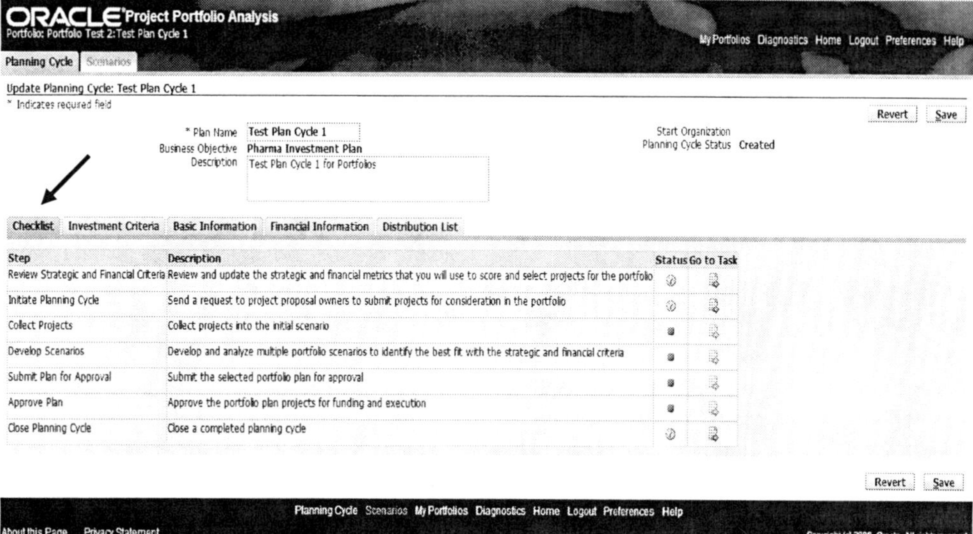

Figure 122 – Oracle Projects provides you with a high level check list. You can track the status of items on the checklist, and you can click on "Go to Task" to add, view or update specific tasks.

In order to begin the basic Planning Cycle, users create a Plan Name. The checklist on the initial tab steps the user through the entire planning cycle. Figure 123 shows the Portfolio Analysis view of the Investment Criteria tab. As part of the required checklist in the Planning Cycle, Investment Criteria allows you to rank or determine weights for each of the investment categories.

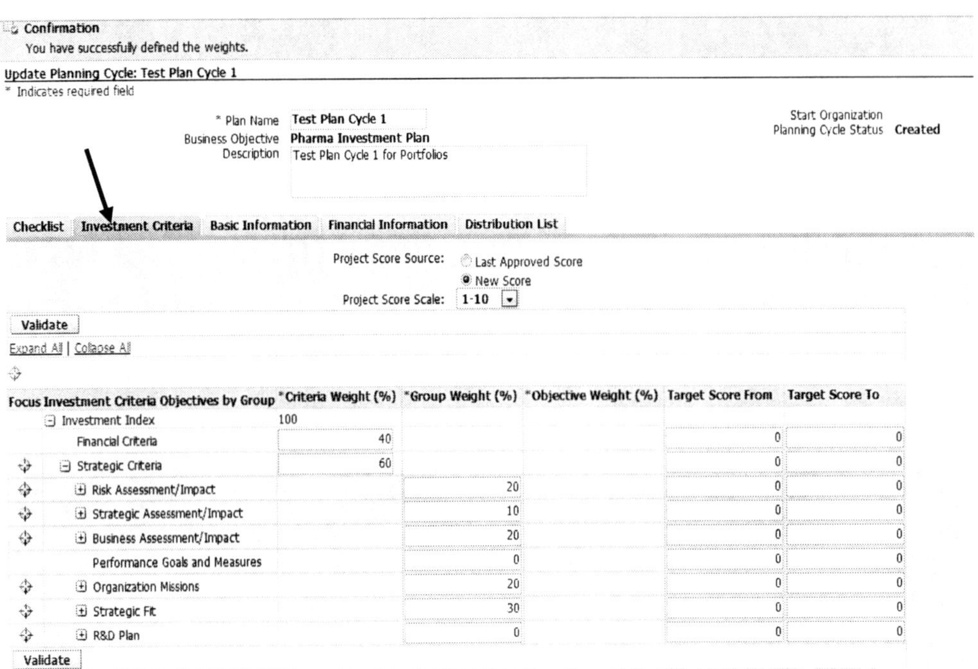

Figure 123 – The Investment Criteria tab in the Planning Cycle

Another required checklist step in the Planning Cycle is the Financial Information checklist (see Figure 124), which provides all of the financial metrics, including the allocation percentage of funds to be used across varying class codes. Some of the class codes include those for board requirements, discretionary spending, governmental requirements (both Federal/Statutory and SEC), overhead, key business objectives and revenue generating.

Checklist | Investment Criteria | Basic Information | **Financial Information** | Distribution List

* Discount Rate 25 **Percent**
The discount rate is applied to the annual rate.

* Funds Available 2500000 **USD**

Display Factor Thousands
Please select a divisor for displaying amounts. For example, Thousands, to display amounts in Thousands.

Targets

Financial Metrics Targets

Financial Metrics	Range From	Range To
Internal Rate of Return (%)	11.6	17.9
Net Present Value (USD)	114111	20661
Payback Period (Months)	8	14
Return on Investment	10	25

Investment Mix

Investment Category - Investment Mix

Previous 1-10 of 19 Next 9

Class Code	Description	Percentage of Funds
Appliances	Appliances	10
Commercial Electric	Commercial Electric	30
Construction Service	Construction Service	0
Consulting Service	Consulting Service	5
No Product	No Product	0

Figure 124 – The Financial Information tab

Figure 125 shows the distribution list within the planning cycle, which allows users to assign a specific person(s) or roles to view the portfolio plan that has been created. This correlates into two specific areas of security. First, from a role-based perspective, no one else except those identified in the distribution will be able to view the plan. Second, no one else except those identified can receive workflow notifications for any changes or updates to the plan, or provide any approval responses to the plan.

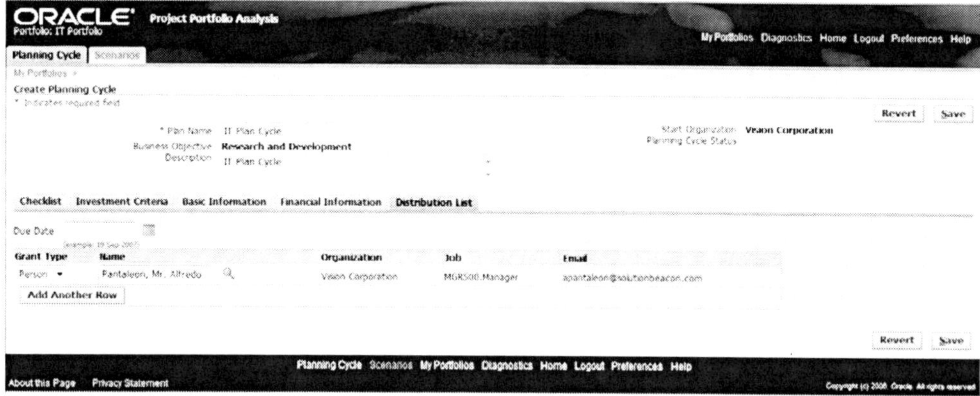

Figure 125 – The Distribution List tab

Once the planning cycle has been initiated, users can then create scenarios. Figure 126 is the Scenarios home page. One of the benefits of what-if scenarios is the ability to perform a side-by-side comparison of multiple scenarios. This enables businesses to make the best decisions for the good of the organization and its strategic goals. Figure 127 illustrates the comparison functionality.

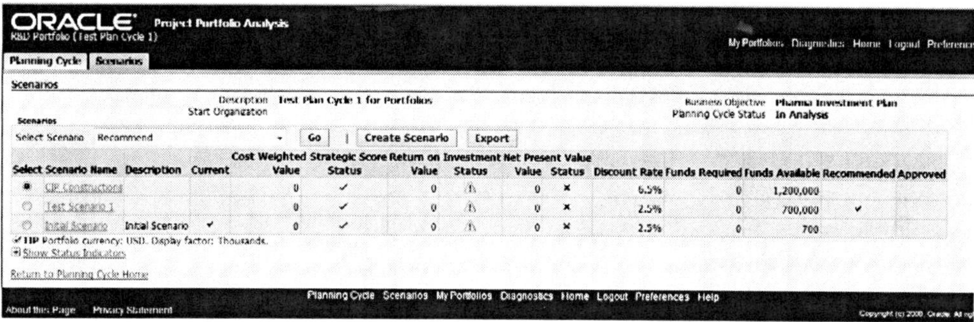

Figure 126 – The Scenarios home page

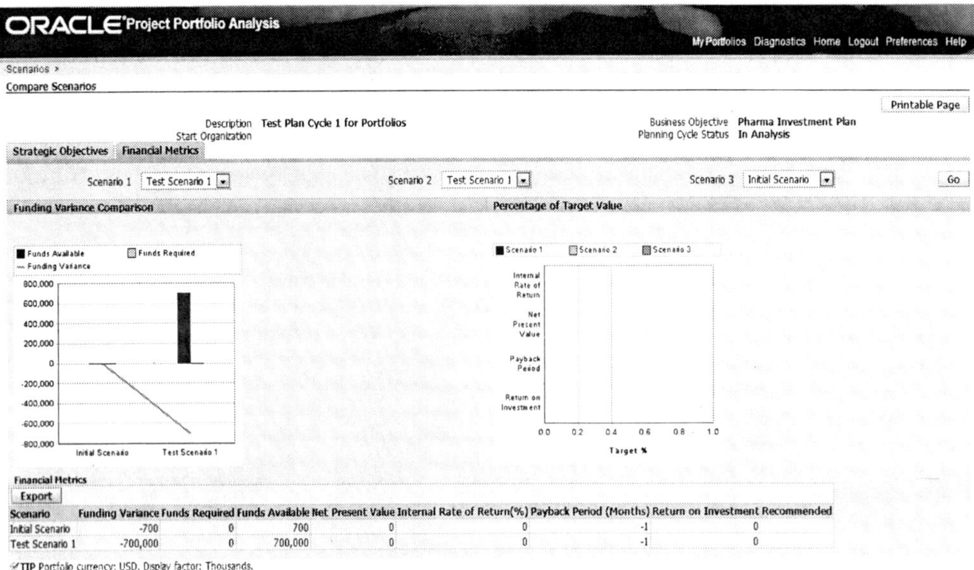

Scenario	Funding Variance	Funds Required	Funds Available	Net Present Value	Internal Rate of Return(%)	Payback Period (Months)	Return on Investment	Recommended
Initial Scenario	-700	0	700	0	0	-1	0	
Test Scenario 1	-700,000	0	700,000	0	0	-1	0	

Figure 127 – Scenarios can be compared side-by-side for good decision making

Project Portfolio Analysis features include the ability to create portfolios, use strategic criteria definition, use criteria weighting and targets, initiate planning cycles, score and nominate projects, model scenarios, compare scenarios, recommend and approve scenarios, and refresh financial data for portfolio analysis.

PROJECT MANAGEMENT

Projects includes a number of improvements that make project management easier. A single repository for all project information includes all elements of the project lifecycle, creating a single source of truth. A number of workplan definition enhancements allow for the defining, tracking and controlling of projects in more detail. These enhancements include support for task dependencies, the ability to assign resources to tasks, and Gantt Chart support for dependencies and resources. Also, task attachments are visible from the workplan view, and users can receive notification of task execution from Workflow.

Oracle's decision to expand Projects' integration with Microsoft Project is also a significant improvement. Projects now includes additional workplan and financial structure integration options that can be used to make project management simpler. Additional enhancements include simplified workplan navigation, the ability to process updates on structure and the ability for multiple users to update multiple task details. Also, an earned value calculation runs after selecting a new baseline version, a mass refresh for conversion rates and cost and bill rates can be run, and the "as of" date for financial percent completion derivation is provided.

While initially released in Oracle Projects, Family Pack M for Release 11.5.10.2, several features in Project Management are new enough to warrant a mention. First, Deliverables Management provides the ability to track any measurable, tangible, and verifiable items that have to be produced to complete a project (items and documents). Also, Workplan and Staffing Plan Integration allows users to leverage a Workplan's task resources to integrate with a project-level staffing plan, thereby tracking resource capacity on the project and their usage on the workplan. By reviewing resource usage on tasks against their planned capacity, users can determine whether they are over or under utilization, and whether they can work on a particular project. Finally, there are now several ways to collect, roll up, and analyze progress on a workplan so it can be accurately managed and communicated. A new client extension is included to track workplan progress that allows tracking for all task types. Users can also cancel tasks and see "as of" date display values.

Budget and Forecasting Enhancements include the ability to perform budget generation and forecast generation from a Financial Plan, Staffing Plan, or Workplan resource; and streamline data entry for budgets with flexible budgeting options for entering and viewing data. Enhancements also include honor bill rate overrides on project assignments, honor billability on revenue budget or revenue forecast generation, the ability to generate a cost budget from a Workplan with cost disabled, and visibility of missing rates for budget and forecast generation. Users can also analyze a forecast and make adjustments, create an initial forecast, and take advantage of new data entry and view options. Other improvements include enhanced budgeting and forecasting spreadsheet integration, and new budgeting and forecasting APIs. Issue and change management enhancements include streamlined ability to create issues and make changes, as well as improvements to how to implement those changes to budgets and forecasts.

In the reporting area, Project Management has addressed both performance reporting and performance exceptions reporting. Project Performance Reporting provides a new centralized view to review all pertinent information for a single project, including Earned Value, Cost Information, and Project Status. Viewing the project and the drill downs of specific tasks can be performed from the "project performance reporting page". Information included on this page includes Project Financial Information, Task, Resource, and Periodic Reporting, multi-currency support for project performance, support for multiple calendars, performance reporting user interface enhancements, and custom measures (metrics). It also includes enhanced supplier mapping for contingent workers, the ability to run concurrent programs by operating unit, the ability to view periodic data for a range of periods, public views for the project performance summarization model, financial planning and Project Status Inquiry (PSI).

With Performance Exceptions Reporting, users have the ability to review the status of all projects, use alerts based on specific issues or criteria of project status, and then drill down to the details to identify the root cause. Users can create rules based on certain factors and can then use these rules to compare against other schedules and financial measures (cost, revenue or profitability) to generate reports and exceptions. These exceptions can be segregated as KPAs (Key Performance Areas) that are scored based on some weighted value or weightings of the associated exceptions. Users can then use the KPAs to drive reporting of the overall status of the project. Use of colored graphical indicators highlights the exceptions, KPAs, and the project status from the standard user interface.

While initially released in Oracle Projects, Family Pack M (PA.M), Projects improves the Earned Value Management (EVM) method of program management. With this method, users manage projects by understanding the mathematical relationships between project scope, work and budget. Leveraging enhancements in progress management, Project Management supports the following EVM metrics: Planned Value (a.k.a. Budgeted Cost of Work Scheduled); Earned Value (a.k.a. Budgeted Cost of Work Performed); Actual Cost (a.k.a. Actual Cost of Work Performed); Schedule Variance, Cost Variance; the Schedule Performance Index, the Cost Performance Index, the To Complete Performance Index; the budget at completion, the estimate at completion, and variance at completion. These metrics are available for all levels of a project and can be integrated in the project status reports. This addition is especially important to government contractors as all government contracts awarded after October 1, 2006 over a certain dollar amount must use EVM.

From the perspective of Program Management, EVM metrics can be applied to the program, but the grouping of those projects in a hierarchy to track progress with aggregate data is most important. You can view both the projects and the programs from your "Project List" page. From there you can drill down from the program to the project details. You also have visibility to rolled up workplan schedule information at the program level or rolled up to the level of associated/related projects. Always keep in mind that analysis using any of the methods discussed in these chapters still requires review to ensure that what is captured is of value to the organization. Modifications outside of EVM to generate additional reporting may need to be considered.

Project Management View

Project Management allows quick project creation without returning to the standard forms for Projects every time. The Project Management dashboard was built with a couple of goals in mind. The dashboard provides single-source accessibility to global information as well as the ability to create information on the fly. Also, Figure 128 shows the Actions LOV where users can perform an alternative type of project search, create a new project based on existing projects or templates, and maintain project sets that have been previously created or those sets users want to create based on personalized groupings.

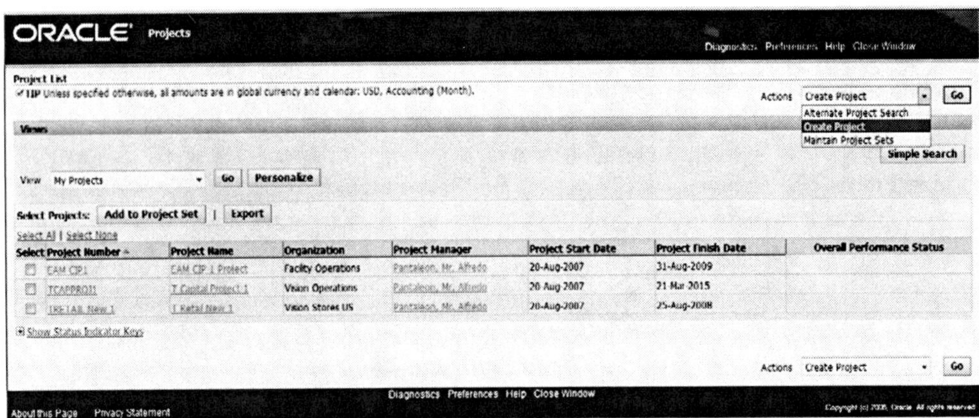

Figure 128 – A user's project list

Based on specific targets that users configure, Oracle uses the KPIs, or Key Performance Indicators embedded in Projects Daily Business Intelligence and derives the scores of user's project(s) in order to rank them based on past and current activities. This view allows users to see each of the Key Performance Areas that are affected by the project activity across the entire project, the tasks and deliverables of a project, as well as any change control items based on issues management and the ability to track project performance.

ORACLE Projects

Diagnostics Home Logout Preferences Help

Project | Resources | Workplan | Control | Financial | Reporting

Home | Overview | Directory | Attachments | Relationships | Setup

Home: T Retail New 1 (TRETAIL New 1)

Shortcuts ---Project--- Go

Organization Vision Stores US Project Manager Pantaleon, Mr. Alfredo
Project Type Construction Target Start Date 20-Aug-2007
Status Unapproved Target Finish Date 25-Aug-2008

General | Tasks And Deliverables | Change Control | Performance

Key Performance Area Summary

Refresh Key Performance Areas

Overall Performance Status

			Score Threshold		Critical		At Risk		On Track		
Key Performance Area	Status	Score	From	To	Count	Score	Count	Score	Count	Score	Last Recorded Date
Schedule		30	20	100	0	0	0	0	3	30	22-Aug-2007 17:02:39

Hide Status Indicator Keys

Keys

Critical

At Risk

On Track

Figure 129 – The Project home page lists the Key Performance Areas (KPA) for a project. KPAs allow better control of forecasting as well as current status of any financial indicators. With these views, key performance elements provide the picture of health for a project.

As the Project Manager, and based on the role assigned (key member), users will only see their specific projects in the Project List. The home view can also be personalized by the users based on requirements in the dashboard. For example, if a manager has requirements that are mostly financial in nature, then the manager can modify the view accordingly. Emphasis is on performance, so the Release 12 Daily Business Intelligence performance indicators are now visible.

The Workplan tab (see Figure 130) provides the ability to control projects tasks, deliverables and resources by establishing initial versions for review and rework. The Workplan is the integral piece for the budgets and overall funding. As with all of the self-service forms, the ability to modify or update current data is as easy as clicking on the appropriate links.

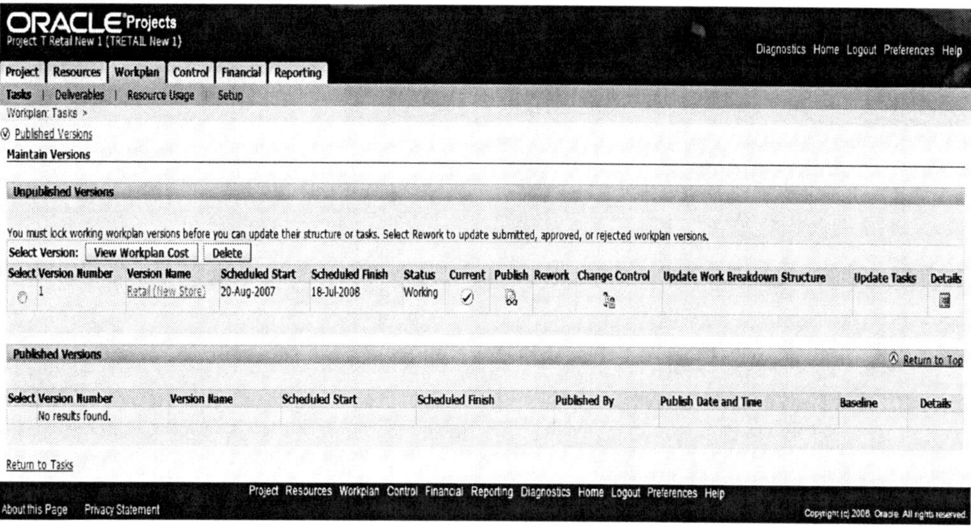

Figure 130 - Projects Workplan tab

Drill down capabilities are more prominent within the Workplan view (see Figure 131). Notice the left side-bar where users can instantly go to the details for a particular task, and the regions to the right allow not only visibility of the task details but the ability to modify specific attribute tabs, with filtering capabilities. Attachments at the task level are another key element. Attachments can be used at all levels of the project.

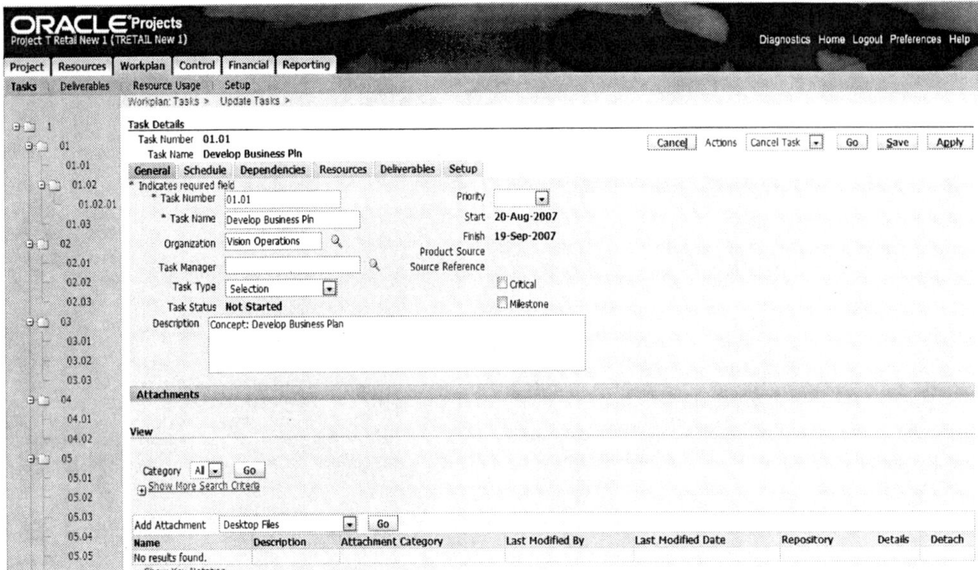

Figure 131 – The Workplan Task Detail form

The ability to maintaining budgets is found in the Financial tab (see Figure 132) where standard budget creation and control functionalities reside. Note: specific plan types must be created prior to building budgets. Users will discover that most of the budget capabilities in the standard Projects form for Budgets have now moved to the use of Plan Types, especially with regard to both Approved Cost and Revenue Budgets. These plan types must exist in the Budget and Forecasts setup within the Financial tab prior to creating a budget. Again, the ease of updating current versions or setup is common in this form as well.

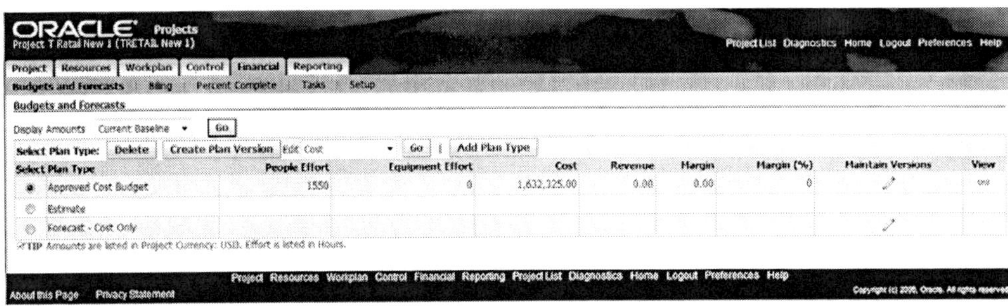

Figure 132 – The Financial tab

Once users have defined a plan type for the specific project, they can view the cost details of the particular plan across the project or across the tasks for that project (see Figure 133). The cost details include the budgeted costs for each level of activity as well as all associated labor hours. Again, with all of these views within Project Management, they can be modified or filtered based on personal criteria. This is also a rolled-up view. The "+" signs indicate that there are more sublevel details available for view. Also, note the "Hide Display Preferences" link at the top left of this Budget Lines window. Users can filter the results either by currency or by factor. If factoring by "2", then the budget cost values will incrementally move by a factor of "2". This allows some ability to forecast based on planned and unplanned events.

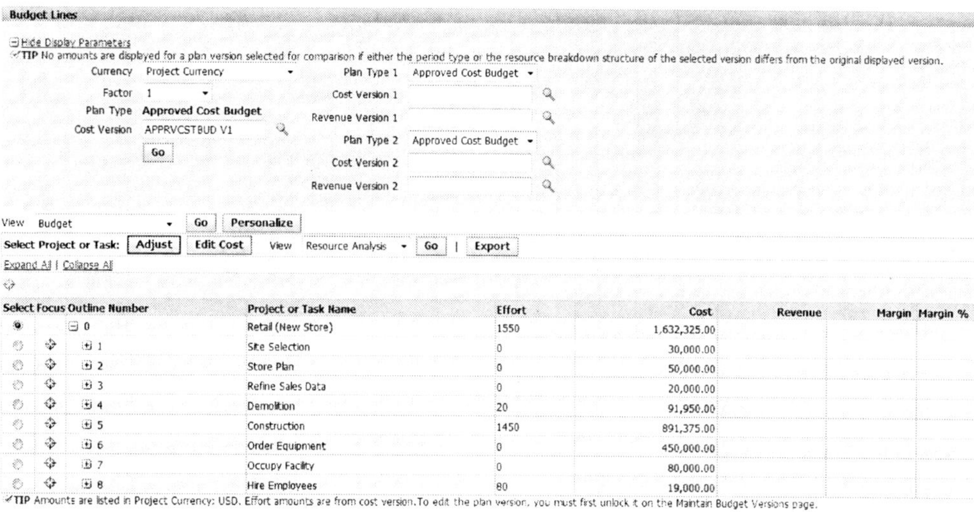

Select	Focus	Outline Number	Project or Task Name	Effort	Cost	Revenue	Margin	Margin %
		0	Retail (New Store)	1550	1,632,325.00			
		1	Site Selection	0	30,000.00			
		2	Store Plan	0	50,000.00			
		3	Refine Sales Data	0	20,000.00			
		4	Demolition	20	91,950.00			
		5	Construction	1450	891,375.00			
		6	Order Equipment	0	450,000.00			
		7	Occupy Facility	0	80,000.00			
		8	Hire Employees	80	19,000.00			

Figure 133 – Budget Lines detail

The Cost Plan and the elements for each task of the project are shown in Figure 134. Planning Elements and/or Resources are defined at this step. This identifies which tasks currently have or will have a budget line defined.

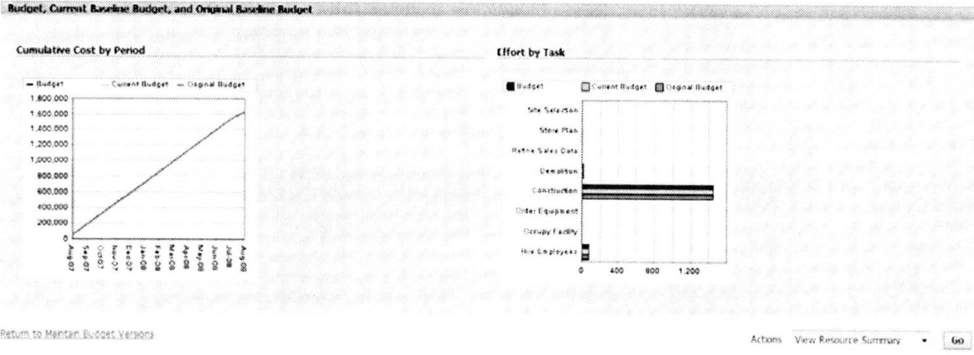

Figure 134 – Cost Plan and Task Elements

Once the Cost Plan, Elements and Resources have been identified for each task, the budget line amounts and labor resource hours can be allocated for each task (see Figure 135). Note: Unless users have predefined burden cost rates/factors, budget costs for both Raw and Burden will be the same. If predefined rates are entered, then variances or the estimated average automatically calculate and are displayed in the appropriate column. Ease of use is the overall theme in every form. Users can edit any value, as well as the budget line details. Users can add or remove tasks as they begin to build a budget across the Workplan.

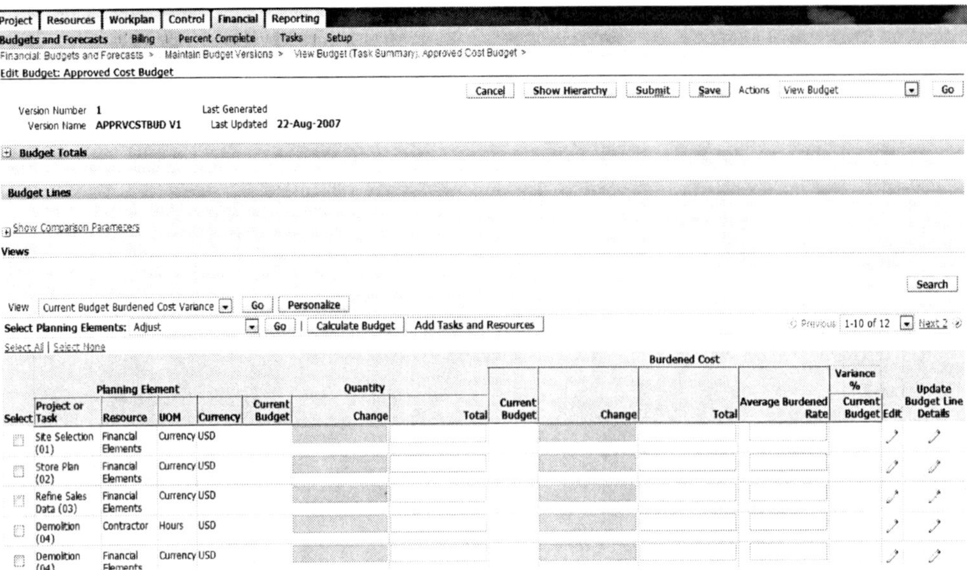

Figure 135 - Form to maintain budgets

Once changes are applied, your budget version is updated with the most current cost for both Raw and Burdened costs. Resource level estimated output is also displayed as People Effort in total. At this point, users can rework the budget, or baseline the budget. The same versions of budgets can be created and monitored in this view. Once users are satisfied with a current budget, a baseline budget can be created for use and reference. From this form, users can also view other versions of the baselined budgets (see Figure 136).

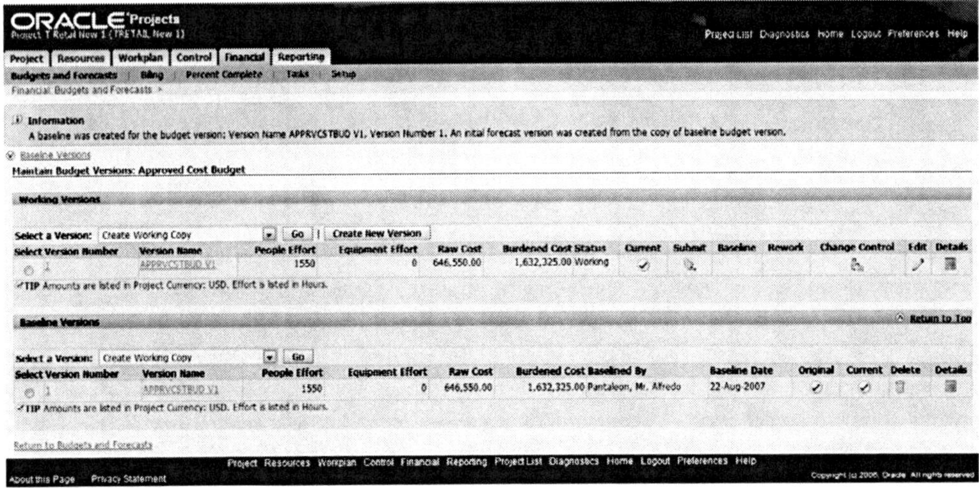

Figure 136 – The Budget and Forecast home page within the Financial tab

On the Reporting tab, the Performance Overview (see Figure 137) allows charts or graphical representations of a particular project's performance based on both cost and effort over time. These details can be made visible or hidden by clicking on the "Hide Details and Parameters" Quick Link. Users can also use any of the Quick Filters to manipulate the charts based on specific viewing requirements, or to look at particular scenarios.

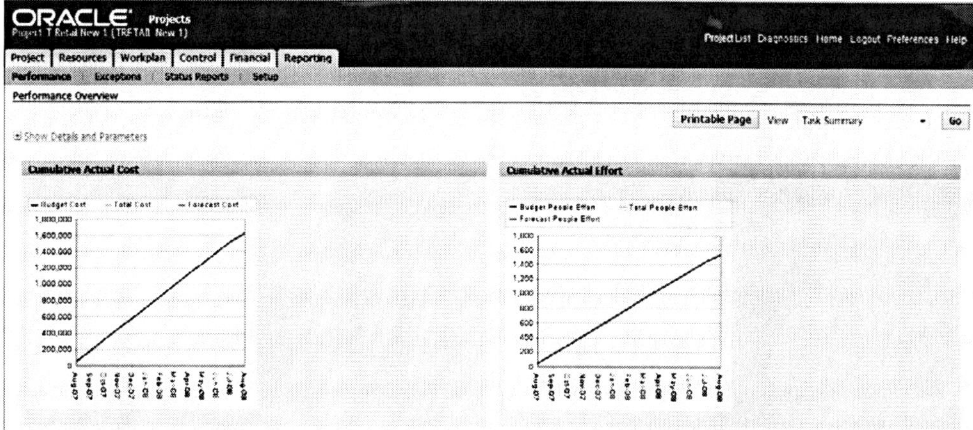

Figure 137 – Performance Overview

Project Management also provides the flexibility to filter or view data in various ways. The view in Figure 138 displays a high level summary of the periodic trend of the project performance based on both period-to-date and year-to-date cumulative planned costs, earned value, and actual costs.

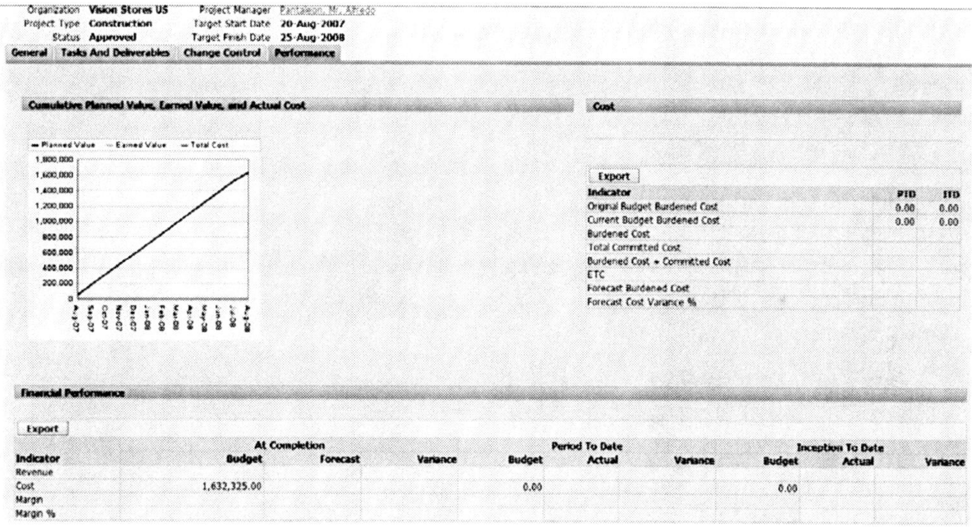

Figure 138 – The periodic trend of project performance

Enabling Project Management

There are a number of Profile Options that need to be set to enable project management:

- The Profile Option "PA: Licensed to use Project Management" must be set to Yes at the Site Level. "Deliverables on Project Templates" must be set to Yes at the Operating Unit Level. If you use Microsoft Project, set "Microsoft Project Integration" to Yes at the Site Level

- Workplan and Progress Management setups are all optional at the Site, Application, Responsibility and User Levels.

- "Financial Plan Types", "Control Item Classifications", "Control Item Types", "Deliverable Types", "Performance Rules", and "Key Performance Area Scoring Rules" need to be defined at the Site Level.

Solution Beacon Recommends: *An important note at this point regarding enabling any of these applications. Configuration of each application varies in content and complexity. Please refer to the latest implementation guides for current setup steps and configurations.*

With Program Management, you can track programs by grouping projects in a hierarchy, which provides visibility of aggregate project data into a program. This allows more drill down capabilities. Advantages include unlimited program hierarchy, program rollup, and program reporting enhancements. Users can now link more than one project to multiple programs so that the project data will be reflected in the rolled up amounts for each program. Program Management also includes Microsoft Project integration for programs.

Project Collaboration

Oracle Project Collaboration enables team members to collaborate more easily and communicate their efforts to review and complete project work. Team members are provided with secure (personalized) access to project information. This information can be shared anytime, anywhere. Visibility to this portal, which contains tasks, issues and deliverables, helps increase team efficiency.

Oracle Project Collaboration includes new regions on the Team Member Home Page, including Assigned Actions and Task Assignments. Task Assignments lists all tasks across projects where a resource has an assignment and owned work. The collaborative progress entry for entering tasks, assignments, and deliverables has been streamlined. Collaborative work planning now allows you to include task managers in the planning process without granting access to the entire project or workplan.

To Enable Project Collaboration, set the Profile Options "PA: Licensed to use Project Collaboration" and "PA: Team Home Page Layout" to Yes at the site level.

Project Costing

Project Costing improves the bottom line of your projects by integrating and controlling all global project costs. Users can manage budgets, streamline processes, automate resource-sharing and capitalize assets more effectively. Project Costing enables the tracking of programs by grouping projects in a hierarchy, providing visibility of aggregate project data into a program. This allows more drill down capabilities.

Project Costing integrates with several new key Release 12 features and derives the full benefits of all of them. First, Project Costing uses the Subledger Accounting Engine to generate accounting entries leveraging all the capabilities described in Chapter 2, *Financials Product Family*. Because Multiple Reporting Currencies (MRC) amounts are now calculated by Subledger Accounting and stored in alternate ledgers, Project Costing can also leverage MRC functionality. With budgetary controls and public sector accounting enabled, users can perform funds checks or generate encumbrance entries, then use the Subledger Accounting

Engine to generate accounting entries. Also, users can perform tasks across operating units with multi-org access control (MOAC).

Integration with Purchasing and Payables now includes Contingent Worker Support. Also known as Contract Labor, it can fill any job role, including a Project Manager. The Procure-to-Pay process provides organizations with improved methods for procuring and managing contingent workers. Enhancements include Labor Cost Processing for Contingent Workers and Expense Report Processing for Contingent Workers.

Finally, since Invoice Lines has now been introduced in Payables, Projects can now capture and transfer the additional information included on the Invoice Lines tab. From Chapter 2, *Financials Product Family*, the invoice line contains data representative of the actual goods and services being invoiced, along with tax, freight and other charges.

Improved Project Costing with Cash Basis Accounting

With Release 12, if Cash Basis Accounting is enabled in the primary account ledger, then payments instead of invoices are interfaced from Payables to Project Costing. This enhancement allows you to recognize partial payments and reverse the cost when the payment is made. Users can now reconcile the cost recorded in Project Costing with the cost recognized in the General Ledger, improving accuracy. Also, Subcontractor Payment Management, which addresses business requirements such as retention, advances, and finance payments, is available.

Supplier costs can now be adjusted in Project Costing if the following set of conditions is true:

- Invoices are fully or partially paid, but the option to allow adjustments is not enabled in Payables
- Payment discounts were taken and distributed to invoice expense distributions
- An invoice is finally matched to a closed Purchase Order
- An invoice is prepaid, fully or partially
- An invoice is selected for payment in Payables
- All adjustment processing is disabled in Payables

If Automatic Offset is enabled in Payables, any adjustments made to the balancing attributes of the charge account will not be allowed. If Cash Basis Accounting is enabled in Payables for both the primary and secondary ledgers, invoices can be fully or partially paid.

A new "Mass Adjust" concurrent program performs adjustments to a larger number of transactions at any given time. A new "Supplier Cost Adjustment" report lists adjusted transactions, and displays original transaction attributes, and the adjusted amounts by project or GL Account. Finally, drill down capabilities from Payables to the Project Expenditure Inquiry Window are available from the invoice workbench. This allows auditable project adjustment activities.

Integration with Project Manufacturing includes Burdening WIP and Inventory Transactions. Another enhancement is the addition of new expenditure item attributes and future-dated people. Users can enter actual project transactions for future-dated people only after they become active. In a future-dated expenditure batch, users can enter people who will be active as of the transaction dates.

Project Billing

Project Billing helps improve cash flow and project profitability by streamlining and managing your billing processes. Flexibility is enhanced by giving users the ability to define top tasks by customer or invoice method. When the customer is defined as the top task, this allows invoicing of customers for specific job work by top task. When the invoice method is defined as the top task, this allows the invoicing of customers at varying levels – fixed price and time and materials within the same project.

Functionally, users can create invoice write-offs at the line-level, which can be applied by prorating an amount across selected lines or entering an amount line by line. This enables the write-off of invoice specific line-items without having to prorate the amount across all lines of the invoice. Users can also manually apply credit amount against a customer invoice, without needing to adjust any supporting transactions. Project Billing also gives users the ability to review and approve invoices. Finally, Project Billing integrates with the new E-Business Tax engine.

Users can view information in several ways to assist in research. Billing Review has a new interface that provides access to Project Billing summary information, with the ability to review and approve draft invoices. All of these functions can be performed from the new interface. Users can also view the billing summary, which includes information regarding revenue, funding backlog, invoice collections, and invoicing status. Finally, the invoice summary can be viewed by customer.

Summary

Projects global benefits include greater efficiencies through automated processes, providing a single point source of both information and configurations, allowing better control of the decision-making process through increased global visibility of the enterprise, ease of configurability and usage, the ability to test and pre-determine scenarios, enterprise analytics shared across the foundation, and collaborative design for efficiency and results.

That concludes the discussion of some of the functional features and enhancements by product family. The next chapter details the technology underlying the Release 12 applications.

Technology

This chapter provides a high level view of the Release 12 architecture. Each section will build on the previous one until you have a full picture of the Release 12 E-Business Suite. We will start by walking you through the tiers that comprise the E-Business Suite. Then we will detail the components and services that implement the business logic, and indicate the tier where they operate. The Technology Layer, which is the "base" set of modules for all the other product modules, is described along with the associated activities and some of the better known functionality. The Release 12 Application Filesystem will be reviewed as well, as this is an area that is significantly different from earlier E-Business Suite releases.

At the end of this chapter, you will understand where the technology components reside, why they belong there and the main reasons Oracle moved in this direction. You will also be familiar with the baseline architecture of Release 12 and, at a higher level, understand how the system works to provide the functionality you need.

These sections are critical for understanding AutoConfig and Cloning. Both the AutoConfig and the Cloning processes will be discussed in this chapter, as familiarity with both of these tools is required to maintain a stable environment. We will briefly talk about Oracle Application Manager (OAM) and will then move on to *i*Repository.

One caution – if you are not a technical person, you may find the sheer quantity of new terminology presented in this chapter to be overwhelming. Take your time, and you will find it is worthwhile to understand what's going on under the hood.

RELEASE 12 OVERVIEW

Oracle Applications Tiers

Oracle's E-Business Suite of Applications (EBS) consists of three tiers. These tiers are logically based, since many customers run multiple physical servers, or nodes, in their configuration, often with several servers comprising a single tier. For example, customers expecting heavy web traffic against their E-Business Suite may deploy upwards of four physical servers to handle the Application Tier's workload. Although there are multiple servers, there is still only a single Application Tier.

An important reason for taking time to thoroughly understand what tiers are involved in the EBS, as well as what service or services are provided by each tier is related to Oracle documentation. Oracle often cites the tier they are referring to or the one with which you should interact. So, understanding what comprises each tier and what service it provides is imperative to getting the most out of Oracle's documentation and MetaLink notes.

A node is another name for a physical server that is just a more powerful computer than the desktop computers some of you use. A tier can consist of multiple logical servers that all do the same type of work. A node houses services – it runs certain types of programs. For various reasons we often split out the Applications Tier across multiple nodes. Some of the benefits include scalability of resources that can be put on a task; availability of the application tied to Service Level Agreements (SLAs); segregation of services for finer control; or perhaps you are trying to achieve a "stretched" configuration where you have Application services nodes, from the same environment, located at different sites. Maintaining multiple servers does have certain drawbacks. Some of these drawbacks include the purchase and licensing costs of multiple servers, troubleshooting problems can be more challenging when attempting to isolate the specific component for repair, and the added human workload needed to maintain the Applications on multiple servers.

You could, however, run the entire Applications suite, Applications Tier and Database Tier, on one server – one computer – one node. Depending on the workload, it could be a very powerful server. The ease of administration alone could make deploying on one node a consideration. Companies that install the Vision database instance (Oracle's demo instance), for example, normally install it on one server. A single server configuration, however, is not a one size fits all configuration. In the end, our best advice is to fully understand what your needs are when determining how many nodes you want to employ.

Desktop Tier

End users work on the Desktop tier. Internet Explorer, Netscape and Firefox all work with Oracle Applications Release 12, as well as Safari for Mac users. The interface is HTML-based and should be familiar to most people that "surf the net".

A user utilizes two different types of "forms" with the EBS. The first "form" is HTML-based and looks just like a web page. The other "form" is the set of Oracle's Professional forms, which have a different look and feel and are accessed using a java applet that is downloaded from the Oracle Applications environment when the form is first accessed. It can also be loaded as a standard image by IT Departments. This java applet, which in Release 12 is the Sun OAJ2SE Java Plug-In, remains installed on the user's machine and houses "jar" files (java archive files), which are necessary for proper forms functionality.

The jar files on the desktop are checked when you access the form, and the most current jar file is downloaded from the forms server and stored on the user's machine if the existing jar file is out of date. These jar files on your desktop can also be a source for problems with forms. There is no simple way to determine if the on-board jar files (the files located on your local desktop) are the source of the problem. If you suspect this to be the case you can simply delete the jar files on your desktop and the newest ones will be downloaded again onto your computer when you next access the forms. You can find these jar files by looking at the java program in your Control Panel. When this program is opened, there is a "settings" button that will show the path to your cache.

Suppose you are going to use the Oracle Applications and you have never used them before. What software do you need on your PC, and who will give it to you? What other information do you need to start using the Applications? First, you will need Internet Explorer, Netscape, Firefox, or some other Oracle certified browser software installed on your PC. Next, you will need to find out which link to follow from your browser to get to the Applications. When you follow that link for the first time, the Sun OAJ2SE Java Plug-In will automatically download to your PC, assuming you don't already have it installed on your PC. Figure 139 is an example of the Java code download you will see on your computer when it is installed.

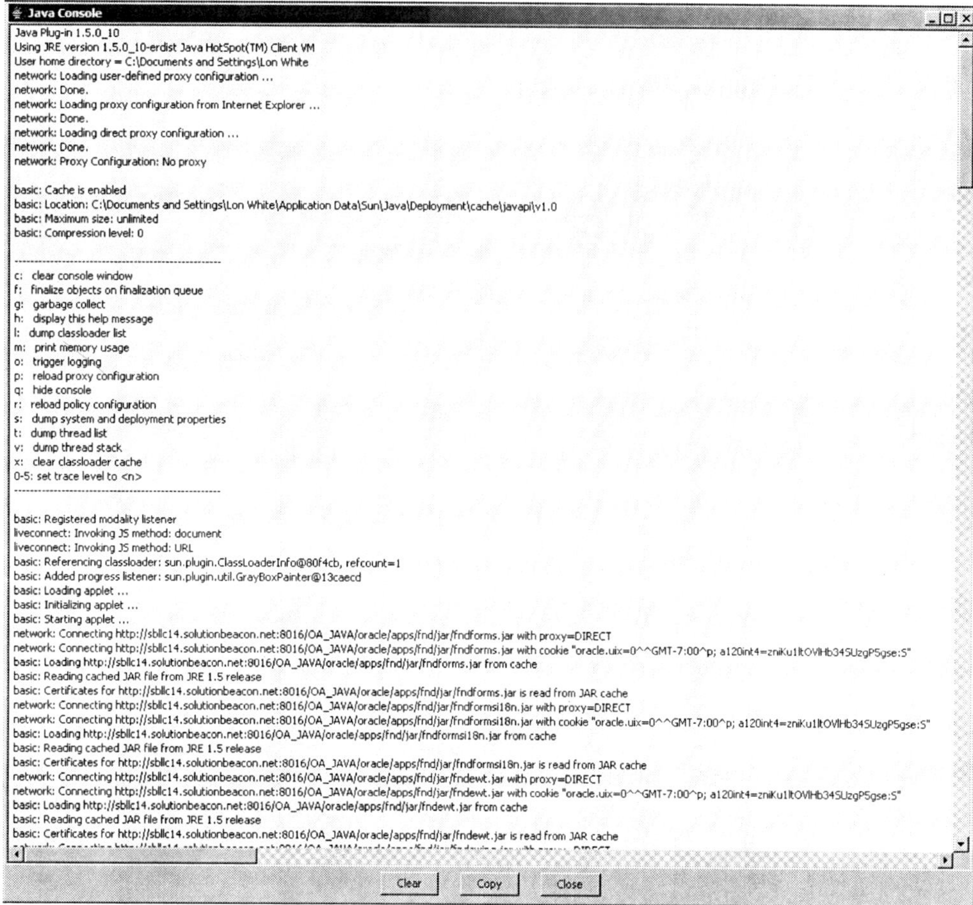

Figure 139 – An example of a Java code download

For organizations thinking of upgrading who are familiar with a previous release of Oracle Applications (11*i*), the OAJ2SE plug-in replaces the JInitiator plug-in. Next, you will need someone to tell you your username and password. Beyond that, if you have never seen the Applications before, you will need some training, because you will be looking at a production database, and you certainly would not want to mess it up by plunking around aimlessly.

Application Tier

The Application Tier is also known as the Middle Tier. It works as a go-between for communications between the user's desktop and the database. It does this by using the components and services it hosts that are responsible for processing business logic. The components and services on this tier are called Web Services, Forms Services, the Concurrent

Processing Server, and the Admin Server. These services are discussed in the Components/Services section, which includes more details about the tasks handled by each service. The application tier is comprised of two different code sets from Oracle's 10*g* Application Server: 10*g*AS version 10.1.3 and 10*g*AS version 10.1.2.

Let's talk about Oracle Home, for a moment, since it is an important concept when dealing with Oracle's software. An Oracle Home, or ORACLE_HOME as it is more often called, is the common name given to the installed binaries for Oracle's software. The database ORACLE_HOME is where you would find the binaries that are used by the Oracle database. These binaries, as the techies often refer to them, are the collection of programs, utilities, library files and related objects that comprise the Oracle product. In the E-Business Suite Release 12, at least three Oracle Homes exist:

- Application Oracle Home (10.1.2 Application Server binary code set)
- Web Oracle Home (10.1.3 Application Server binary code set)
- Database Oracle Home (10.2.0 RDBMS binary code set)

Database Tier

The database tier is where the Oracle RDBMS Server resides. This is the tier that the applications services connect to via SQL*Net for fulfilling queries and transactions. Oracle Database 10*g*R2 is the version of the database that is installed with Release 12. At the time of this writing, the latest certified version number of Oracle Database 10*g*R2 for Release 12 is 10.2.0.3. This version is also certified for use with the Release 11*i* Applications. Keep the Oracle Database version certification in mind when making decisions on which version to upgrade your database to because that could affect your timeline for an E-Business Suite Application upgrade. You can deploy two distinctly different configurations on the database tier. The deployment of the database is traditionally installed as a single instance. Conversely, you could deploy the database using multiple instances and this is known as Real Application Clusters (RAC).

The Oracle database stores most of the data in the Oracle Applications, including online help files. We say most because some data can be stored in external tables called "flat files" that exist on your application's filesystem, which is outside the database. We have seen this more from third party software vendors as their way of integrating their product into Oracle's Applications rather than "out of the box" from Oracle. The major point here is that some of the data your system depends on may exist outside of the database. This means that the Applications DBAs need to insure that the filesystem of their Applications environment needs to be backed up along with their database. This may be a change in thinking for some Applications DBAs while others have seen this and are already backing up their filesystem routinely. An in depth discussion of backups and the various methods to complete them is outside of the scope of this book.

When people talk about "loading flat files" or "loading interface tables", they are generally talking about taking data that is in spreadsheet format and loading it into Oracle's tables. We often load this data when a different type of database holds information that we want incorporated into Oracle tables or while establishing interfaces between other application environments – say an interface between an Oracle Financials environment and a PeopleSoft HR, or a SAP supply chain environment. During a new rollout, Data Conversions are the first major process to load data into the Oracle Applications database via APIs or interface tables. The simplest way is to pull the data out of the source system in a format that Oracle can convert into its table format.

Components / Services

The Applications Tier is made up of Web Services, Forms Services, the Concurrent Processing Server, and an Admin Server that handle business logic. The logic contained in these components provides the guiding principle for actions in a given field or transaction. In other words, the Oracle Developers wrote code that governs the fields and transactions, how they handle data and what they do. Release 12 uses and depends on "services", which is a change from earlier E-Business Suite releases. The direction towards "services" will help Oracle tie in disparate systems and enable them to work together as a cohesive unit. Another service is the java desktop client that resides on the desktop tier. We have already talked about the java desktop client – it is the code that automatically downloads to your PC the first time you log in to the Release 12 Applications from your web browser.

Web Services

Web Services handles requests from the user by means of HTTP requests (the Web), and are comprised of several components: the Web Listener, the Java Servlet Engine and the Oracle Process Manager and Notification Server, more commonly referred to as OPMN. The web services run out of the 10.1.3 Oracle Home code set.

The Web Listener is an Apache web server wrapped for Oracle's environment. This component "listens" for incoming http traffic from the client and will fulfill the request itself if possible. These are simple requests such as retrieving the HTML needed to produce a web page. Code that is "wrapped" is a means used to take existing code and force it to react the way you want it to without changing the source code. Oracle did not make Apache but they "wrap" all their programs and utilities around it so it does what Oracle wants it to do.

The Java Servlet Engine handles the more advanced requests and works directly with the database server. This is really an OC4J (Oracle Components for Java) container that runs Java Server Pages (jsps). We will cover OC4J containers in more detail toward the end of this chapter, in the "OAS 10*g* Technology" section. These jsp pages contact the appropriate database and then render the HTML-based page that the end user sees in their web browser. Think about the page that is displayed after clicking on a specific responsibility. The request pulls information from certain tables that determine which menu functions are associated with that responsibility. The function's prompts are then combined into the HTML user interface, which was picked up from the metadata dictionary, so that they can be rendered by the web server and read from the end user's browser. This access path looks like this:

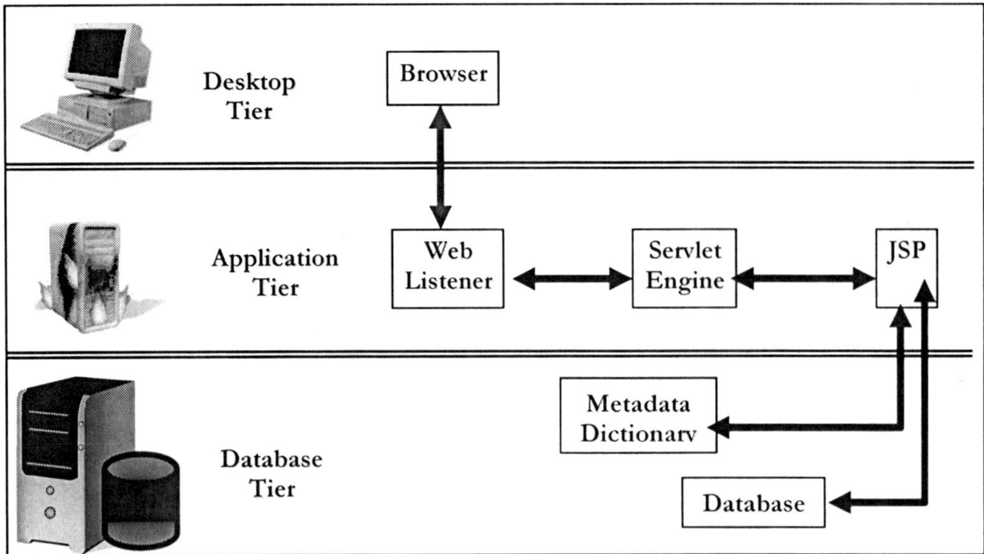

Figure 140 – Release 12 Tiers – Java Servlet Access

Java on the Server

At the core of the Java changes in the Release 12 environment is the replacement of JServer (JServ) on the Application Tier with the Application Server 10*g* (AS 10*g*) product. This move is an excellent change for the environment, as it not only brings a new level of functionality to the application server, but also allows us to begin working with some of the Fusion Middleware that will be at the heart of the Fusion Applications when they are released.

Oracle Application Server 10*g* Features

Let's start by looking at the features and functionality of AS 10*g*, before we delve into some of its inner workings. First, it is important to understand the differences between AS 10*g* and its predecessor, JServ. The JServ product was a simple Java applications server that supported JSP and Servlets, and little else. This was representative of other early generation Java application servers, so JServ was generally competitive with the market when it was released. However, the Java Enterprise Edition marketplace has since matured significantly, as can be seen from the plethora of new(ish) programming interfaces that it offers.

So the first feature of note in AS 10*g* is that it supports Sun Microsystem's Java Enterprise Edition version 1.4 (Java EE 1.4) programming standards. For those who are writing custom applications to deploy into the Oracle environment, this is very worthwhile. But even for those that aren't writing custom applications, this is of some importance, as it helps to set the stage for Fusion by showing us some of the tools that Oracle has at their disposal. Features of note in the Java EE 1.4 standards include a variety of new toolkits for creating user interfaces, and inclusion of some that help make the client's web browser experience a little more pleasant. Also included are some new tools for helping to make the movement of data between relational database tables and active Java objects in memory much more seamless for developers. This should help shorten some development processes, and help make the resulting code more resilient in the future.

In terms of Oracle products and features that are part of AS 10*g*, we discuss several of them in Chapter 10, *Fusion Middleware*, later in this book. But let's explore a few of the more relevant ones here to introduce the concepts and stir some thought. The first is important to anyone running Release 12, regardless of what your stance on Fusion might be: Oracle BPEL Process Manager. Considering Oracle's statement that the current Workflow technology is going to be replaced by BPEL in the Fusion Applications, now is the time to begin learning about the new technology on the block.

For larger or more sophisticated deployments, the inclusion of Oracle Identity Management in the OAS 10*g* means that integration into corporate security infrastructure such as LDAP directories should be that much easier. Also, there is a group of products that all focus on providing the infrastructure for the Service Oriented Architecture design that Oracle is using for the Fusion Applications: Oracle Web Services Manager, Oracle Enterprise Service Bus, and Oracle Application Server Service Registry. Together these tools provide the means to access Services, secure them, and locate and manage them on remote servers.

OAS 10*g* Technology

At the heart of OAS 10*g* is the Oracle Containers for Java (OC4J) product, the engine that drives the larger application server. OC4J, as it is commonly known, takes the form of an application running in its own Java Virtual Machine. In fact, OAS 10*g* uses multiple instances of OC4J running concurrently to provide all of its functionality. For those of you familiar with the underpinnings of E-Business Suite Release 11*i*, we need to stop you before you equate this to the Release 11*i* environment running multiple copies of JServ. JServ allows multiple copies of itself to run to provide scalability: you can execute one copy of JServer for every X number of users that you expect to have logged in simultaneously. That was done partly because the JVMs of the day had limited scalability and a single one could not handle all the users that the Release 11*i* environment was likely to see.

With OC4J and the newer JVMs that are available, scalability is first achieved by increasing the resource pool available to the JVM. Resources in this case mean both CPU processing power and server memory, both of which are consumed for every user that is logged in and doing work. When the sever itself cannot scale to provide additional resources, or when the operating system imposes limits of its own, then scalability is achieved by adding an additional server and creating a clustered OAS 10*g* solution. Those familiar with the Applications call this "throwing hardware at a performance problem."

So then the question remains, why does OAS 10*g* have multiple copies of OC4J running, if not for scalability? The answer is quite simple: for division of processing. Each instance of OC4J is used as a compartment to contain one portion of the OAS 10*g* functionality. This allows the individual instances to be tuned for their actual workload, and helps to prevent them from competing for resources. The instances that you are likely to find running in the average Release 12 deployment are:

- The oacore instance – for HTML based applications
- The oafm instance – for web services
- The forms instance – for Oracle Forms
- The Application Server Control instance – an optional component, for managing the application server itself

OC4J Logfiles

Even with regular monitoring, it is possible for your Oracle environment to go through an unanticipated spike in activity, such as during a periodic close process, which could make the server run out of memory. In this instance, your first indication of trouble could well be the dreaded calls from your user community, who are helpfully telling you that Oracle is down and their world is ending. If you see that one of the normal OC4J instances is not running, your first course of action should be to check its logfile and look for errors.

You will find this logfile under the `Instance Top` directory structure that we will look at in more detail later in this chapter. Specifically we will go to:

> `$INST_TOP/logs/ora/10.1.3/j2ee/oc4jname` (or 10.1.2 if it is the reporting instance that is having an issue).

In this case, `oc4jname` is the name of the OC4J instance. Here we'll find an `application.log` file, and at the end of it we'll find the last messages that OC4J wrote before shutdown. If it is the dreaded `java.lang.OutOfMemory` error message then we know that we must go into our memory tuning exercise. Note that as a quick fix you can simply restart the Oracle environment by running the script `adopmnctl.sh,` for instance; and do the memory tuning, with its potentially lengthy AutoConfig step, when it is more convenient. Just don't be surprised when the same thing happens a few hours later!

The Oracle Process Manager and Notification Server (OPMN) manages Application Server components. It is responsible for starting, stopping and death detection of the OC4J container processes. It also sits between the Oracle HTTP Server and the OC4J Containers and passes notifications between the two.

Forms Services

Forms services deliver the ability to run Oracle Forms, and are handled by a java servlet known as the Forms Listener Servlet. This servlet corresponds to the Java Applet on the Desktop Tier and handles communications between the end user and the database server over HTTP/HTTPS or TCP/IP connections.

Use of the Forms Listener Servlet allows data to be cached and returned to the end user when the user is ready to act on the requested information. For example, Figure 141 shows that if you query information on all users of the Oracle Applications from the Security >Define screen, you will only see one record at a time, even though there may be hundreds or thousands of records returned. The remaining records have been returned and are available for you to scroll through because they have been cached.

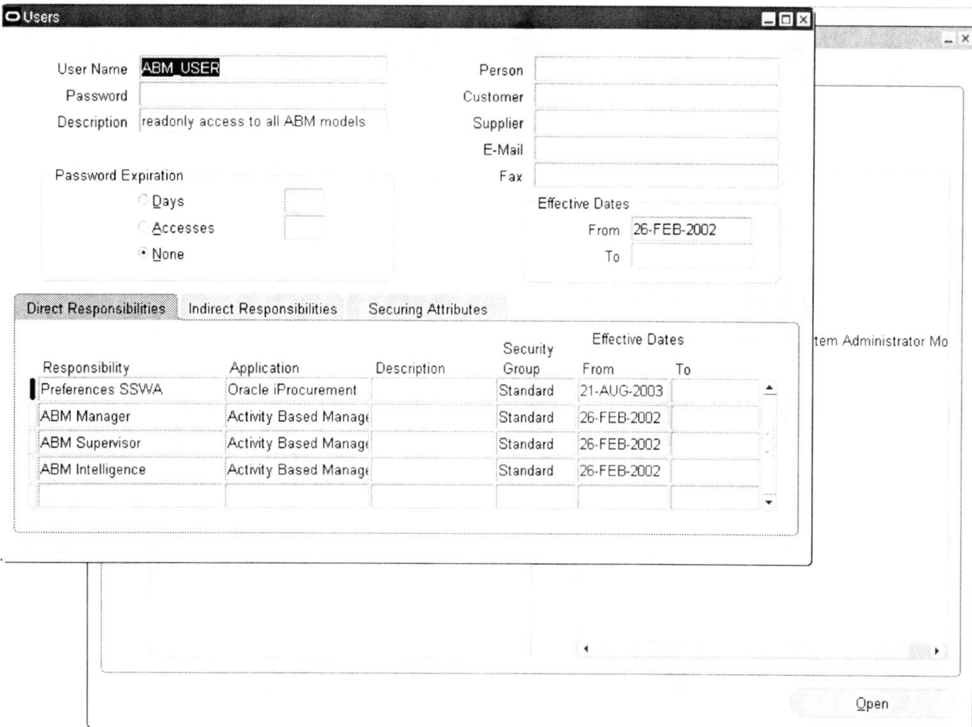

Figure 141 –This shows the screen for defining security for users. While our query requested information on all users, the information is cached so that we can page through the results one record at a time. In this case, we are looking at the user ABM_USER's security profile.

To step though an example, here we see the Define User screen as mentioned above. Using the <ctrl> - f11 key combination would execute an open query and would return every user in your system that had been defined as an applications user. As you can see from this screen shot, only one record is viewable at a time even though there are many more (at a minimum there are several default "seeded" users for the applications). Using the <down arrow> key on your keyboard will move to the next record. The results of your open query have been cached and are therefore immediately available as you move from record to record.

Forms, by the way, are run from a different code set than the HTTP services. The executable program, known as `frmweb`, is run out of the Version 10.1.2 Oracle Home. Interestingly enough, the Forms Listener Servlet runs out of an OC4J container that is under the 10.1.3 codeset and can be seen by running the following command (assuming your *i*AS environment is sourced):

```
opmnctl status -l
```

The process-type, as you can see in Figure 142, is listed as "forms".

```
a120int2@sbllc12 > opmnctl status -l

Processes in Instance: a120int2_sbllc12.sbllc12.solutionbeacon.net
-------------------+--------------------+---------+----------+------------+----------+-----------
ias-component      | process-type       |     pid | status   |        uid |  memused |    uptime |
-------------------+--------------------+---------+----------+------------+----------+-----------
OC4J               | oafm               |   29013 | Alive    |  974353527 |   147940 | 379:52:33 |
OC4J               | forms              |   28922 | Alive    |  974353526 |   105192 | 379:52:40 |
OC4J               | oacore             |   28745 | Alive    |  974353525 |   184808 | 379:53:06 |
HTTP_Server        | HTTP_Server        |   28650 | Alive    |  974353524 |    91480 | 379:53:07 |
ASG                | ASG                |     N/A | Down     |        N/A |      N/A |       N/A |
```

Figure 142 – use the `opmnctl status` command to see the Forms Listener Servlet

Release 12 runs Forms in either Socket or Servlet mode. For Release 12 the default is Servlet mode. MetaLink Doc. ID: 384241.1, "Using Forms Socket Mode with Oracle E-Business Suite Release 12" describes the differences between the Release 11*i* socket mode and the Release 12 servlet mode. Oracle MetaLink Doc. ID: 311091.1 "Understanding the Network Overhead Of Forms Servlet Listener Architecture Compared to Forms Server" details the performance considerations related to each of these modes, including:

- The Socket mode performs better over WAN(s)
- The Servlet mode is based on standards that make working with load balancing, proxies, and firewalls easier.

The Release 12 Forms Mode is illustrated in Figure 143:

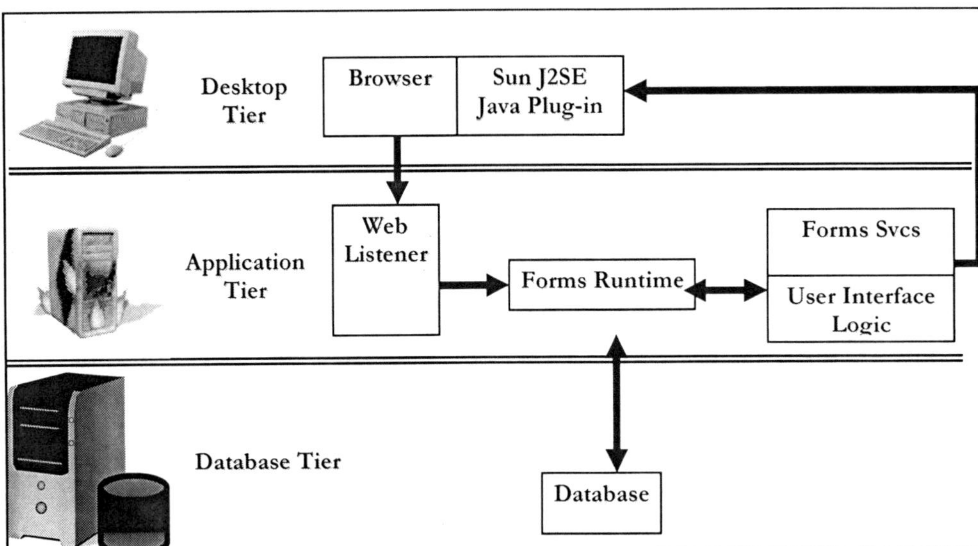

Figure 143 - Release 12 Tiers - Forms Socket Mode

You might wonder at this point why you should care if you are running a form or an HTTP service, and why you might want to know the `opmnctl` command. Knowing the difference between an Oracle Professional Form and an HTML based screen is mostly helpful in your troubleshooting efforts. This knowledge will also help you better understand what is happening in your system as you interact with it. What components are involved with a form versus an HTML screen? Which code set does this functionality belong to? If a screen is acting strange, is it a form with a forms base object (`.fmb` object) or is it a collection of java server pages? OPMN, and its controlling utility `opmnctl`, are a new part of the E-Business

Suite because Release 12 now uses the 10*g* Application Server software, and OPMN is used to control the 10*g*AS components. It is also used on the command line to interact with the application server. The `opmnctl` utility allows you to start and stop components and subcomponents individually or as a group.

Concurrent Processing Server

The concurrent processing server allows reports or programs to run in the background. It provides the framework for a user to request a report or submit a program to be run and then continues working in other areas as those requests run behind the scenes. This increases efficiency for the end user, as they can continue working on other tasks while their request is processed. This server also facilitates scheduling these requests to run once or periodically, as well as providing the ability to choose when the requests will run. A series of tables house all the information needed to handle this processing, including how many resources are claimed from the operating system. The Concurrent Managers (CCMs) also run requests that are generated by Oracle Forms and Workflow as part of their processing architecture.

Requests run for Forms or Workflow can be run in an "immediate" mode depending on the setups. These "immediate" requests require the use of a "Transaction Manager" and are hooked to each node where forms services are run. As an end user, though, you will likely be oblivious to transaction managers unless one of them stops working for some reason. In that case, you could be in the middle of a form, trying to enter data, and see unusual error messages. The best thing to do in this case is to call your Help Desk.

The Concurrent Processing Server by and large regulates itself. It is comprised of control type managers like the Internal Concurrent Manager (ICM), which starts and stops the other managers; the Conflict Resolution Manager, which handles conflicts between requests, the transactional managers that run programs for forms and workflow processing, as well as a Standard Manager that runs everything else. Companies can create their own concurrent managers to suit their processing needs. Concurrent managers are versatile in that they can be configured to run SQL, PL/SQL, host shell scripts, C programs, Oracle Reports, Oracle Load programs and Java programs.

Release 12 has an additional subtle change in that there is no Report Server, as we knew it. Oracle Reports are now run through the Concurrent Managers or, where necessary, the `RWRUN` utility is executed directly.

Solution Beacon Recommends: *Characterize the run times for your requests and then create time-based concurrent manager queues to house them. We like to see fast requests in a fast queue, long running requests in a long queue, and everything in between in a middle queue. We leave the Standard Manager active and use this queue to characterize the running requests, which leads to the assignment to one of our time-based queues. We do this because there is nothing more frustrating than having a three-second request queued behind a three-hour request. Note, though, that end users generally are not tasked to "tune the concurrent manager" – that's a job your Applications System Administrator and your Applications DBA will work on together. They have scripts available to them that can help gauge which concurrent managers are running efficiently, and which need to be adjusted.*

Concurrent Managers always produce two types of output files: log files and out files. Log Files show information (including error messages) about running the concurrent request. At times, they may not contain any information other than standard header type information. Out Files contain the "results" of the concurrent request. This is "data retrieved" as a result of running the program. This file may not be produced if there is no mechanism for the program to return results, or may be a zero length file if no results are returned. These directories can be reached by using the `$APPLCSF/log` and `$APPLCSF/out` paths respectively. The `$APPLCSF` is set when your Applications environment is sourced. When you source a file, you are executing or running it. So when we say that `$APPLCSF` is set when your Applications environment is sourced, we mean that a program was run that set the variable for `$APPLCSF`. If you want to look at the `out` file (the report) that was generated for a concurrent request, you can either look at the concurrent request screen within the Applications, or from UNIX you can go to `$APPLCSF/out` and look for the request that way.

The E-Business Suite has certain variables that need to be set, along with certain paths to key directories and programs, for proper operation and ease of navigation at the OS level. Oracle keeps all the items that need to be executed into environment files managed by AutoConfig. When working at the OS level we often source files by using the "dot" construct followed by a space and a filename. In Oracle Applications Release 12 we use the "`APPSdb sid__host.env`" (the Release 11*i* equivalent is named "`APPSORA.env`") file to house all of these requisite settings for the applications environment. So the syntax for us to source the "Apps" environment would be:

```
. <path-to-file>/APPSsid_host.env
```

In our Solution Beacon Vision instances, this would look like:

```
. /a120int2/apps/apps_st/appl/APPSa120int2_sbllcXX.env
```

Using this "dot" construct tells the operating system to execute all commands contained in the specified file in the current shell. This last piece is important because it means the results of the executed commands are still applicable even after the file has been executed. So, one command that is executed in this file is to set the context name for the Applications Tier. As written in the Solution Beacon `APPSORA.env` file it looks like this:

```
CONTEXT_NAME="a120int2_sbllcXX"

export CONTEXT_NAME
```

Now, for the remainder of our time in this shell running the command `echo $CONTEXT_NAME` will return the value `a120int2_sbllcXX`. Make sense? So, we now know that `$APPLCSF`, from above, has been assigned a directory path in the `APPSsid_host.env` file that will be usable after you source the Application Tier environment file.

If you are an end user, you might think that the only file location of interest to you should be the Out Files, where your report output is stored. In actuality, you will want to be able to see the Log Files as well. Sometimes a program fails for deeply technical reasons, and sometimes they fail for simple reasons. In either case, it helps if you've looked at the out file to see if there's something obvious that you can do to fix the problem, or if the problem needs to be called in to your Help Desk. Now, we've told you where to find the files if you are a UNIX guru, but you should also know that when you run a concurrent request, afterward you can look up the result and see the logfile and output file from your concurrent manager screen.

Admin Server

The Admin Server is responsible for handling the Oracle Applications data model and the data in the Oracle Applications database. Mainly we are speaking of Patching and Maintenance. Patching is Oracle's way of releasing code fixes, functionality enhancements or new functionality. Patches update or create new file system objects like forms, reports and sql scripts as well as executing code within the database to change seeded data.

Seeded data is data that is preloaded by Oracle. For example, after you first installed the Oracle Applications, the table `APPLSYS.FND_CONCURRENT_QUEUES` was already populated by the installation process. The information contained in this table helped to define concurrent managers (queues). As you did not need to load this data yourself, it is referred to as "seeded" data.

Patches must be applied from the Admin Server using a tool called ADPATCH. This is a toolset written by Oracle that allows your DBA or Applications System Administrator to apply a patch. Maintenance tasks are not relevant to all services on all nodes but most tasks requiring maintenance are performed on the Admin Server node.

Java Desktop Client

One of the simplest changes in Release 12 is also one of the most telling, namely the replacement of JInitiator with Sun's Java Runtime Environment. Let's start with a quick review of what JInitiator was, and then we'll tackle its replacement and the significance thereof.

JInitiator was Oracle's version of a Java applet viewer that ran in the end user's web browser. Remember the E-Business Suite is composed of two core client technologies: html/javascript for most of the Applications, and Java applet technology for the Forms-based Applications. Rather than depend on Sun's Java Runtime to provide the applet viewer in the end user's browser, Oracle chose to provide their own, in the form of JInitiator. It gave Oracle complete control over the applet viewer's Java language version, and allowed them to have complete control over patches and bugs. This makes JInitiator Oracle's licensed version of the applet viewer, and another custom component that had to be deployed in the environment.

In the Release 12 environment, things are much simpler: JInitiator is gone, and you can simply use versions of Sun's Java Runtime environment that Oracle has certified. Well, that's the goal, and if your environment is patched current then that's the reality. For the initial base build of Release 12 Oracle required the use of a patched version of Sun's Java Runtime, so in effect it was JInitiator by another name. Oracle has since switched to Sun's version, so this is a good reason to bring your shiny new installation of Release 12 up to the latest patch level before ever logging into it!

In June of 2007, Oracle certified the environment on top of the unpatched Sun 1.5.0_12 Java Runtime and its applet viewer. With the removal of the need for Oracle patches to the Java runtime, JInitiator was truly gone both physically and in spirit. To use the 1.5.0_12 runtime you will need to apply Patch Number 4377566 entitled "Applications Interoperability Patch for JRE1.5.0_x Plug-in". All of this, as well as the simple procedures that you'll need to go through to apply the patch are detailed in MetaLink Doc. ID: 393931.1, "Upgrading JRE Plugin with Oracle Applications R12".

The move from JInitiator to a particular version of the Java environment directly from Sun may seem like a trivial improvement, but actually, it's not. For one thing, it shows Oracle's commitment to standardization, but much more importantly, it opens the door to incremental improvements in the applications desktop. There are multiple initiatives underway at Sun to improve Java on the desktop, including efforts to improve its performance, to reduce its startup time, to reduce how long it takes to install, and to reduce its disk and memory footprints. Most of these improvements will appear in the Java 1.6 environment, so they are a just a line on a project plan right now. But they should move into production much quicker if we can get them directly from Sun, rather than waiting for them to be incorporated into JInitiator.

We would be remiss if we left you thinking that by using Sun's Java software that you won't encounter any problems connecting to your Release 12 environment. In fact, Solution Beacon supports a very large free test environment for the user community, and we regularly hear from first time users that are experiencing difficulties. The issue here, it turns out, is that your PC likely has all kinds of different pieces of software installed, many of which may be incompatible with the Applications for one reason or another. If you experience difficulties logging in or find yourself kicked off your E-Business Suite environment, you should contact your Help Desk to see if there is anything obviously wrong.

Solution Beacon Recommends: *You can also try out the set of fixes that Solution Beacon recommends to new users by accessing the following document:* http://www.solutionbeacon.com/logintips.pdf

Technology Layer

The Technology Layer is the supporting layer for all of the modules in Release 12. This layer has existed in previous versions of Oracle Applications but it existed as a disparate collection of modules that were treated as separate products unto themselves. Beginning in the latest release of 11*i* this layer has been consolidated into the Applications Technology Group (ATG) and is supported, maintained and patched accordingly. This section breaks down the ATG and provides information about what each module does. It should be noted that Oracle can still release a focused patch that deals with only one of the modules in this layer. For example, one upgrade in one of our Release 12 environments called for an Applications DBA rollup patch as a prerequisite.

If you are an end user, you might wonder just how much you need to understand about the technology layers. It is worthwhile to have a general idea of the acronyms that we are about to explain, primarily because if a module that you use needs to be upgraded, the technology layer will often need to be upgraded as well. This increases the scope of the upgrade effort, and will require more testing than you as an end user might anticipate, since changes to some or all of these modules would need to be tested as well. Keep in mind that these modules are the very heart of the Oracle Applications – they affect every module, so changes to them are incredibly important to all users.

From a technologist's perspective, the modules that make up the Applications Technology Group make up the majority of their workload. The DBA, the Applications System Administrator, the Workflow Administrator and the Reporting Administrator all care deeply about what goes on with these modules.

AD (Application DBA)

The Application DBA module provides the administrative tools used to install, upgrade, maintain, and patch the Oracle Applications environment. It does this through the following programs and utilities:

- AD Administration is the ADADMIN utility for maintenance
- AutoPatch uses the ADPATCH utility for applying patches
- AD Merge Patch is used to consolidate multiple patches into one patch
- AutoConfig is used for configuration management
- Rapid Clone is used to clone (duplicate) an Applications environment
- Rapid Install is used when installing and upgrading the Oracle Applications

AK (Common Modules)

The Common Modules, also known as the AK modules, is an active data dictionary used to define HTML-based Applications components. It generates runtime characteristics of the Applications, is used to develop inquiries for the HTML-based Applications without strong programming knowledge, and it stores language translated data field labels

When upgrading to Release 12, you will need to run the Personalization Migration Tool, CustMigrationTool, via java. Several parameters need to be passed to this tool so it can accurately migrate the AK repository to the new MDS repository. More information on these parameters can be found in the Oracle Application Framework Personalization Guide Release 12 Part No. B31347-01 in your Release 12 Document Library.

AU (Application Utilities)

The Application Utilities module is actually just a location used to maintain the Oracle Applications environment. It provides a standard, shared location for certain files copied from other products and is located on the file system at `$AU_TOP`. Among the objects stored there are:

- Forms base files, also known as `.fmbs`
- Shared PL/SQL library files, or `.plls`, as needed for common objects like forms
- Discoverer end user layer objects and components
- `.ogd` graphics objects
- Java class files are here as well as in other locations like the `$JAVA_TOP` and `$<PRODUCT>_TOP`s
- `.ldt` files, which are Data Loader Datafiles, can also be here in the patch directory

FND (Application Object Library)

The Application Object Library, or AOL, is a key component in the Technology Layer. It provides common or uniform functionality across all products or modules. It ensures:

- Concurrent Requests are submitted in the same fashion between product modules. A Concurrent Request is a program, usually submitted by a user that usually produces a report (though it could just change some data and complete without producing a report)
- A standard look and feel
- Common Value Sets are provided for use between product modules. A Value Set is a list of values for a parameter. For example, you might create a Value Set for valid zip codes. Any module could use this Value Set if needed.
- You can use the same GUI and coding standards for custom development as Oracle's Developers use.
- Many customizations can be seamlessly integrated into Oracle Applications
- Flexfields are processed in the same manner by every module. A Flexfield is an Oracle Applications construct used to display a single field made up of several segments. They can be described as a single "field" of data that is made up of several other fields

  Figure 144 shows a screen shot from Solution Beacon's Release 12 Vision environment where we used an HR responsibility to navigate to this screen. In this graphic, we see what looks like a standard field (highlighted). However, clicking on this screen opens the second graphic, which contains a series of fields. In Figure 144, the Flexfield appears to be a standard field until activated and then it becomes a special screen allowing additional information to be entered.

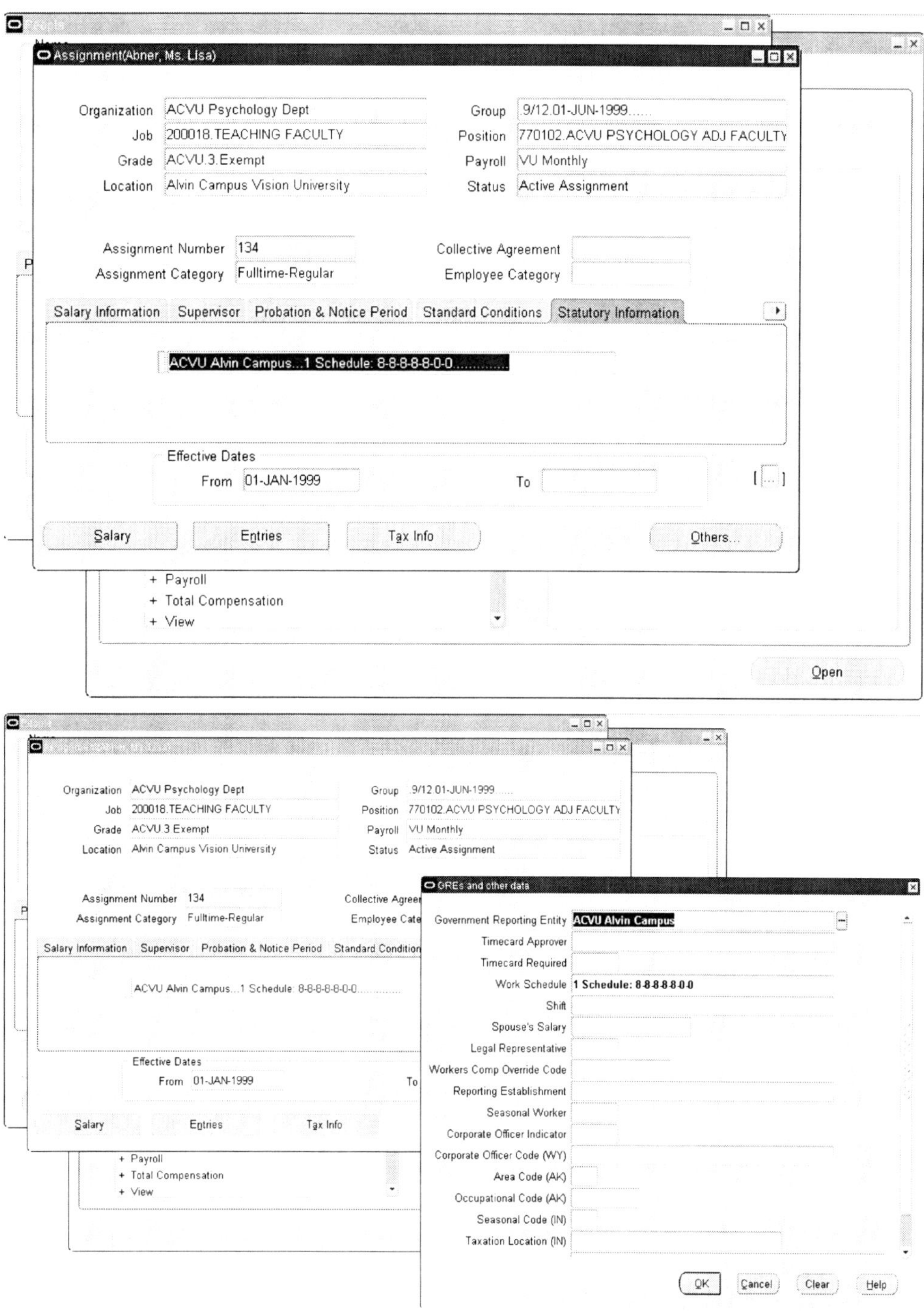

Figure 144 – An example of a Flexfield

The AOL also provides System Administration functionality encompassing all product modules:

- Access Control - this is the common interface for defining a new user and assigning responsibilities that provide the required menus, which in turn allow access to the functions necessary to complete a job

- Administration of System Profiles - these system profiles govern much of the Application's capabilities and are set through AOL-provided functionality

- Administration of the Concurrent Managers (CCM) - this allows monitoring, starting, stopping, creating new concurrent managers, and setting options for each CCM, like the number of processes to run, the cache size and workshifts

- Administration of Flexfields and Value Sets - all Flexfields and value sets are available to all Applications modules and are created and administered through AOL functionality

- Registration of Custom Products - custom product "tops" that house specific company customizations are also registered with AOL functions. A "top" is a directory where all the code for a particular module is stored. So the code for the General Ledger is stored in "GL_TOP". Oracle recommends that customers keep all of their customizations to code in its own custom "top" rather than mixing the code in with Oracle's code. So if you modified one of Oracle's General Ledger programs, you would store the modification in your custom top rather than in GL_TOP

The AOL provides the administrative framework for creating and managing functions, menus, and responsibilities

OWF (Workflow)

Workflow is a framework for transactional flows that provides step-by-step processing of transactions that are automated. Workflow transactions can be fully autonomous or require user intervention. Workflow has several components:

- Workflow Builder

- Workflow Engine

- Business Event System

- Workflow Event Manager

Oracle's Workflow plays an important role in the Oracle Applications and needs to be well understood if you are going to work with the E-Business Suite. An in-depth look at all of its capabilities is not possible within the scope of this primer. However, you can think of workflow as a flowchart of actions that need to be taken for a transaction or business process. These actions take specific steps based on derived answers that either come from the processed data itself or from user inputs. Some simple examples are: If more than 5 orders exist, do something… If user A answers yes, then do something else… Continue processing next step after sending a notification to user B…

Again, using simple explanations that belie the capabilities and advanced processing the workflow system can do, the workflow components have these tasks:

- The Workflow Builder component is used to model the transaction or business process

- The Workflow Engine is used to monitor and react to the derived data at decision points

- The Workflow Event Manager is used in a trigger like fashion; for example, when a new user is created, send an email to the system administrator

- The Business Event System uses Oracle's Advanced Queuing technology to communicate between systems, which means it propagates messages between agents using specific protocols

A business event is an occurrence that has an impact on objects in a system. For example, hiring a new employee is an event. An action that must occur following a business event is defined as a subscription to that business event. For example, a subscription might be a notification to the benefits department to prepare paperwork for the new employee. The Event Manager executes any subscriptions on the event.

Solution Beacon Recommends: *We simply can't do justice to the complexity of Workflow in this Primer, so we recommend that you look at other material if you plan to support Workflow or want to know more about it. Solution Beacon's* *The ABCs of Workflow* (available at http://stores.lulu.com/store.php?fAcctID=83172) *provides a detailed explanation of Workflow's features.*

ALR (Alerts)

The next technology layer component is Alerts. It notifies defined entities when an exception occurs and can execute a code set when it encounters an exception. The Alerts module uses the concurrent managers to process "periodic" exceptions and uses trigger type code to process "event" exceptions. In Release 12, as with later 11*i* releases, the workflow mailer is used by the alerts module to send emails/notifications. It can be effective for users that do not have strong programming skills who want to know of exceptions, since it is Screen/ Form driven (point and click, then fill out the data field).

Oracle Alerts can be used to monitor activities that you may want to know about with little effort. Some examples are:

- When a tablespace is almost out of space

- When a Profile Option is altered

- When a patch is applied

- When a new employee is hired

- When a supplier's email or address is changed

In addition to handling notifications, Oracle Alerts can also take action on an exception (i.e., run a script to extend a tablespace when it is almost out of space; or perhaps submit a concurrent request to gather statistics when a patch has been applied)

FWK (Application Framework)

The Application Framework module is next on our list. The Applications Framework (FWK) is Oracle's development framework for HTML applications and is a way to shorten development time while maintaining consistency. Several components comprise the Applications framework but the two primary components are the bc4j (business components for java) and the aol/j (Application Object Library Java Services). bc4j is used to create java procedures directly linked to the application tables but separated from the user's interface. aol/j handles the database connection and its integrated security along with E-Business Suite specific functionality

You can read more about the Application Framework in the Oracle Application Framework Personalization Guide Release 12 Part No. B31347-01. This manual includes tie-ins to the Application Developer Guide and the System Administrator Guide on Configuration.

XDO (XML Publisher)

The XML Publisher layer is a Java product based on the W3C's Extensible Stylesheets Language specs. It uses the XSL-FO standard to change XML data into a formatting object and uses data definitions and templates to produce output reports in the desired format. It includes the following core components: the FO Processor, PDF Document Merger, PDF Form Processor, and RTF Template Parser.

- The FO Processor generates the required output document from the "formatting object". Currently only PDF is supported, but rtf and html will be supported soon
- The PDF Document Merger uses a mapping to merge XML Data into fields in a PDF document
- The PDF Form Processor adds attributes to a PDF document (for example: it can add a "Draft Only" watermark as a comment)
- The RTF Template Parser converts RTF templates to an XSL-FO that can then be applied to XML data

XML's Template Manager features include:

- Data Source Registration, which is the registration of sources that can output XML data
- Template Registration, which is the registration of templates used to format data
- XML Publisher APIs, which are APIs provided that allow direct communication between underlying processes and Applications products

Application Filesystem Primer

A full Oracle installation is a large and complicated beast. To help tame that beast, it is important to use standards wherever possible. In this case, Oracle has created a standard application filesystem layout that, while it may seem complicated in and of itself, helps to simplify the support of the installation. The paradox of simplifying something by adding more to it appears repeatedly in enterprise software with varying degrees of success. In this discussion, we will detail how the application filesystem is laid out, why it is done that way, and how you can benefit from this configuration.

In the traditional RDBMS Version 9*i* E-Business Suite, Oracle uses a few conventions to structure the installed software. This serves dual goals: it makes it easier for the Applications DBA to navigate through the installation, and it groups resources into logical categories. In Release 12, Oracle builds on this architecture and makes the division of resources more clear cut, making it easier to navigate the directory structures and easier to share them between servers.

For the sake of completeness, let's begin by looking at the filesystem structure on the database tier, which is represented in Figure 145. In Oracle's default layout, the directory structure begins at the `$ORACLE_BASE` directory, which would commonly be a keyword denoting something like the instance or the project name. Below this would be the `apps_st` directory, which would contain the database's various kinds of data files, and alongside that would be the `tech_st` directory, which would contain the 10.2.0 Oracle Home for the database software.

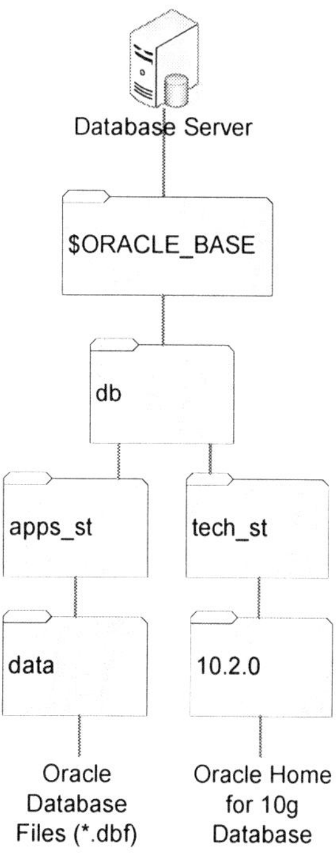

Figure 145 – The filesystem structure on the database tier

Next, let's move to the applications tier as shown in Figure 146, which has two major directory structures. Again we will begin the directory structure at the `$ORACLE_BASE` level. Under it, let's start with the `apps_st` directory tree, which contains the product files and HTML files. There is also the `tech_st` directory, which is where things start to get complicated. It contains a 10.1.2 Oracle Home for the Concurrent Managers and Forms, and a 10.1.3 Oracle Home for the Apache and OC4J product files. This directory tree therefore houses most of what is needed for the application server, but one thing we haven't seen yet are configuration files or log files.

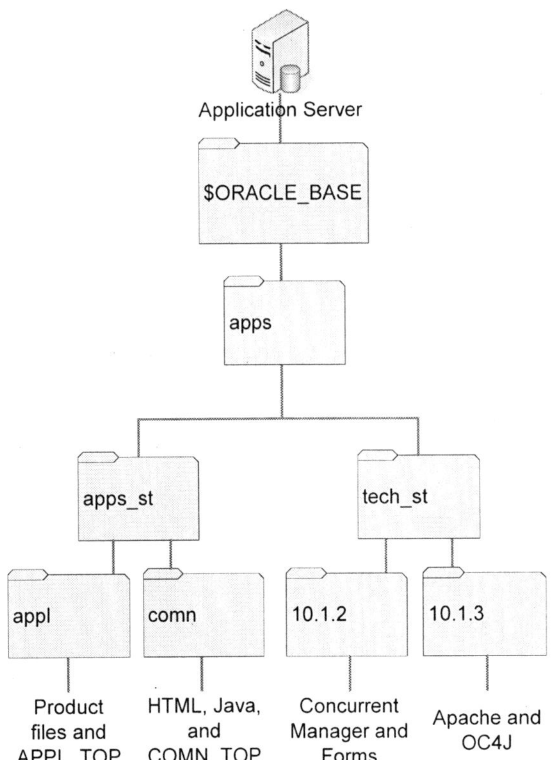

Figure 146 –The filesystem structure on the applications tier

Now is the time to locate the missing resources by introducing a new concept in the application filesystem standard: the Instance Home. This structure, illustrated in Figure 147, is new for Release 12 and is denoted by the `$INST_TOP` variable in UNIX. It resides under the `$ORACLE_BASE/inst/apps/`*context_name* directory, where *context_name* is the name of your dbsid_host.

First things first: we need to see what we will find in the Instance Home, and then we can examine why that is the case. Figure 147 shows the contents best, but let's cover some of the highlights here. First we have the logs directory (stored in `$LOG_HOME` variable), which contains directories to hold the Apache and OC4J log files, as well as the concurrent manager's output (out and log files). This is important because these are the files that DBAs are most often looking for. We have the `ora` directory, which holds the configuration files for the various Oracle products and the `admin` directory that houses the inventory files and the administrative scripts. The `appl` directory here also holds the `dbc` file along with the context xml files. There are additional directories here, but let's move on.

What is the common theme to the content of the Instance Home structure? It's rather simple: all of the files in it are specific to *this* running instance of the Oracle environment. They are logfiles that are written at runtime, they are configuration files that contain instance-specific entries, and they are commands (scripts, generally) that contain instance-specific entries such as directory paths and context names. All of these entities are written to either at configuration-time when AutoConfig is run, or at runtime when the applications are actively processing work; in other words, this content is variable in nature. Contrast this with the previous directories housing product files and the like, content that is static in nature, except of course during a patch or installation process.

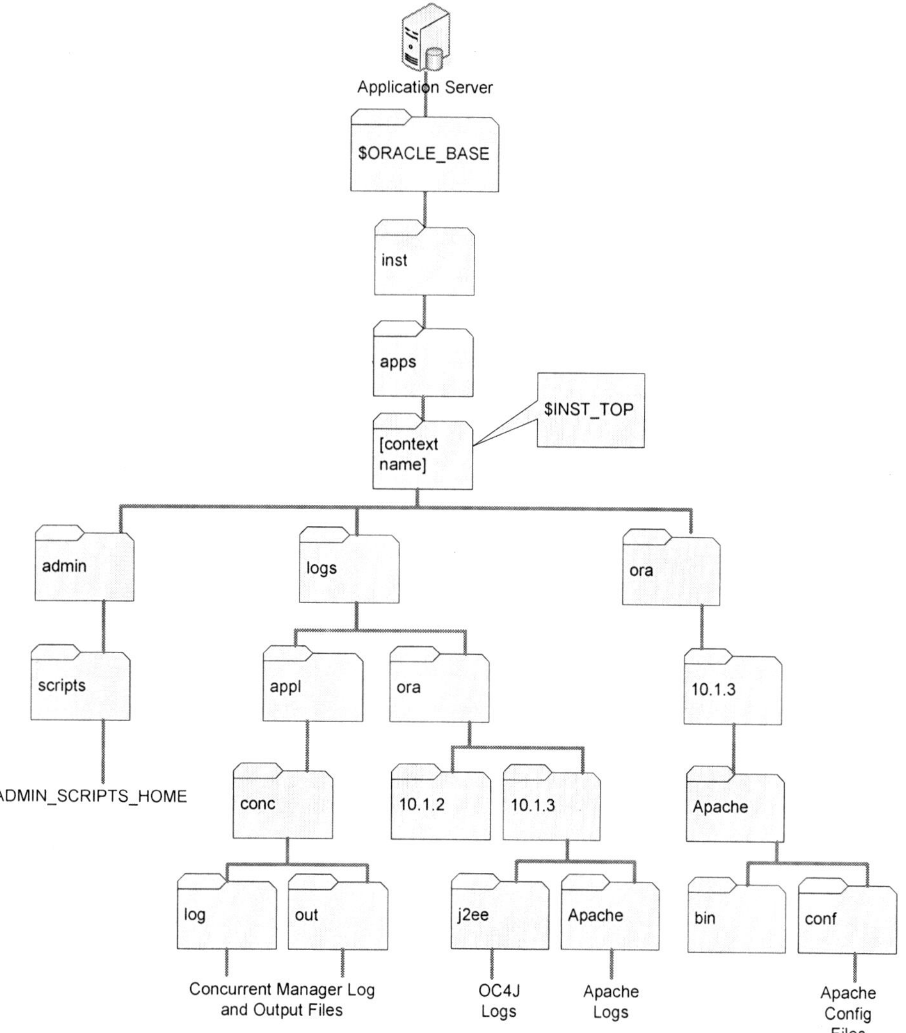

Figure 147 – The Instance Home

So what have we seen so far? We've seen that the applications tier places all of its binaries and other non-variable product files into the `$ORACLE_BASE/apps/apps_st` and `$ORACLE_BASE/apps/tech_st` directories, while the variable content is stored in the new Instance Home structure.

If you haven't already guessed, the major reason for this is to facilitate sharing the product files between multiple servers that are commonly used to create an Oracle implementation.

There are many reasons that multiple nodes might be used in an implementation, ranging from scalability to security to segregation of workload. If the Oracle software is installed individually on each server, not only does the amount of disk space that it consumes go up, but so does the amount of time that the Applications DBA must spend applying patches to it. If the prospect of repetitively applying patches to one server after another doesn't appeal to you, then the Shared Applications Filesystem (see Figure 148) is for you.

In this architecture the non-context specific content, the `apps_st` and `tech_st` directories, are placed on shared storage, such as an NFS filesystem in the UNIX world. All nodes then mount this filesystem and can access the same content. Also, each node has its own Instance Home structure located on private storage that only it can access. This means the Applications DBA can apply patches once, and they will instantly be seen by each node in the shared environment, greatly reducing the maintenance effort and downtime.

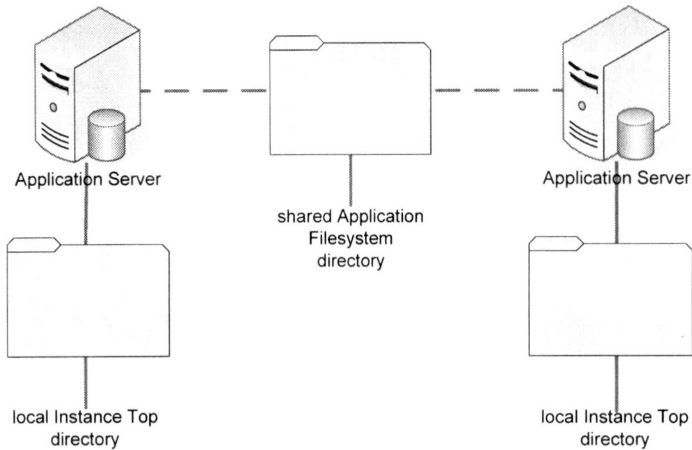

Figure 148 – Shared Application Filesystem

Does this sound like something that you want to have in your environment? If so, there are only two simple, but extremely important conditions that your architecture must meet. First, all the servers that will access the Shared Applications Filesystem must be of the same hardware architecture and must be running the same operating system. Note that they don't have to be the same hardware model, but merely the same hardware architecture, because it isn't possible to run Solaris SPARC binaries on an Intel or AMD based Solaris system.

As for the second requirement, it's also simple: your shared storage must have a level of fault tolerance that is equal to what you require in your applications. Simply put, the shared storage becomes a single point of failure in the environment because it is shared among multiple servers. If you require 24 x 7 availability from your Oracle implementation, and you make sure that every server has redundant components (power supplies, network cards, SAN cards, and so on) then you probably don't want to have the entire implementation shutdown because your NFS, or Network File System, server is down.

While this requirement is simple enough, the solution to it can become very complicated. The easiest way to solve the problem is to start at the database tier. Is your database clustered in some way, either using traditional host based clustering (active/passive) or via Oracle's RAC technology? If it is, then you must have stringent availability requirements; if not, then your requirements are more relaxed and your solution is easy. How easy? If you have a single database server, then you can simply use it as the NFS server for your environment.

If you have clustered database servers, then you need to have an external NFS server, preferably in the form of an add-on to your SAN, or Storage Area Network. Most SAN vendors have a component that can be added to provide NAS (Network Attached Server) capabilities to their product line. Just as SAN hardware typically contains redundant power supplies and processors and fibre cards and of course disks (RAID anyone?), NAS hardware contains all the same concepts. This means that when it is coupled with redundant network infrastructure it should be able to provide a level of fault tolerance that matches what you've achieved with your clustered database servers.

If you are an end user, you might wonder how much of this file system jargon you need to understand. It is worthwhile for you to understand that if a vendor or a consultant or your IT staff recommends a change, whether it is adding another node to improve performance, switching to SAN to make cloning faster, or changing to a different RAID level to improve redundancy and performance, these types of changes are a big deal.

AutoConfig

Now that you have a feeling for how the file system is laid out, let's look at the tools your DBA will use to configure and make changes to your environment.

AutoConfig is a tool that manages the storage and propagation of configuration information for an Oracle Applications system. Items that may need to be configured include which components are active; the locations of certain programs, utilities or files in your environment; port numbers; local display settings, and timeout values. The exact workings of AutoConfig are beyond the scope of this primer, but we have used the following "household" explanation so you will have some idea of how AutoConfig works:

Why do we shop for groceries? Simple, we need to get new items or replace old or out-of-date items. So, we make our list of new things we need or are out of, and we look at the items that are out-of-date. We pick these items up during a shopping trip and then bring them home. If we just throw them in the front closet, we would know where they are but our family members might not. So, we put the new items where we wanted them to go and we replace the old or out-of-date items with the fresher ones. This is a household version of AutoConfig.

In Oracle Applications what we would see is that some value changed as the result of a patch being applied or direct user activities and that a change or changes needs to be made to our system. If we made the change but did not run AutoConfig then the change would be there but the system would not know about it. So, we run AutoConfig, which will take the changes and update the correct template and context files (see below for a more detailed picture of what template and context files are). Now, the entire system has that change in place and the system is "AutoConfig'd".

AutoConfig is used for both the Application Tier and Database Tier, but, thankfully, it does not interact with the Desktop Tier, since there are no configuration files stored on the Desktop Tier

AutoConfig uses a central "context" file and template files to store settings needed for the instance. The context file is located in the `$INST_TOP/appl/admin` directory and is named `<DB SID__HOST>.xml` (for our Solution Beacon external vision instance it would be `a120vis1_sbl1cXX.xml`). Template files are located in a template directory under the `$<PRODUCT>_TOPs` for the Application Tier and under `<rdbms_oracle_home>/appsutil` for the Database Tier.

Important AutoConfig scripts:

- `adautocfg.sh` - runs AutoConfig
- `adchkcfg.sh` - produces a report that details the differences found in the AutoConfig environment at that time and what changes AutoConfig will make when it runs (`output = cfgcheck.html`). This can be a very useful report if

you are new to AutoConfig or if you are making system changes and want to know which files are touched by those changes

- `adcfginfo.sh` - lists all the product modules maintained by AutoConfig. This report can be a shortcut to determining what Applications modules you have licensed and whether you are over-licensed or under-licensed. We worry about licensing because Oracle expects its customers to implement only those modules that they paid for. It is easy to accidentally install more modules than intended. The repercussions to installing too many modules is that you might end up wasting time patching modules that you don't care about, and Oracle may audit you at some point and demand payment for these unnecessary modules.

- `adtmplreport.sh` - finds the template files for a given configuration file. This can be helpful if changes you make for local needs keep getting overwritten, i.e., if an additional directory needs to be listed in the `LD_LIBRARY_PATH`, hunting down which template file sets the `LD_LIBRARY_PATH` (the needed variable in this case) can be difficult if you are not using this report.

Cloning

As defined by Oracle, cloning is creating an identical copy of an existing Oracle Applications system. Why clone? You use cloning to create a copy of your production system to test upgrades, patches, and configuration changes – this is a best practice recommended by Solution Beacon. You don't develop or test in production do you? Cloning can also be used to change the server that your production environment is installed on – this can be done when upgrading your operating system (OS), changing vendors, or upgrading hardware.

Basic steps for cloning:

- Run `adpreclone.pl` – this program gathers information about the source system's Database Tier and Application Tier, which is then stored in a clone directory for each tier.

- Next, copy the entire application file system to the target system. This assumes you are doing a complete clone and not just a database refresh. Rapid Clone does allow for just the refresh/clone of the database from the source to the target. When copying the source system you can use utilities like `Rsynch`, disk to disk copies, the operating system `cp` command, or SAN/NAS-based utilities like `snap copies` or `BCV copies`.

- Run `adcfgclone.pl` - This script reads the clone files created from running `adpreclone.pl` and prompts you to enter new information that will need to be changed, like port numbers, the name of the host, and instance specific information.

- Start the new Applications environment.

OAM (Oracle Application Manager)

Oracle Application Manager (OAM) is an HTML-based GUI tool that is included in the installation of any Oracle Applications system. OAM extends your Applications management capabilities:

- Monitor your system - OAM allows you to monitor your system for security problems, usage characteristics, configuration changes and performance.

- Manage maintenance and patching activities - OAM also has a Patch Wizard that can recommend patches recently released from Oracle as well as provide detailed information about what objects a patch will specifically change. In addition, OAM will allow you to see what patches have modified a specific file.

- Manage configurations within your system - OAM is the recommended method for making changes to your `context_file.xml`. This tool will also let you see previous configuration changes to the system, like other context value changes and Profile Option changes.

- Administer concurrent managers and workflow components - OAM allows you to start and stop concurrent managers as well as submit concurrent requests. OAM also provides performance characteristics about the concurrent manager environment. Also, workflow services can be controlled through OAM. Services include background engines, notification mailers, and listeners.

- Provides access to troubleshooting and Diagnostic Wizards - OAM has wizards that can be used to step through Concurrent Manager Recovery, Service Infrastructure, GCS and Forms Monitoring, CP Signature and Dashboard Collection Signature. It also provides a menu-driven system to set up diagnostics, schedule the running of those diagnostics and then view the output.

The two main screens in OAM are the "Site Map" (see Figure 149) and the "Applications Dashboard" (see Figure 150). These screen shots come from one of Solution Beacon's Release 12 Vision instances:

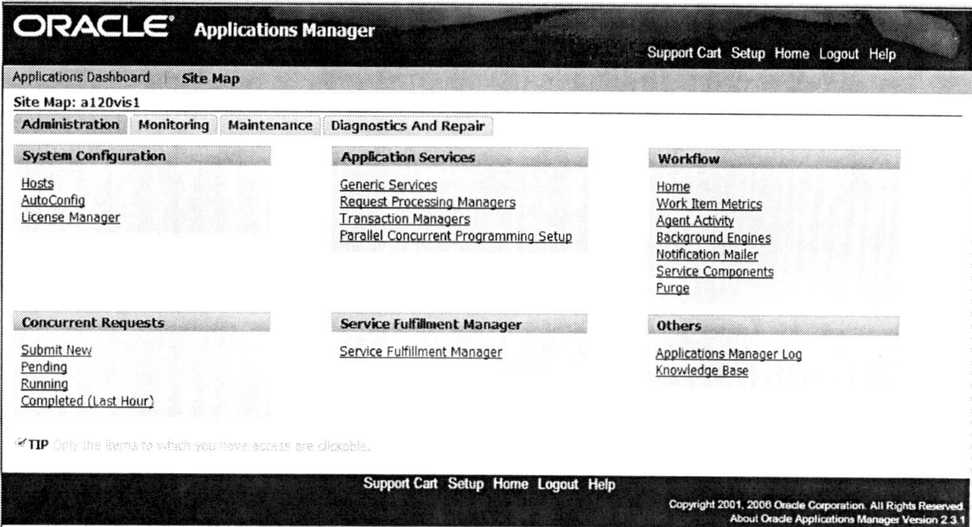

Figure 149 – The Site Map screen in OAM

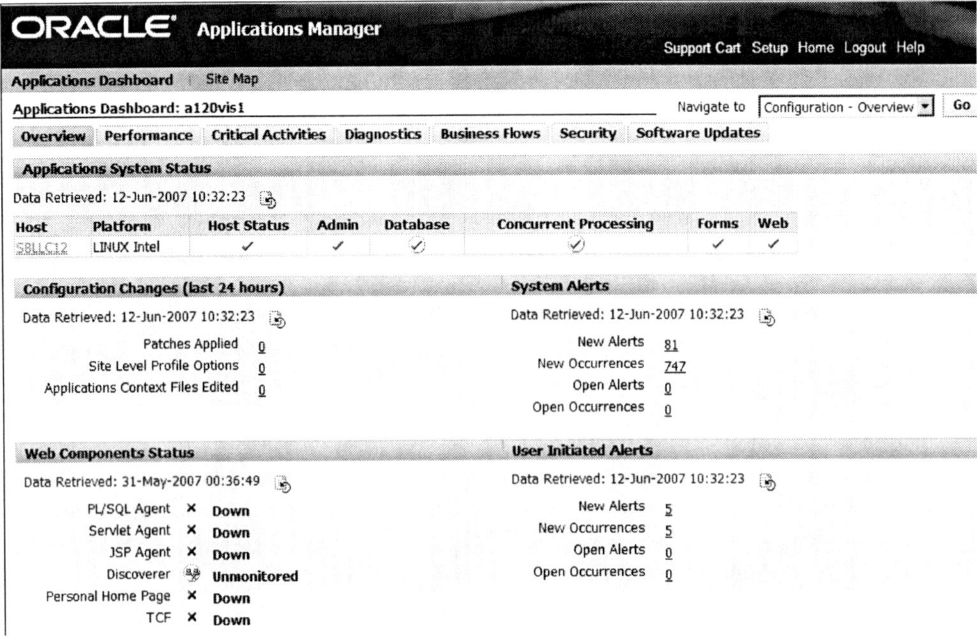

Figure 150 – The Applications Dashboard screen in OAM

Oracle Integration Repository (*i*Rep)

Have you always wanted to be able to view all the interfaces in the E-Business Suite in one convenient location? Oracle has developed a comprehensive integration repository that serves as the single source of truth and comes packaged in Release 12. This repository describes all of the Oracle endpoints whether they are Business to Business (B2B) or Application to Application (A2A). With the appropriate responsibility, users are able to both view and deploy the interfaces as needed. The following interface types are described in the repository:

- **PL/SQL** – includes a list of procedures and functions that are part of the interface package. Clicking on the procedure/function takes the user to a detailed description including the signature and parameter list.

- **Concurrent Programs** – information includes description and parameter list.

- **Open Interfaces** – always tied to a concurrent program, these interfaces include a parameter list and the associated tables/views. Users can further drill down to the tables or views to see a complete list of columns, including type, length, and description.

- **Interface Views** - details the source file information and the columns that make up the view.

- **Electronic Data Interchange (EDI) Message Transactions** – this is an industry standard that facilitates interfaces between the Oracle e-Commerce Gateway and Trading Partners. The repository provides a description and source file information.

- **XML Gateway Message Maps** – includes links to online documentation and the associated Method. If the map can be exposed as a Web Service, it is documented on a tab on this page and details the Web Services Description Language (WSDL) used.

- **Java Methods** – contains the description, source information and methods of a Java package. Drilling down on the method lists the signature and parameters of the method.

There is an additional interface type that can only be accessed if a user has the appropriate responsibility (typically the SYSADMIN login) because services can be deployed from within the repository for this interface. The Java Service Interface supplies access to service oriented architecture (SOA) services to enable the integration between Oracle Applications and trading partners. They can be used directly or exposed as Web services.

Interfaces can be queried in two different ways. The program opens up in browser mode where users can drill down to specific interfaces by product family or interface standard. Note: if accessing internally, users can also view by interface type. If viewing by product family, interfaces are arranged by product family, then product and finally business entity. Figure 151 show the interfaces associated with the Payables Invoice business entity. Figure 152 shows the drill down to the Payables Open Interface Import.

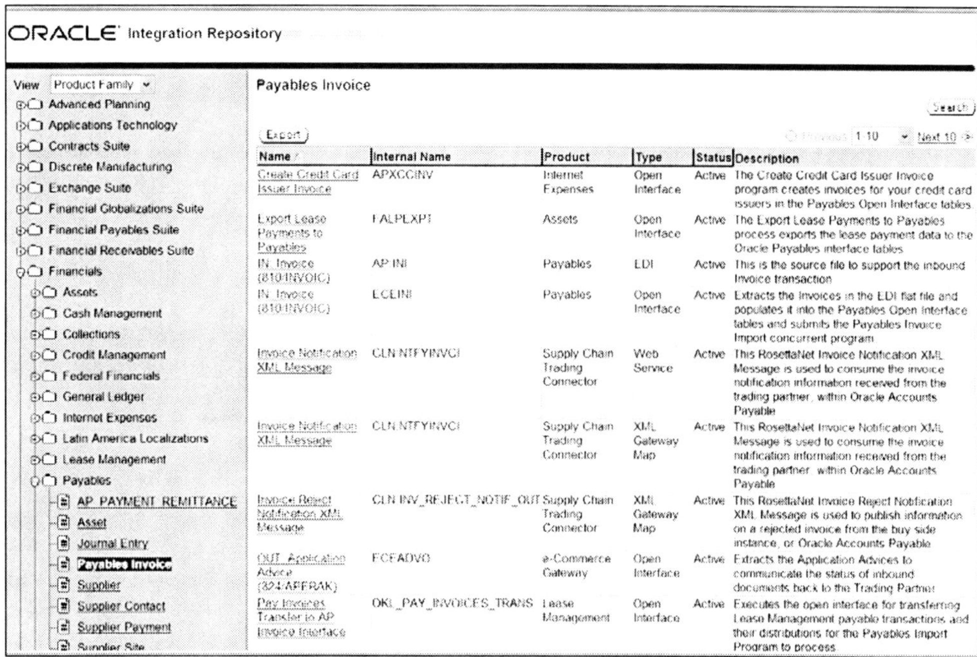

Figure 151 – Payables Invoice business entity screen in *i*Rep

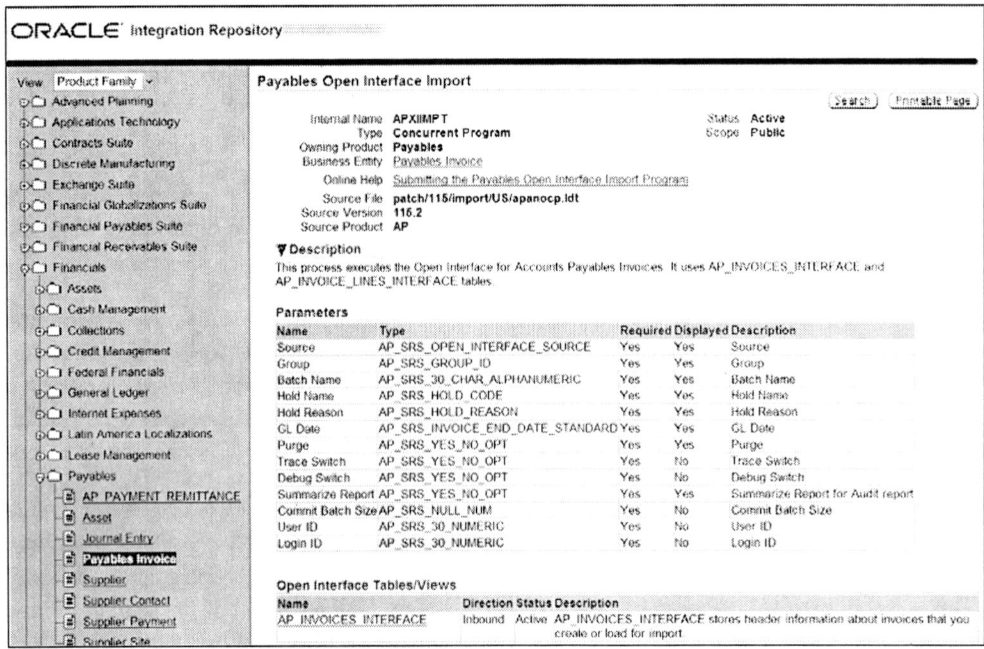

Figure 152 –Drill down to the Payables Open Invoice Import in *i*Rep

Users can access the Search screen by clicking on the Search button on the Browse page. Figure 153 shows all the Interface Views in the Financials product family

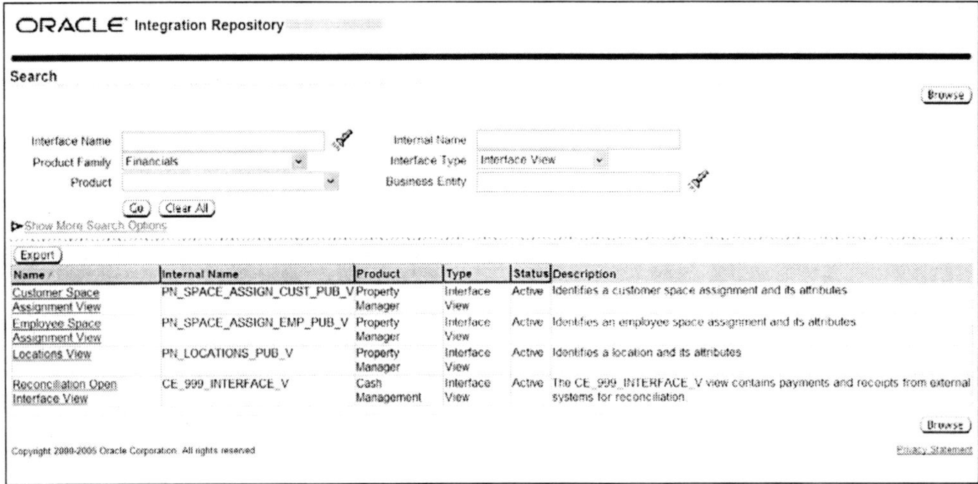

Figure 153 –All the Interface Views in the Financials product family

The repository can be accessed via the Integration Repository responsibility. Profile options can be set to allow users to view externally all interface types except the Java Services Interface.

SUMMARY

So, to wrap it all up, we have covered the three Tiers of Release 12 Oracle E-Business Suite as well as the components on each of those tiers that are responsible for all of the technological business logic. We talked about the Technology Layer, which supports all of the product modules and provides commonality in process, functionality and look and feel for Release 12. We then described the Application Filesystem that laid the new directory structure for the Applications. We also discussed how the environment gets set up for variables and contextual values, which in turn sets up the groundwork for how AutoConfig works. We also showed that AutoConfig is a cornerstone of cloning. And, speaking of cloning, we reviewed the basics of cloning and why it is necessary. We also discussed OAM, the Oracle Applications Manager, and the new Release 12 *i*Repository. With this information, you are ready to tackle Chapter 8, *Security*, since it is easier to understand the issues around security if you understand what you need to secure at the technical architecture level.

Security

Security. The word can conjure up feelings of warmth and protection or it could have connotations of austerity, locked perimeters and bulked up guards with mean and unaccommodating demeanor. Why is security an issue at all? Why is security a multi-billion dollar a year industry – is it because everyone is not to be trusted? And what is so valuable within the confines of a suite of applications to warrant a separate and distinct security discussion?

The first day after E-Business Suite Release 12 is implemented and the business owners begin to create transactions against any number of subledgers and ledgers, the lifeblood of an enterprise begins to flow. Information entered by users defines the vitality, health and profitability of the enterprise. What is the value of being able to produce accurate financial statements at quarter's end? How high are lost opportunity costs should sensitive data (i.e., employee benefits information, bank accounts or customer credit card numbers) mistakenly become part of the public domain? All are valid questions that warrant some level of discourse on security as a topic.

Consider the undercurrents in Corporate America today. Outsourcing is up – benefits are down – employee loyalty is at a comparative low point when compared to decades past – all these elements create a fertile environment for internal threat and risk. It is not unusual for project teams to be comprised of both onshore and offshore elements. As the world, let alone project teams, becomes a much more integrated place, brick and mortar no longer provides adequate protection over critical enterprise data. Corporations invest significant funds securing their perimeter from external threats, but what about the internal environment where integrated project teams are active through VPN tunnels and highly skilled contractors are onboarded for internal staff augmentation?

Over the next few pages, we examine E-Business Suite Release 12 security and give recommendations to minimize that internal threat; however, understand that any automated process is only as secure as management's posture and appetite for risk.

WHO ARE YOU...?

For E-Business Suite Release 12, or any automated process for that matter, authentication of the person desiring access is critical to protecting very valuable enterprise data. So let us explore some techniques and mechanisms that the E-Business Suite Release 12 uses to authenticate or verify identities.

Are You Unique?

Unfortunately, identity theft is a fairly common occurrence today; in fact, chances are most of the readers of this book will either have first or second hand knowledge of someone who has had their identity misappropriated, redirected or just plain stolen. The underlying issue of identity theft is simple; someone has obtained certain unique characteristics or vital statistics about another person and then proceeds to portray themselves as someone they are not. Once that act of identity hijacking occurs, the victim's identity is no longer unique. E-Business Suite Release 12 uses the combination of a userid and an associated password to ensure uniqueness for all users, so which userid is used and how passwords are constructed and protected are of utmost concern for preventing identity theft.

E-Business Suite Release 12 Application Generic Userids With System Administration Responsibility				
OSC	SYSADMIN	OSM_ADMIN	APPSADMIN	OSCUSER
ASGADM	BSC	MOBADM	MOBDEV	MOBILEADM
E-Business Suite Release 12 Application Generic Userids Without System Administration Responsibility				
IEXADMIN	OP_SYSADMIN	ADSFWK	ASGUEST	IRC_EMP_GUEST
GUEST	IRC_EXT_GUEST	WIZARD	ADSADMIN	OSOADMIN
IBE_GUEST	ABM_SYSADMIN	ABM_USER	IBEGUEST	PRM_ADMIN
AME_INVALID_APPROVER	IBE_ADMIN	OP_CUST_CARE_ADMIN	APPSMGR	PROFILEOPTIONS

Figure 154 – E-Business Suite Release 12 Application Generic Userids

As part of the installation of E-Business Suite Release 12, certain generic application userids (see Figure 154) are created that are used by various automated processes and initial administration tasks during installation. Due to the extensive integration in the E-Business Suite, several of these userids may be created for applications that are not fully installed. This can be quite an unexpected surprise. Distribution and use of these application userids are NOT recommended and their usage after initial installation should be audited. Even with auditing, the dilemma presented by generic userids is that the identity of the person who is actually entering the keystrokes cannot be determined.

CTXSYS	DBSNMP	MDSYS	ADSADMIN	AD_MONITOR
ANONYMOUS	HTMLDB_PUB	MGDSYS	MOBILEADM	ODM_MTR
ASGUEST	OLAP_SYS	ORABPEL	OPMOR	ORDPLUGINS
ORDSYS	OUTLN	OWAPUB	ORASSO	ORASSO_PUB
IBE_GUEST	PORTAL_PUB	REPADMIN	SCOTT	TRACESVR
TSMSYS	UDDISYS	WCRSYS	WKSYS	WKPROXY

Figure 155 – Oracle10*g* Database Generic Userids

Generic userids (schemas) are also installed at the Oracle10*g* database level (see Figure 155) as part of the installation process for both the E-Business Suite Release 12 and the Oracle10*g* database. Many of these generic userids have been around for quite some time and their default passwords (passwords set at installation) are widely known in the public domain. Some of these generic userids have significant (read DBA level) privileges and could result in catastrophic destruction or modification of E-Business Suite Release 12 if they are used in an unauthorized or unintended manner.

Solution Beacon Recommends: *Never use generic userids – always audit the use of all generic userids – assign specific, unique userids to each and every user of E-Business Suite Release 12 and make sure that company security policy authorizes the use of specific userids only. Oracle Workflow requires that the SYSADMIN userid remain active in order to receive certain error conditions that may be encountered; therefore, do NOT end-date the SYSADMIN userid.*

The TNSLISTENER is the SQLNET or network mechanism that sits like a sentry or guard post waiting for someone to ask for access to the database. Therefore, it is very important to the overall health of the database that all access requests originate from trusted sources. Any unauthorized administration of TNSLISTENER could put the underlying enterprise data at risk.

Part of installing E-Business Suite Release 12 includes establishing the "Oracle" user at the operating system level, and beginning with Oracle10*g*, the "Oracle" user owns the administration of TNSLISTENER. Any other operating system userid (remote OS authentication) that attempts to perform administration is denied access. There is an option to set a password, which would then allow other operating system userids to perform administration as long as they know the password. From a security perspective, it is best to administer TNSLISTENER through the "Oracle" operating system userid only and not allow remote authentication to other operating system level userids.

Solution Beacon Recommends: *Administer TNSLISTENER through the "Oracle" operating system userid only and do not allow remote authentication to other operating system level userids. Further, while you can use the default "Oracle" operating system userid, Solution Beacon recommends that the userid include the database SID in its name and that each Oracle instance have its own unique Oracle account following this naming standard. The "Oracle" operating system userid is commonly used by third party vendors, so should be avoided for that reason and because it is widely known in the public domain. Including the SID in the name helps prevent DBAs from inadvertently performing actions against the wrong Oracle database.*

The `init.ora` file is a configuration file that specifies startup information to the Oracle10*g* database and it contains the parameter REMOTE_OS_AUTHENTICATION. It is recommended that this parameter be set to false to ensure that access to the database does not come through non-secure protocols (i.e., TCP) at the operating system level or from some other remote client/host.

Solution Beacon Recommends: *Make sure the parameter REMOTE_OS_AUTHENTICATION is set to false in the init.ora configuration file.*

Direct connections between desktops/laptops and the Oracle10*g* database may be allowed at most companies by using developer tools such as TOAD, Oracle SQL*Plus and Oracle SQLDeveloper. First, this type of access should be limited to read only access, and only non-generic database userids should be authorized. This type of access can be further restricted by setting the TCP node checking parameters (as shown below) in the `sqlnet.ora` configuration file to only allow certain and specific I/P addresses to establish direct connections to the database. If possible and if direct database connections are allowed, then I/P level restrictions should be deployed.

- `Tcp.validnode_checking = Yes`

- `Tcp.invited_nodes = (I/P address 1, I/P address 2, …)`
- `Tcp.excluded_nodes = (I/P address 1, I/P address2, …)`

Solution Beacon Recommends: *Modify the TCP valid node parameters in sqlnet.ora to restrict direct database connections to specific and approved I/P addresses.*

Does this mean we are saying that no one can work from home or from a hotel? After all, aren't most companies allowing more and more remote work these days? Customers who lock down their SQL*NET to ONLY allow connections from known, trusted IP addresses or where DNS services can change the assigned IP address may still need a way to provide remote access for system, Oracle Database and Applications Administrators working from home or on business trips. Generally, this can be done using VPN connections for such users to connect to either UNIX/Linux or Citrix/Windows Terminal Server systems running inside the customer firewall. Using this approach, it is the UNIX/Linux host, or the Citrix/Windows Terminal Server system whose IP address needs to be known and authorized to access the database, as they are the systems where administrative applications and database network clients will run. The road warrior's IP address will still vary, but the systems to which they connect are trusted to access the database. Of course, the protection of those trusted systems becomes paramount to the security of the database, and appropriate measures to secure them and the connections to them must be taken.

What Keeps You Unique?

Aging, strength and construction sound like attributes associated with a construction site, or maybe coin collecting – but passwords? How do passwords and these attributes help keep your identity unique to E-Business Suite Release 12? E-Business Suite Release 12 provides a series of Profile Options (see Figure 156) that contain these password attributes. These settings should align with company password security policy.

Profile Option	Recommended Setting	Impact
Signon Password Case	Sensitive	Requires both upper and lower case characters
Signon Password Failure Limit	3	Maximum of 3 attempts at forgotten password
Signon Password Hard to Guess	Yes	➢ Must contain at least 1 number and at least 1 letter ➢ Cannot have any repeating characters ➢ Cannot be set = to userid
Signon Password Length	8	Minimum password length
Signon Password No Reuse	180	Number of days before a password can be reused

Figure 156 – Recommended Settings for E-Business Suite Release 12 Password Profile Options

Password construction speaks to the length, alpha/numeric character combinations and character repeatability restrictions. Password aging considers the life of any given password, or in other words, how long can any given password live until E-Business Suite Release 12 requires a new password to be assigned? Password strength revolves around the "guessability" factor should hacking occur against a password, and how easy would it be to figure that password out. Also, avoid the following when determining what that next password should be – any number of co-workers and password cracker programs know of the following and can hijack a password in fairly quick order:

1. family member first names
2. city, state names
3. calendar dates - birthdates in particular
4. setting the password equal to the userid

Solution Beacon Recommends: *Set E-Business Suite Release 12 password Profile Options as specified in Figure 156 and ensure alignment with company password security password policy.*

Is There Any Opportunity to Lose Your Uniqueness?

The most non-secret place in the corporate workspace is beneath the keyboard or on the back of the PC monitor. How many times have auditors taken an after hours cruise through their client's work area to find any number of keyboards shielding the "hard-to-find", "nobody will ever look here", "this is my assigned space – nobody else sits here" yellow sticky note from the light of day?

Passwords can be strongly constructed and aged appropriately, but if discovered by someone else, bingo – E-Business Suite Release 12 identity theft has occurred. How many times a day is any given workspace vacated by the principal, perhaps leaving a logged in E-Business Suite Release 12 session up and running? Screen saver and E-Business Suite Release 12 timeout Profile Options (see Figure 157) can mitigate this "away from my desk" risk.

Many times, you may encounter an organization's end users pushing back on implementing timeouts. Should this be a debatable topic? Does user productivity benefit from not having to login again upon returning from lunch or a 2 hour meeting? Does the organization have policies or provisions in place for temporary or contract staff? An important issue and potential risk comes from employees sharing their logins with contractors or having contractors sharing amongst themselves with logins possessing varied privileges.

Profile Option	Recommended Setting
ICX:Session Timeout	30 minutes
ICX: Limit time	4 hours
ICX: Limit connect	2000
JTF_INACTIVE_TIMEOUT_SESSION	30 minutes

Figure 157 – Recommended Settings for E-Business Suite Release 12 Timeout Profile Options

Solution Beacon Recommends: *Change Profile Options per Figure 157, ensure screen saver timeout setting is in the 5 to 10 minute range, avoid storing passwords in the work area and avoid first names, city names, state names and birthdates as part of password construction.*

WHAT CAN YOU DO ...?

Now that your identity has been checked at the E-Business Suite Release 12 level, by the Oracle10*g* database, and at the network and OS level, different Applications users will be able to do different tasks within the Applications - some users, for example, might be allowed to enter payments while others are permitted to enter journals. Hopefully, these allowed behaviors are aligned with authorized job roles/responsibilities. You might ask how E-Business Suite Release 12 provides for varying degrees of responsibilities. Continue reading and those techniques will be examined.

...in the Application?

There are two online access frameworks within E-Business Suite Release 12, Oracle Forms and Oracle Application Framework., Oracle Forms is the older cousin, a technology that has existed in ever evolving fashion since the early 90's. The basic elements of the Oracle Forms technology are menus, functions, data groups, request groups and responsibilities.

E-Business Suite Release 12 comes packaged with seeded menus, data groups, request groups and responsibilities that usually are designed with "great privilege" from a security perspective. "Great privilege" means that Oracle groups every conceivable function across the many Oracle modules that may be required to perform a specific job responsibility. Consequently, there are typically a significant number of segregation of duties issues when Oracle's "great privilege" meets up with authorized duties within an enterprise. Care should be taken to review and analyze all the functions grouped together in any menu, request group and responsibility to make sure duties are segregated per the enterprise's requirements. It is not considered a good practice to use seeded Oracle responsibilities due to this out-of-box design. When E-Business Suite Release 12 job responsibilities align with the enterprise's segregation of duties, consider the underlying tables (see Figure 158) as candidates for audit.

FND_MENUS	FND_MENU_ENTRIES	FND_RESPONSIBILITY
FND_RESP_FUNCTIONS	FND_FORM_FUNCTIONS	

Figure 158 – E-Business Suite Release 12 examples of tables that are audit candidates

Now let's turn our attention to the other online access technology within E-Business Suite Release 12, and that is Oracle Applications Framework, which has its roots in the self service applications. Some E-Business Suite Release 12 modules have seen both technologies in that they were originally delivered using Oracle Forms and have since been rewritten in E-Business Suite Release 12 using Oracle Applications Framework (e.g., Cash Management).

With advances in technology and increasing demands for regulatory compliance provided by Sarbanes Oxley asking so many questions about role-based security, Oracle has embraced Role Based Access Control (RBAC) as a new standard for authentication and authorization. RBAC is an ANSI standard that supports the mapping of user access control based upon the role the user plays within the organization rather than upon the user's individual identity. Oracle User Management (UMX) is the E-Business Suite Release 12 application that delivers RBAC functionality that uses roles, data security policies and grants to define what a user can do across the E-Business Suite Release 12 modules. Roles can contain responsibilities and data security policies that can restrict access to specific rows and columns within any given application table. Conversely, responsibilities can only restrict down to the function level and unless personalizations are implemented, have a difficult time restricting access within a table structure. UMX/RBAC is not very pervasive throughout E-Business Suite Release 12 (yet), but it is definitely the direction Oracle will follow to manage authorized user accesses.

Solution Beacon Recommends: *All responsibilities, menus, request groups, UMX roles, UMX grants and UMX data security policies should be analyzed to ensure alignment with the enterprises' approved job roles/responsibilities. New responsibilities must always be established to avoid Oracle's delivery of "great privilege" and to ensure alignment with the authorized segregation of duties.*

...in the Database?

There are desktop tools such as SQL*Plus, SQLDeveloper and TOAD that allow direct connections into the Oracle10*g* database. Hopefully these connections, if allowed, use unique and user-specific database userids. Database privileges should be examined for all database userids found in the `DBA_USERS` table by looking at the following tables:

1. `DBA_SYS_PRIVS`
2. `DBA_ROLE_PRIVS`
3. `DBA_TAB_PRIVS`

Privileges give the database userid the right to perform a particular action against specific database objects. Privileges such as ALTER, CREATE, DROP, BECOME USER, UPDATE, EXECUTE, LOCK and INSERT can all have catastrophic impact if performed against an E-Business Suite Release 12 Applications table. For example, the DROP privilege removes whatever object is specified – so if the GL schema is dropped, then Oracle General Ledger is destroyed. The EXECUTE privilege allows any procedure, package, trigger or any executable piece of code that resides in the database to be executed. This command could have catastrophic consequences outside the context of E-Business Suite Release 12. Privileges can also exist at the table level, which can be seen by examining the `DBA_TAB_PRIVS` table. You should check to see if any E-Business Suite Release 12 application table is specified and be very concerned if the privilege is INSERT, DROP, UPDATE or ALTER.

One last noteworthy item is that database roles can have privileges assigned and then roles can be assigned to database userids – so make sure any inheritance of privileges that database userids have gained through the assignment of role privileges is well understood. Needless to say, updates at the database level are no laughing matter and should only be performed under the auspices of Oracle Support to avoid the E-Business Suite Release 12 functioning incorrectly, or having your Support License Agreement with Oracle jeopardized.

Solution Beacon Recommends: *Ensure that all direct connections to the Oracle10g database (if allowed) use unique and specific userids. For every non-generic database userid found in DBA_USERS, examine the three privileges tables (DBA_SYS_PRIVS, DBA_ROLE_PRIVS, and DBA_TAB_PRIVS) to make sure the following are not assigned to anyone: ALTER, CREATE, LOCK, UPDATE, DROP, BECOME USER, EXECUTE and INSERT. Also, don't forget about roles that can have privileges inherited by other than the intended database userids.*

...at the OS Level?

At its most discrete level, the Oracle10*g* database is comprised of physical files. Permissions and ownership of these files are critical to understand to be able to avoid unauthorized access at the operating system level. Ownership should be either by the DBA or SYSTEM group, which means that the physical files are locked down and only available to the Oracle DBAs. Directories of interest are defined by the environment variable `$APPL_TOP`, or beginning with E-Business Suite Release 12, `$INSTANCE_TOP`. These environment variables will point to specific physical directories that contain all the physical files that comprise E-Business Suite Release 12.

Specific UNIX file permissions are specified in Figure 159, where each number represents what three different communities can perform against the contents of the physical file and directory. Let's take 751 as an example: the first number, 7, indicates what the owner of the physical file or directory can perform. The second number, 5, indicates what the group that the owner belongs to can perform. Finally, the 1 indicates what actions the rest of the world can take. The masked attribute value for each number is determined as specified in Figure 160. Therefore, 751 indicates that for a file or directory owned by the DBA group, that group can perform all actions against the file or directory. The DBA group can read and execute the file or directory while the rest of the world can execute against the file or directory only.

Physical File/Directory Path	**Recommended Setting**
`$ORACLE_HOME/bin`	751 or less
All Other `$ORACLE_HOME`	750 or less
`Listener.ora`	600 or less
`TNSNAMES.ora`	644 or less

Figure 159 – Recommended UNIX File Permissions

Permission Mask Value	**Permission Attribute**
0	All types of access denied
1	Execute access only
2	Write access only
3	Write and Execute access only
4	Read access only
5	Read and execute access only
6	Read and write access only
7	All access allowed

Figure 160 – UNIX File Permission Attribute Values

Solution Beacon Recommends: *Ensure permissions are as specified in Figure 159 for all physical files/directories/subdirectories that comprise E-Business Suite Release 12.*

WHAT CAN YOU SEE...?

With our enterprise data, there are ever increasing penalties and loss of goodwill facing most enterprises should their sensitive information fall into the wrong hands. What considerations are made for access to sensitive production data when new non-production environments are created? Where does sensitive data reside across the Release 12 E-Business Suite? To answer these questions, we will examine a few techniques that might help.

Obfuscate, Obfuscate, Obfuscate!

To obfuscate means to confuse, bewilder or otherwise mask what is real. Each company needs to go through the exercise of identifying all data that is sensitive to them and then understand where that data comes to rest, especially across E-Business Suite Release 12, but also including legacy applications as well.

There are no short cuts on this exercise, but Figure 161 provides a list of data elements that commonly have sensitive connotations to most companies.

Bank Accounts	Credit Card Numbers	Payroll Salary Information
Social Security Numbers	Employee Birthdates	Employee Phone Number
Employee Gender	Payroll Deductions (medical)	Employee Vendors

Figure 161 – Commonly Sensitive Data Elements for E-Business Suite Release 12

Obfuscation is not only a good idea but also a requirement in some areas. The Payment Card Industry (PCI) Data Security Standard (DSS) covers areas from network security and data protection, vulnerability scanning and maintaining policy. Major credit card companies and those merchants processing payments collaborate on the practices necessary to secure customers' data and transactions and try to minimize identity theft. Those found not to be in compliance might be restricted or removed from card acceptance programs.

Within the context of non-production E-Business Suite Release 12 environments, most are created from a clone (copy) of production and then turned over to a project team. Consider including into the delivery process of these non-production environments some type of obfuscation mechanism to go out and destroy or otherwise mask/alter the sensitive data. Solution Beacon provides a PLSQL package at http://www.solutionbeacon.com/security that is available for download that will replace sensitive data with meaningless data. Please understand that there are no short cuts in identifying data that is sensitive to any given company – discussions must be held with the HR and legal departments and key business groups to gain this understanding. Once the sensitive data has been identified, then steps can be taken to search and destroy the sensitive data in non-production environments.

Solution Beacon Recommends: *We recommend that each company identify their sensitive data and then understand where that data comes to rest across the E-Business Suite Release 12 application suite.*

A data obfuscation mechanism (i.e., http://www.solutionbeacon.com/security) should be incorporated into the delivery process for non-production environments whereby sensitive data is destroyed, masked and/or altered.

Personalize Those Forms!

E-Business Suite Release 12 provides personalization mechanisms and enhancements, one for forms that use Oracle Forms and one for forms that use Oracle Application Framework. Both of these personalization mechanisms will allow specific data on the form to be hidden based on predefined criteria that can provide an option for keeping sensitive data from being displayed to unauthorized parties. A word of caution though - personalizations only mitigate unauthorized viewing of sensitive data within the context of E-Business Suite Release 12, they do nothing to mitigate unauthorized viewing at the Oracle10*g* database level. Should users be perceptive enough to know which E-Business Suite Release 12 tables contain sensitive data and if they are allowed to establish direct connections from their desktops/laptops to the database, then sensitive data can be queried and extracted out to those desktops/laptops, further exacerbating the answer to the question, "Do you know where your sensitive data resides?"

Oracle Applications Framework personalizations are controlled by the following Profile Options:

- Disable Self-Service Personalizations
- FND: Personalization Region Link Enabled
- Personalize Self-Service Defn

Oracle Forms personalizations are accessed through the Help pulldown menu. Choose Diagnostics > Custom Code > Personalize. The APPS password is required to gain access. Take care to change the APPS password for all non-production environments so that the production password is not jeopardized by development work being conducted on Oracle Forms personalizations.

Solution Beacon Recommends: *Develop and deploy personalizations to hide sensitive data from unauthorized user populations and/or responsibilities. Be advised that personalizations are only effective within the context of E-Business Suite Release 12 and do nothing to mitigate direct connections to the Oracle10g database. Change the E-Business Suite passwords for non-production environments so they are not the same as the production environment, or your obfuscation and forms personalization efforts will be wasted!*

Scrub Those Database Privileges!

To mitigate direct database connections from querying up sensitive data, especially in the context of the production environment, it is recommended that separate sensitive database read roles be established for each E-Business Suite Release 12 application that has been identified as containing sensitive data. These sensitive database read roles should be prefixed with XX as part of the naming standard to protect against any future conflict with seeded E-Business Suite Release 12 database roles. Incremental authorization should be obtained from the respective/owning business group for any userid requesting access against any of the sensitive database read roles and evidence of authorization should be filed away as audit artifacts.

All existing database roles should be examined to see if any have access to E-Business Suite Release 12 tables containing sensitive data. If any are found, access to the sensitive tables should be removed in favor of the new sensitive database read roles recommended above.

Solution Beacon Recommends: *E-Business Suite Release 12 access to E-Business Suite tables containing sensitive data should be removed from existing database roles and established in separate sensitive database read roles where incremental authorizations for access are obtained from the owning business group.*

Batten Down Those Application Roles and Responsibilities!

Application roles and responsibilities are a bit easier to analyze in light of sensitive data since they are mostly broken out along application boundaries; however, it is still worth the exercise to understand what sensitive data is available to which application roles and responsibilities. Remember that responsibilities contain request groups that specify which concurrent programs can be submitted and those concurrent programs may reach out to other applications and may in fact report on data that has been deemed sensitive. Don't fall victim to creating query-only roles, only to find that those users can accidentally, or otherwise, run a Payroll process or depreciate assets. Oops! Always review the request groups that are associated to responsibilities or set into menus directly.

Solution Beacon Recommends: *Review/analyze/examine all active job responsibilities and roles to understand if sensitive data is being displayed/reported. We recommend that all users associated with those sensitive job responsibilities/roles obtain incremental approval by the business owners of the sensitive data.*

Encrypt Those New TCA Entities!

Bank account numbers, routing numbers and account holder names are sensitive information for any enterprise – occurrences of bank fraud and wire theft are on the increase – just see how many hits are received from searching the web for "bank fraud". Beginning with E-Business Suite Release 12, banks and their associated sensitive data are elevated and integrated with the Trading Community Architecture (TCA) module through the new Oracle Payments application. One of the features of Oracle Payments is that it provides for the encryption of bank account information – encryption should be in force and used and consideration should be given to include the underlying bank account table (`IBY_BANKACCT`) as an audit candidate.

Credit card numbers are another source of sensitivity for most enterprises. Regulatory agencies are interested in how their credit card numbers are protected from unauthorized viewing and are not hesitant to assess severe penalties that can include losing the right to transact with their credit card. This could remove a healthy chunk from the revenue line for some companies. Oracle Payments does make encryption available for credit card numbers and its use is recommended. Further consideration should be given to including the underlying credit card table (`IBY_CREDITCARD`) as a candidate for auditing.

Solution Beacon Recommends: *Make sure encryption is turned on and functioning properly for bank account and credit card information, and include the application tables mentioned above as audit candidates.*

Don't Forget About Secondary/Tertiary Datastores!

For our purposes, it is important to understand what process pipelines extract, transport and deposit sensitive E-Business Suite Release 12 data. Most companies develop various inbound and outbound processes to receive and send data to and from their business partners, and these processes should be examined to understand what, if any, sensitive data is being processed. A common technique for these inbound/outbound processes is to deposit the interface data in work table(s) and then provide a transport mechanism between the work table(s) and the desired E-Business Suite Release 12 API. Check those worktables! Sensitive data could be sitting there in clear text format without a lot of security protecting the data.

What about ad hoc query environments? Tools like Oracle Discoverer and Business Objects create meta-data repositories that sit on top of production data and then access is provisioned through separate and distinct permissions through the tools themselves. Examine the end user layers and universes to understand what sensitive data is being mapped and then who has query access. Make sure other ad hoc tools such as Microsoft Excel or Microsoft Access have appropriate security enabled and that steps are taken to secure data that is exported or stored in these applications.

At startup, the Oracle10*g* database uses a configuration file called `init.ora` that contains the `UTL_FILE_DIR` parameter, which indicates what server directories can receive flat files created out of E-Business Suite Release 12. Check to make sure the wildcard character ("*") isn't specified as a valid receiving directory, as this means that flat files can be created in any server directory, and could end up in a directory where security permissions are not locked down. All flat files created from E-Business Suite Release 12 data should be examined for the presence of sensitive data and the server directories receiving the flat files should be secure from unauthorized viewing at the operating system level.

One last word of caution – check to make sure `SYS.LINK$` is secure from unauthorized viewing within the Oracle10*g* database. This particular table contains connect strings for any DBLINKS established within the E-Business Suite Release 12 environment and often times the APPS password can be found there.

Solution Beacon Recommends: *Ensure that the wildcard ("*") isn't specified in the* `UTL_FILE_DIR` *parameter within the init.ora file. Examine ad hoc end user layers and universes to understand if any sensitive data is being mapped and require incremental authorization for all users with access to mapped sensitive data. Analyze all inbound/outbound processes to see if sensitive data is being sent or received and where it comes to rest – make sure associated work tables are secure from unauthorized viewing within the Oracle10g database. Finally, make sure* `SYS.LINK$` *table is secure from authorized viewing because the APPS password is often times held there as part of* `DBLINKS` *that have been established for the E-Business Suite Release 12 environments.*

What Did You Do…?

Auditing examines artifacts to detect and derive conclusions about certain behaviors – kind of like some of the forensic shows on television, but for our purposes all the forensics are conducted within the safe confines of E-Business Suite Release 12. Let's examine some of the options for performing that audit detective work for E-Business Suite Release 12, shall we?

…to the Apps?

Application level auditing is controlled by the following Profile Options and should be set to the recommended settings as depicted in Figure 162.

Profile Options	Recommended Setting
Sign-on:Audit Level	Form
AuditTrail:Activate	Yes

Figure 162 – E-Business Suite Release 12 Audit Profile Options

Form level auditing allows for tracking from the initial user login and allows all actions to be captured. The audit reports listed in Figure 163 are provided as part of E-Business Suite Release 12 and should be audited at least quarterly with evidence of the audit review filed away as audit artifacts. More frequent reviews of the audit reports should occur within the context of actions against sensitive data – remember an enterprise is only one unauthorized query away from loss of goodwill from a public relations perspective.

Signon Audit Concurrent Requests	Signon Audit Forms	Signon Audit Responsibilities
Signon Audit Unsuccessful Logins	Signon Audit Users	

Figure 163 – E-Business Suite Release 12 Audit Reports

Solution Beacon Recommends: *Ensure application level auditing is turned on at the form level and that standard audit reports are reviewed at least quarterly, or more frequently within the context of actions against sensitive data. Evidence of audit review should be filed away as audit artifacts.*

...to the Database?

Database level auditing should also be deployed as a way to mitigate risk over trusted roles, most notably DBAs, Applications System Administrators and Operating System Administrators. Activity can occur against key E-Business Suite Release 12 tables through direct connections to the Oracle10*g* database, allowing database level auditing to capture this activity and present it in a meaningful format. Sarbanes Oxley has called into question the controls (or lack thereof) surrounding trusted roles such as DBAs, Applications System Administrators and Operating System Administrators. Database level auditing provides some level of oversight to any activity conducted against E-Business Suite Release 12 tables. Figure 164 contains some key E-Business Suite Release 12 application tables that should be considered as audit candidates depending on which applications are installed.

IBY_BANKACCT	IBY_CREDITCARD	PER_ALL_PEOPLE_F	DBA_AUDIT_TRAIL
DBA_STMT_AUDIT_OPTS	DBA_PRIV_AUDIT_OPTS	PO_VENDORS	AP_SYSTEM_PARAMETERS_ALL
AUD$	GL_CODE_COMBINATIONS	GL_PERIOD_TYPES	GL_PERIOD_SETS
GL_PERIODS	GL_LEDGERS	FND_ID_FLEXS	FND_FLEX_VALUES

Figure 164 – E-Business Suite Release 12 tables that are audit candidates

Care should be taken to create the audit trail logs to a directory where segregation of duties can be insured. If the goal of the audit is to mitigate activity by the DBAs, then create the audit log file to a directory that cannot be accessed, or at least updated, by the DBAs.

Solution Beacon Recommends: *Turn database auditing on for certain key E-Business Suite Release 12 tables and make sure the audit trail log is readable, reviewed at least quarterly and created in a directory where the trusted roles (e.g., DBA) do not have update access.*

SUMMARY

With your business' data safeguarded, it is now time to consider another vital resource – the people who will support the Release 12 E-Business Suite of Applications. Chapter 9, *Resources*, describes the roles and responsibilities for some of the support staff who will keep your Applications environment running smoothly.

Resources

The objective of this chapter is to describe the various roles and responsibilities needed to support the Release 12 Applications in a typical environment. While this chapter does not go into detail about how to set up a help desk or how to build an IT organization, it will address the roles and skill sets that may be beneficial in the ongoing maintenance and support of Release 12. Although many of the roles fall within the Information Technology area, there are also roles required of the business and user community. Particular focus is given to the new or evolving roles and responsibilities for Release 12.

SUPPORT INFRASTRUCTURE HISTORY

When the early releases of Oracle Applications were introduced, it was adequate to have a DBA (who often played the Applications System Administrator and Operating System Administrator roles as well), a development team and some functional experts within a specific module. The Applications have become much more complex, requiring considerable changes to the Oracle Applications support infrastructure.

The Oracle Applications have evolved significantly over the past two decades and so has the personnel infrastructure needed to support efficient operations in the typical organization. Some of the roles that we describe in this chapter fall outside of mainstream IT organizations. With Release 12, we see not only the continued evolution of existing roles; but we also see a few new roles.

READ THE INGREDIENTS

Based on information from Oracle Corporation, there are well over 1,500 new features added when moving from Release 11*i* to Release 12. The online documentation library weighs in at 400 MB. Moving to Release 12 requires using the 10*g*R2 database and Oracle Application Server 10*g*. Advances in technology and changes in specific components of Release 12 have created a need for a changing support environment that will likely cross organizational boundaries.

SAMPLE ROLE DESCRIPTIONS

Following are sample role descriptions we see evolving with the introduction of Release 12. The following roles include breakouts of key tasks that must be performed to support the ongoing day-to-day operations of the Applications. It is entirely possible that one person will handle more than one of the roles. Depending on the organization, a role may be performed by an individual or multiple people, and an individual may perform one or many roles. If an individual performs multiple roles, the security implications regarding segregation of duties and SOX compliance should be carefully understood for publicly traded companies.

Reporting Administrator

The majority of reporting will move to XML Publisher with Release 12, and will emerge as a replacement for Oracle Reports with Fusion. Since the Reporting Administrator may handle much more than just XML Publisher, it is also important to consider other technologies such as Discoverer, OBIEE, and Hyperion, depending on which additional tools your organization uses.

Responsibilities

Responsibilities of the Reporting Administrator may include:

- Migrate existing Oracle Reports (both seeded and custom) to XML Publisher
- Control access to the XML Publisher development environment
- Maintain report source files and Concurrent Program files within the Applications
- Create and maintain XML Publisher report templates for producing report publishing check writing, EDI, etc.
- Create and maintain XML Publisher data templates to extract XML data from various sources.
- Create and maintain data definitions for associating report templates with various data extraction mechanisms.
- Define concurrent programs for executing XML reports
- Develop report delivery mechanisms (email, fax, FTP, etc) using advanced XML Publisher techniques
- Gather and analyze user reporting requirements
- Monitor reporting results and distributions
- Maintain related documentation

Requires

- Proficiency with common markup languages including XML, HTML, DHTML, XHTML
- Experience using Extensible Style Sheet languages such as XSL and transformations using XSLT and rendering/formatting techniques with XSL-FO
- Familiarity with localization transformations and XLIFF
- Understand Document Object Models (DOM) and Document Type Definitions (DTD)
- Experience using commercial XML development tools and graphic design tools
- Familiarity with EDI and EFT data transmission
- Working knowledge of Java programming language
- Understand conditional formatting using if-then-else logic and data driven formatting
- Working knowledge of MS Word with XML Publisher Add-in to build and modify report templates
- Understand Adobe Portal Document Format (PDF) usage, properties, font management, etc.
- Knowledge of E-Business Suite concurrent manager processing, concurrent program definition and design, and output format
- Experience with SQL language and functions, query design and development, along with understanding of AOL infrastructure
- Experience with SQL X to generate XML files from SQL and PL/SQL code
- Development experience with Oracle Reports
- Familiarity with typical reporting requirements, including financial statements, payment documents, MICR, image watermarks, etc.
- Knowledge of image formats such as GIF, JPEG, BMP, etc.

Breakdown by Category

XML Templates

- Create custom report and data templates using MS Word, Adobe Acrobat, hand-coded XML and XSL, plain text, etc.
- Modify existing PDF template files such as government tax forms for integration with XML Publisher
- Register and maintain templates using Oracle Applications interface

- Associate templates with appropriate XML data source

XML Data Extraction

- Create XML Data Templates to extract data from various sources including Oracle Applications infrastructure, external applications, database programs, text files, etc.
- Register and maintain Data Definitions using Oracle Applications interface
- Create appropriate mappings for templates
- Modify existing processes (PL/SQL routines, Oracle Reports, scripts, etc) to produce XML output for use with XML templates
- Develop custom data extraction processes using data templates, SQL, PL/SQL, Java, etc.

Report Delivery

- Create and maintain concurrent processes to execute XML Publisher reports
- Design and develop report delivery process using concurrent processes, XML Publisher APIs, Java, PL/SQL, email, etc.
- Assist in providing report accessibility via web portals
- Use intelligent design and best practices to minimize data extraction and maximize data re-usability

Workflow Administrator

The Workflow Administrator role has changed with the sheer number of Workflows used in Release 12. Release 12 includes over 1000 workflow item types and over 4500 individual workflow processes.

The Workflow Administrator plays a key role in the ever-increasing requirement to provide up-to-date information at any given time. More and more, we see executives using dashboards to track key performance indicators throughout the business day and using this data to make timely decisions to meet corporate goals. Much of this information is kept up to date and flowing freely, indirectly, by the Workflow Administrator. When the Workflow process is not working properly, the impact on reporting and business intelligence is significant. Workflow Administrators use the workflow page in OAM (Oracle Applications Manager) to perform this function. The Workflow page includes dashboards and key performance indicators.

Because Workflow is such a complicated product, we cannot do justice in this book to all that it entails. Solution Beacon's Oracle Workflow Handbook provides much more detail about the nuances of Oracle Workflow.

With Release 12, Workflow is the obvious tool of choice for processes that are contained within the E-Business Suite. BPEL will ultimately be the go-to tool for processes that cross multiple systems (Oracle and non-Oracle). Ultimately, BPEL will replace Workflow.

Responsibilities

Following are some of the responsibilities that fall within the role of the Workflow Administrator:

- Ensure that the technology (database, Advanced Queuing, propagation, notification mailer, agent listeners) is working, and ensure that patches are applied as directed by Oracle Support or the business management team
- Work with the Applications DBA to ensure that current Oracle Diagnostics patches are applied quarterly or per Oracle's published release schedule
- Work with the Applications DBA to update AutoConfig to reset the workflow administrator to the correct responsibility rather than the SYSADMIN user default
- Ensure that all aspects of cloned environments accurately point to the cloned instance
- Work with DBA to develop and enforce the methodology for maintaining and testing the mailer in cloned instances
- Ensure that the parameters on the global administration page remain accurate
- Finish workflow technology setups not completed by any upgrade, patch, or install
- Configure and maintain Workflow Administrator security
- Assist Super Users in understanding the workflows in each module and the setups that are required to make them work. Ensure that any required setups are determined, documented, and applied in all instances
- Monitor MetaLink for new patches and ensure that patches are applied and tested at both the database and PC level (for those developers who are creating or maintaining workflows using the Workflow Builder)
- Monitor `WFSTD.wft` workflow for additions added by developers that should either be placed in a specific workflow or in a company or application standard library workflow
- Set up and maintain the scheduling of the background engine(s)
- Set up and maintain the purge schedule(s) for runtime history (completed workflows)
- Ensure that appropriate directory services synchronization programs are scheduled
- Monitor concurrent processes, managers and containers to ensure that all required processes are scheduled and run at appropriate intervals. These programs include, but are not limited to:
    - Control Queue Cleanup
    - Purge Obsolete Workflow Runtime Data

    - Oracle Application Manager statistics programs (optional)
    - Workflow Agent Activity Statistics Concurrent Program
    - Workflow Mailer Statistics Concurrent Program
    - Workflow Work Items Statistics Concurrent Program
- Monitor Business Event queues to ensure that listeners are scheduled, propagations are scheduled and messages are moving through the queues
- Ensure that "Synchronize Product Licenses and BES" is executed whenever a family pack, point release, or cumulative update is installed or whenever a new product is implemented
- Monitor status of running workflows and overdue notifications
- Monitor status of the mailer and ensure that notifications are delivered. In the event of failure, ensure that the appropriate notifications are rescheduled for email delivery
- Troubleshoot workflows that are stuck or in error status
- Ensure that the issues raised in notifications to SYSADMIN are resolved and that the notifications to SYSADMIN are subsequently closed
- Ensure that notifications sent to SYSADMIN are available to workflow administrators through various methods such as assigning a group email address to SYSADMIN, setting up vacation rules, and/or worklist access.
- Ensure that the folders used by the workflow mailer are periodically cleaned and that messages sent to the discard folder are not sent there in error
- Ensure that the mailer tags are complete and that they handle messages from out-of-office assistants or email servers bouncing emails due to invalid server or invalid email addresses
- Periodically run the workflow diagnostics and other administrative scripts and report/repair any issues
- Assist users/developers in the use of the Workflow Builder tool
- Develop original or customize Oracle-supplied workflows as necessary to enable optimization of business processes
- Ensure that workflow customizations (workflows and associated pl/sql packages) are accurately migrated from instance to instance according to policy
- Ensure that custom workflows are documented and stored in a repository for protection.
- Ensure that workflow development standards are followed for events, workflows, PL/SQL procedures and other components

- Ensure that the directory services remains clean (no assignment of multiple users to same employee)
- Work with HR to ensure that email addresses are specified for each employee linked to a user and that appropriate hierarchies and approval limits are set up and do not violate control procedures
- Re-assign notifications and/or establish vacation rules for persons unavailable to act on pending workflow tasks such as sick time, leave of absence, or vacation
- Provide feedback to management if there are any issues in the management or operation of workflow

Requires

- Procedure Builder tool such as TOAD
- SQL tool such as TOAD
- Responsibility with access to workflow administrator functions, run/monitor concurrent programs, set Profile Options,
- Administrator access to Oracle Applications Manager (OAM)

The Junior Workflow Administrator

The Junior Workflow Administrator is a relatively new role for the Applications that allows the Workflow Administrator to share some of the workflow administration responsibilities with others. This role would only be found in larger Oracle Applications implementations. Starting with 11.5.10.2 RUP5, administration can be granted by workflow item type. For example, the Payables Superuser can be granted access to perform workflow administration tasks only for the Payables Approval workflow. This allows the strong functional "super users" to monitor and troubleshoot workflows in their area of expertise. Tasks that a Junior Workflow Administrator might take on include:

- Understand the workflows in all assigned modules and ensure any required setups are determined, documented, and applied in all instances
- For assigned modules, monitor the status of running workflows and overdue notifications
- For assigned modules, troubleshoot workflows that are stuck or in error status
- For assigned modules, ensure that the issues raised in notifications to SYSADMIN are resolved and that these notifications are subsequently closed
- Periodically run the workflow diagnostics and other administrative scripts and report/repair any issues
- For assigned modules, assist users / developers in the use of the Workflow Builder tool

- For assigned modules, work with the Developers to ensure custom and/or customized workflows are documented
- For assigned modules, work with the Developers to ensure workflow development standards are followed for events, workflows, PL/SQL procedures and other components
- For assigned modules provide feedback to management and the Workflow Administrator if there are any issues in the management or operation of workflow

All Users

Administrators are not the only individuals who need to ensure certain tasks are performed. Every user of the applications has certain tasks they need to perform. These tasks can be performed from any responsibility that has a worklist screen, such as Workflow User. This responsibility will allow end users to view workflows they own, view and respond to notifications as well as perform the following recommended functions:

- Set up worklist access for their immediate supervisor to ensure notifications can be processed in the event of illness
- Set up vacation rules and ensure effective dates are changed whenever vacation or leave of absence is scheduled
- Inform the Help Desk whenever a workflow problem is detected

Skills Needed to Support Workflow

Except for help desk, security, and end users, persons involved in the administration/development of workflow must be able to define components in the workflow builder, must have access to MetaLink, and must know how to research issues and file Service Requests with Oracle Support.

Developers, the workflow administrator, and DBAs should have strong SQL and PL/SQL skills, and knowledge of the directory services tables, the queue tables, and the workflow design and runtime tables.

Junior Administrators must have a good knowledge of their assigned area and be able to facilitate discussions about the setups required to configure the seeded workflows.

Applications System Administrator

The Applications System Administrator performs administrative tasks for the Release 12 E-Business Suite environment. This role requires managing security by granting users access and defining their application privileges, registering custom applications, executing programs and reports using Standard Request Submission, and auditing and monitoring system processing. Managing the concurrent manager environment and creating and maintaining the custom Applications environment are key roles. The Applications System Administrator will work closely with the Applications DBA, developers, the Workflow Administrator, the Reporting Administrator and users.

Responsibilities

Responsibilities include:

- Document customizations including file locations and/or file entries. Ensure that all customizations are reproducible in the event of loss
- Control Applications system security
- Assist in managing SOX compliance, strategies and audit evidence
- Coordinate user security
- Define user security and Applications responsibilities
- Define and implement terminal security as necessary
- Add, modify, or delete Applications responsibilities
- Set and update Applications Profile Options
- Customize end user interfaces
- Create custom menus, forms, and reports
- Create roles and role hierarchies in Oracle User Management/RBAC
- Manage user registrations and approvals in Oracle User Management/RBAC
- Manage permission sets/grants in Oracle User Management/RBAC
- Create and manage forms personalizations to ensure appropriate and approved read-access
- Create and manage report groups, report sets and custom menus
- Ensure that sensitive data is identified and obfuscated in non-production environments
- Manage security profile for Multi-Org Access Control (MOAC – Release 12 only)
- Help define Concurrent Managers, including workshifts and specialization rules
- Manage concurrent processing files
- Assign runtime options for concurrent programs
- Create runtime dependencies
- Create and customize help text
- Define, register, and install peripherals

- Monitor Applications with standard administrator reports
- Help determine Applications upgrade/migration strategy
- Track Applications usage over time
- Monitor Concurrent Manager log/output destinations and purge outdated reports.
- Monitor Concurrent Managers and results
- Update documentation
- Define printers, printer types, and printer drivers for user with the Applications. Coordinate naming of printers with the Operating System SA to ensure correct coupling between the operating system print queue and Applications printer.
- Ensure the directory services remains clean (no assignment of multiple users to same employee)
- Work with HR to ensure email addresses are specified for each employee linked to a user and that appropriate hierarchies and approval limits are set up and do not violate control procedures
- Review setups for all used workflows to ensure compliance with contractual and legal obligations
- Provide backup to the workflow administrator for re-assigning notifications and/or establishing vacation rules for persons unavailable to act on pending workflow tasks due to sick time, leave of absence, termination, or vacation

Breakdown by Category

Applications Superuser Login

- Define Applications users
- Define user security levels and Applications responsibilities
- Define and implement Applications file access security
- Set, update, and maintain user Profile Options
- Add, modify, or delete Applications user responsibilities as needed
- Create custom end user interfaces to Oracle
- Create custom menus, forms, and reports
- Create and customize help text

- Define and create usable comprehensive Flexfield error messages that display the actual Oracle "rule" that created the error message, and ALL the necessary field value to meets to meet the "rule" requirements
- Create and maintain custom Applications environment as necessary
- Manage concurrent processing files
- Assign runtime options for concurrent programs
- Create runtime dependencies

Oracle Security

- Control overall Oracle Applications security

Paper Administration

- Determine Oracle Applications upgrade/migration strategy with Database Administrator
- Maintain comprehensive log of all Oracle configurations, modifications, errors, procedures (test, backup/restore, user setup, detailed listing of each individual software setting used).
- Adhere to Company network standards - naming conventions, security and user groups
- Monitor Applications with standard administrator reports
- Define concurrent managers, work shifts, and specialization rules for Oracle Applications with Database Administrator

Requires

- Procedure Builder tool such as TOAD
- SQL tool such as TOAD
- System Administrator responsibility
- Responsibility with access to workflow administrator functions
- Administrator access to Oracle Applications Manager (OAM)

Applications Database Administrator

The Applications DBA that manages a Release 12 environment now has added Java watchdog responsibilities, increased security awareness and must coordinate efforts with the Operating System Administrator, the Applications System Administrator, the Workflow Administrator, developers and the Reporting Administrator. The Release 12 Applications DBA will work with the Applications System Administrator to tune the concurrent manager, but will also become a master at installing and supporting third party applications, database diagnostics, and tools like the Oracle Applications Manager (OAM), which is full of new features for Release 12.

The Applications DBA must also master new cloning techniques based on significant technology architecture changes, and design an instance synchronization strategy as well as backup and disaster recovery plans based on the relationship between the database and the Applications. The Applications DBA will also assist in Workflow maintenance as well as daily proactive monitoring of multiple indicators across the technology stack. It is the Applications DBA's job to understand the relationship between the Release 12 Applications and the entire technology stack.

Responsibilities

Responsibilities include:

- Responsible for initial and on-going database modeling and design
- Understand system architecture and processing flow
- Install, upgrade, and maintain the database server and tools
- License and install modules and languages
- Create and maintain primary database storage structures and objects
- Customize and modify the database structures
- Allocate initial database storage and plan future storage requirements
- Configure new features including the multi-threaded server and database triggers by adjusting database parameters
- Reduce unnecessary and/or redundant storage through space management
- Enroll users by assigning appropriate roles and profiles at the RDBMS level
- Maintain and guarantee database security using standard database audit tools
- Control and monitor user access to the database objects and data
- Monitor and optimize database performance using cost and rule-based optimizers and compare performance to predetermined baselines
- Manage and monitor health of database objects
- Load bulk data using conventional and direct path loads
- Guarantee data integrity and consistency
- Facilitate the sharing of data among users

- Implement regular and frequent database backups required to recover and/or restore the database objects and data
- Recover and/or restore the database objects and data as needed due to software failure, media failure, or disaster
- Maintain the database to the highest availability state required by users
- Liaison with Oracle, users, management, and other vendors
- Assist in managing SOX compliance, strategies and audit evidence
- Primary source of Oracle information for users and developers
- Review interface and bolt-on code for standards and performance
- Migrate and manage interface and bolt-on code
- Keep abreast of new technology directly impacting database activity, including diagnostic tools, RAID technology, tape arrays, and data storage devices
- Determine server and tools upgrade strategy
- Provide scripts to automate pinging the database and SQL*NET to make sure they are up and running
- Monitor the size and content of log files and storage destinations. Backup and purge logs and storage destinations
- Compile database statistics and health reports
- Manage snapshots
- Ensure that the technology necessary to support Workflow (database, Advanced Queuing, propagation, notification mailer, agent listeners) is working, and apply patches as directed by Oracle Support or the business management team.
- Apply current Oracle Diagnostics patches quarterly or per Oracle's published release schedule
- Apply Oracle Applications patches
- Ensure that the workflow administrator responsibility is properly reset after each execution of AutoConfig (unless custom code has been written to reset automatically)
- Ensure that all aspects of cloned environments accurately point to the cloned instance
- Work with the Workflow Administrator to develop and enforce the methodology for maintaining and testing the workflow mailer in cloned instances

- Work with the Workflow Administrator to ensure that the parameters on the Global Administration page remain accurate
- Migrate workflow customizations (workflows and associated pl/sql packages) from instance to instance according to policy.
- Work with the Workflow Administrator to ensure that the folders used by the workflow mailer are periodically cleaned and that messages sent to the discard folder are not sent there in error
- Monitor MetaLink for new patches and ensure that patches are applied and tested at both the database and PC level.
- Ensure that proper maintenance is performed on a routine basis
- Use `patchsets.sh` to insure knowledge of which modules are not patched current.
- Logical database design
- Physical database creation
- Database modification
- Database backup and recovery plan procedures including disaster recovery
- Database performance tuning and troubleshooting
- Database resource tracking
- Manage developer tools access
- Review Applications performance (design)
- Resource forecasting
- Data conversion assistance

Breakdown by Category

Console Operation

- Install, upgrade, and maintain the Oracle database, tools, and Applications software
- Create the primary database file system
- Create and maintain database software structures and objects
- Install bug and patch software

Database Maintenance

- Monitor and optimize SQL database performance using cost and rule-based optimizers
- Responsible for initial and on-going database modeling and design
- Customize and modify the database structures
- Allocate initial database storage and plan future storage requirements
- Configure new features including the multi-threaded server and database triggers by adjusting database parameters as required
- Test, recover, and restore the database objects and data as needed
- Implement regular and frequent database backups required to recover and restore the database objects/data files in production
- Reduce unnecessary and/or redundant storage through space management
- Perform regular database maintenance to provide the highest availability state required by users
- Keep abreast of new technology directly impacting on database activity including diagnostic tools, RAID technology, tape arrays, and data storage devices
- Determine server and tools upgrade strategy
- Perform maintenance activities like compiling invalid objects; gathering statistics; recompiling forms/reports when necessary, and using ADADMIN to keep snapshots current

Database Security

- Maintain and guarantee Oracle database security using standard database security and available audit tools
- Safeguard data integrity and consistency
- Control and monitor user access to the database objects and data files
- Enroll users by assigning appropriate roles and profiles (limited need in Applications instance)

Workflow Support

- Ensure that the technology necessary to support Workflow (database, Advanced Queuing, propagation, notification mailer, agent listeners) is working, and apply patches as directed by Oracle Support or the business management team.

- Apply current Oracle Diagnostics patches quarterly or per Oracle's published release schedule

- Ensure that the workflow administrator responsibility is properly reset after each execution of AutoConfig

- Ensure that all aspects of cloned environments accurately point to the cloned instance

- Work with the Workflow Administrator to develop and enforce the methodology for maintaining and testing the workflow mailer in cloned instances

- Work with the Workflow Administrator to ensure that the parameters on the Global Administration page remain accurate

- Migrate workflow customizations (workflows and associated pl/sql packages) from instance to instance according to policy.

- Work with the Workflow Administrator to ensure that the folders used by the workflow mailer are periodically cleaned and that messages sent to the discard folder are not sent there in error

- Monitor MetaLink for new patches and ensure that patches are applied and tested at both the database and PC level.

Paper Administration

- Understand system architecture and processing flow

- Document and maintain written RDBMS setup, backup, and recovery procedures

- Develop recovery plan to include salvage of data lost due to software or media failure

- Liaison with Oracle, users, management, and other vendors

- Serve as primary source of Oracle information for users and developers

- Determine SQL database software upgrade strategy

Operating System Administrator

The Operating System Administrator manages the hardware and operating system environment for the Applications.

Responsibilities

Responsibilities include:

- Configure hardware

- Install hardware and software

- Maintain system disk space

- Configure system parameters (kernel)
- System tuning
- System utility and software builds for implementation
- Responsible for UNIX / Linux security
- Accessibility of hardware using standard protocols (TCP/IP)
- Configure home directories
- Enroll users and set up accounts at the operating system level
- Implement, coordinate, and track backups at the OS level
- Debug user system problems
- Network file system configuration and maintenance
- Implement, coordinate, and track user and system accounting
- Configure and maintain UNIX / Linux mail
- Design and implement CRON scripts for system cleanup and performance
- Shell (Korn, Bourne, and C) programming maintenance and support
- Configure printers
- Keep abreast of new technology directly impacting on database activity including diagnostic tools, RAID technology tape arrays, and data storage devices
- Determine server and tools upgrade
- Monitor print queues for problem Applications print jobs.
- Monitor finite system resource utilization including CPU, Memory, and Inode allocation

Breakdown by Category

Console Operations

- Configure operating system parameters (UNIX / Linux kernel)
- Accessibility of hardware using standard protocols (TCP/IP; IPX)
- Design and implement CRON scripts for system cleanup and performance tuning
- Implement, coordinate and track backups at the O/S level

- UNIX / Linux Root/Superuser Login:
- System performance tuning
- Maintain system disk space
- Enroll users and set-up user logins and home directories
- Debug user login, program access, and printing problems
- System utility and software builds for implementation
- Network file system configuration and maintenance
- Configure and maintain UNIX / Linux mail
- Shell (Korn, Bourne, and C) programming maintenance and support
- Customize end user interfaces to UNIX / Linux
- Monitor runtime options for concurrent programs - work with RDBMS Administration
- Monitor runtime dependencies - work with RDBMS Administration
- UNIX / Linux Security:
- Responsible for operating system security (C2, E2 level security)
- Implement dial-in access restrictions

Paper Administration

- Determine server OS, UNIX / Linux server hardware, and tools upgrade strategy
- Implement, coordinate, and track user and system resource accounting
- Monitor resource usage and plan growth as necessary
- Insure consistency of UNIX / Linux and network naming conventions, system definitions, and documentation
- Work with Network Administrator for all network operation issues
- Keep abreast of new technology directly impacting on database activity including diagnostic tools, RAID technology, tape arrays and data storage devices
- Interface with hardware vendor in determining maintenance schedules
- Determine how to respond to hardware vendor "alert" paging

Technical Installation

- Install and configure all UNIX / Linux hardware and UNIX / Linux OS software
- Define, register, and install UNIX / Linux peripherals
- Configure printers - Co-op responsibility with Network Administrator for UNIX/Linux-to-Network LAN printing
- Assist Database and Oracle Administrators in maintaining a custom application environment

WHERE DO WE GO FROM HERE?

Clearly, the task of managing the Release 12 E-Business Suite environment requires highly trained personnel. Staying on top of the technology changes can be challenging. With the introduction of the Fusion Applications in late 2008, even more changes to the Applications will likely cause even more changes to these roles. As consultants, we have an opportunity to see multiple client organizations over a short period of time compared to an employee of a specific organization. One of the best ways you can keep up to date on best practices with the resources and staffing areas in the Oracle Applications area is to speak with other members of the community through participation in Oracle Applications User Group (OAUG) meetings.

Fusion Middleware

Fusion Middleware and Applications? With all its futuristic promise, the title might as well be "Flying Cars and Robotic Butlers". The mystery gets especially deep for Fusion Applications. How will they work? They have been promised for a while now and we've heard the planned release of the first Fusion Applications Suite is sometime towards the end of 2008. What new features will these Applications have and how will we benefit from migrating to it? We cannot answer all of those questions today because Oracle Corporation is keeping the information close to the vest, with good justification from a competitive advantage standpoint. We can, however, provide the latest information about the latest release of Fusion Middleware, as well as how Fusion Middleware and E-Business Suite, Release 12, are currently integrated. That should give you a clearer understanding of how best to leverage these new technologies and features for your own situation.

This chapter attempts to clearly define the term Fusion and its various meanings, with the goal of helping everyone involved in an Oracle E-Business Suite (or other ERP packaged environments) gain an understanding of where things are going. Further, we'll help you gain some insight into what tasks your organization will need to consider acting upon further down the road to this mysterious and shiny future.

Whether your role is that of an Applications DBA, a business analyst, a business owner or even a C-Level executive, this chapter should offer valuable information without overwhelming you with more detail than you need.

Because the actual release of the Fusion Applications Suite is far in the future, relatively speaking, this chapter will focus more on the concepts underlying its architecture and its design. We will also cover some of its technical underpinnings to provide context. This strategy will best provide you with the information that you will need to prepare for the future.

What is Fusion?

Fusion is many things, depending upon the reader's perspective. But there are four basic perspectives we will consider here:

- The Vision for Fusion
- The Fusion Architecture

- The Fusion Technologies
- The Fusion Applications Suite

Regardless of your role in the organization, the information we can gain from these perspectives on Fusion will give you a well-rounded picture of how it will affect organizations.

THE VISION

Arguably, the most important thing to understand about Fusion is that it is representative of Oracle's vision for changing the way Enterprise software works.

When you examine Oracle's statements, you will regularly hear the message that Fusion is about protecting, evolving and extending applications. Rather than encouraging radical change, Fusion is about enabling the Oracle applications that you already have as part of the effort to improve applications so they produce more business value. This vision is radical because it is not about replacing legacy applications but extending them and leveraging their value. That is a big change from the message of the past.

At a technical level, Fusion is intended to enhance Enterprise applications by moving them to a new programming model, a shift that is as drastic and as significant as the shift to distributed-computing was. Fusion has the ability to bring disparate application solutions together into a common design and technology set, so they can be combined to create a best of breed solution for your organization's needs. Fusion is also designed to promote the unity of your applications and your business processes so they become one coherent entity, supporting each other to better adapt to the changing business climate.

Traditionally a business application is selected to support a business process, and then that application is adapted to meet the business requirements. Often times, this means modifying both the application and the business requirements to produce a solution that is technically cumbersome and difficult to maintain over time, as the application and business processes change. Where the application doesn't offer a specific piece of functionality, it might be extended (or worse, customized); creating a new piece of software that must be carefully designed and maintained throughout the solution's lifespan. Or the business process might be adapted to limit its workings to what the application can provide. Neither solution is ideal; with each new piece of custom software, maintenance of the environment becomes more complex and more critical. With each change to the business process, the organization compromises, taking the focus away from the most effective business model.

The promise of Fusion Middleware is a change to that traditional model. With Fusion, applications are no longer a series of monolithic packages that are integrated to approximate the desired goal. Applications are now viewed as a plethora of small blocks, called "Services" that are combined to make a much finer-grained implementation of the business process.

This means that a software suite, such as the upcoming Fusion Applications Suite, will now be architected as a collection of Services that combine to provide a full-featured system. When a Service doesn't fully meet a particular need, it can be extended or even replaced to provide what is needed. As business needs change, the combination of Services used to meet those changing business requirements is altered to match. If you've seen the acronym SOA or Service-Oriented Architecture, then you've already been introduced to this concept. This approach to building applications also provides a new model for interconnections between businesses, wherein each can present Services that the other can invoke remotely without the need for extensive interface programming efforts.

To work most efficiently these software Services will work best when they are "loosely-coupled". This term means that each Service is designed to work independently from other Services around it. Loosely-coupled Services offer several benefits. First they are easier (and faster) to modify since there is a lower risk of creating unexpected problems. A second benefit of loosely-coupled Services is that they can be distributed across multiple Servers for load-balancing and scalability. Using the network, they can communicate just as if they were on a single server.

This illustrates where the primary business value of Fusion comes from: the ability to quickly adapt the software so it meets the actual requirements of the business. Consider these examples. If a regulatory requirement necessitates additional steps in performing a process, they can be inserted rapidly by adding new Services. If a business model changes to favor outsourcing a particular task, such as performing a credit check, the chain of Services previously used in the solution can quickly adapt, and just as importantly, it can be expected to provide a reasonable collection of metrics about the performance of the outsourced components.

For the astute readers who are wanting to know more about this, we applaud you, and encourage you to hold on to that question and look for answers to it throughout the rest of this chapter.

It is important to keep in mind that Oracle did not invent this way of thinking; it is in fact responding to what has been happening in the enterprise applications marketplace over the last few years. With many of the web and distributed application technologies that originated in the 1990's reaching a high level of maturity, they are beginning to become more accepted, particularly as standards have arisen.

In the case of Fusion, Oracle is adopting a variety of application technologies and standards taken from Sun Microsystem's Java Enterprise Edition architecture, which means that the Fusion applications should readily integrate into many environments, and make use of skill sets that are available in the marketplace.

THE ARCHITECTURE

Now that we know about at least one definition of Fusion, let's look at the architecture that will be used to create it. For those who aren't involved in the day-to-day technical aspects of the E-Business Suite, don't panic! As stated at the beginning of the chapter, we will avoid the low level technical discussions here, so keep reading!

Architecture is important to all of us whether we realize it not, because it influences everything from how long a project takes to execute to the frequency and duration of planned outages. A solid understanding of the Fusion architecture will make it so much easier to embrace the coming changes to the E-Business Suite.

The Technology Stack

At a high level, Figure 165 displays the stack of components that will go into making the Fusion Applications Suite. This is a comfortable level of detail for our discussions, although we will dive a little bit deeper in upcoming sections. Let's begin with the bottom of our diagram and work our way up from there.

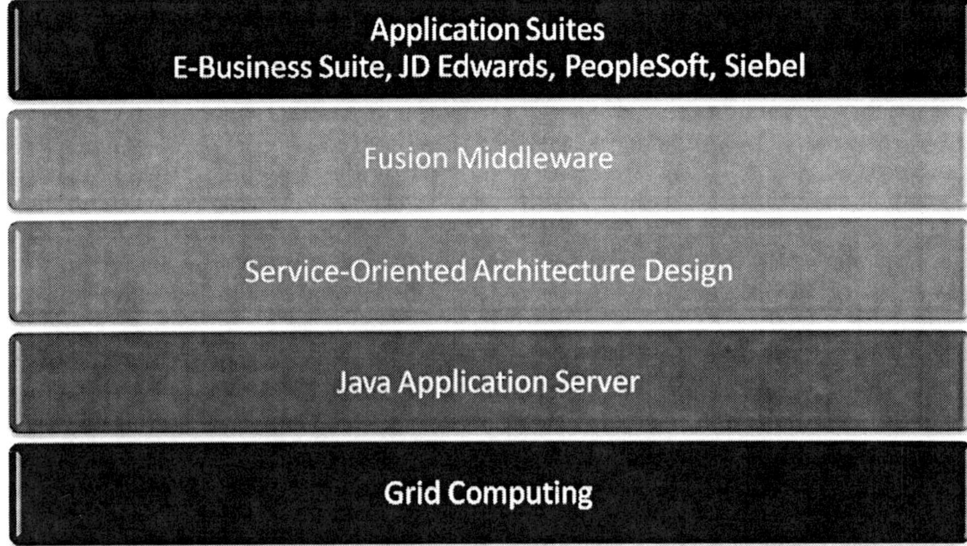

Figure 165 – The components in the Fusion Applications Suite

Grid Computing

Grid Computing has been a popular buzz term over the last few years, and like so many terms it is not only overused, but physical examples of it that we find around us often leave us puzzled and disappointed. Grid Computing includes the components of the Infrastructure, Application and Information Grids. The Infrastructure Grid includes the hardware resources that enable processing. The Application Grid includes business logic and process flow. The Information Grid describes the ability to view all of an organization's information holistically regardless of location.

In its pure form, Grid Computing describes an architecture where processing can be dynamically shifted to meet business requirements. To do this Grid Computing must rely on virtualization and provisioning. Virtualization is done by combining multiple physical resources into a single virtual pool. Whether this is a group of servers, processors, disk drives or databases, the key to virtualization is having the software tools to manage different environments.

Oracle's approach to Grid Computing is enabled by the capabilities of the Oracle database (Version 10*g* and 11*g*), Automated Storage Management, Oracle Enterprise Manager, Real Application Clusters and even the Fusion Middleware.

In reality, few applications have been designed for this environment, and the complexities that it brings. If your grid consists of ten servers, how do you get the applications software onto all ten of them? Do you install it separately on each of them? If so, then how do you handle patches? Clearly, patching ten application installs is not an acceptable solution. And if the solution is to have some form of shared storage for the applications, that makes your hardware architecture just a little more complicated.

That's a simple example, but we hope that it gets you thinking about the true complexities of Grid Computing. These complexities are the reason why there are few examples of general purpose applications that make good use of Grid Computing. There are plenty of examples of specialty applications that use it to great advantage, such as supercomputing tasks like analysis of cancer cells, but these are hardly general purpose applications.

As for the promise it offers, and the reason that it has been such a buzz term in the industry, we need look no further than our own desktop computer. It is well known that each new generation of desktops is much faster than its predecessors, and this has been the case since the industry's inception. But, consider the fact that whatever your favored hardware platform, PC, UNIX, or mainframe, there are limits on the maximum performance of a single CPU. Everything from the laws of physics to human laws of market economics state that a server cannot have an infinite amount of processing power. So if infinite scalability is not available in a single box, then Grid Computing is one way to combine many servers together to achieve enough scalability to meet our business needs. Through careful application design it is possible to create a solution where workload can be distributed horizontally across multiple servers, and where the failure of any one server can be masked by having unused capacity of other servers assume additional workload.

An offshoot of Grid Computing, and another one of its goals, is improved application availability. If an application makes good use of the Grid's infrastructure, it should be entirely possible for the application to survive the failure of a single server. Certainly, any work that was in progress on that server will be lost and the transaction will have to be restarted or continued on another node. But what is important is that the application as a whole is still available to the user community.

Some aspects of these scalability and availability enhancing features are available in today's clustered applications. How then is Grid Computing different? It takes these features to the next level, integrating them deep into the software, instead of adding them on as an afterthought. In fact, many applications today are capable of being clustered largely through sheer luck, not through good design. In an application truly designed for the grid, we can see subtle changes throughout its design and implementation so that it can actively exploit the grid to its advantage. This is especially true as it relates to maintaining the applications running on top of the grid. Grid computing should allow us to patch various components of the applications without shutting the entire application down for maintenance.

Java Application Server

Let's move up the diagram one level, to the Java Applications Server, where we see many of the Grid Computing concepts embodied. With a solid foundation of shared resources, the Applications Server must now be designed to exploit those resources, and to marshal them to support the needs of the applications. Oracle's use of Java in the environment is well known, and well suited to the design of grid-enabled applications, since Sun's Java Enterprise Edition development suite provides many of the programming models and tools needed in an open, standards-based environment. In the context of the Oracle product suite, we need to know that the application server is in fact the cornerstone of a suite of products, called the Fusion Middleware, which we'll discuss later in the chapter.

Service-Oriented Architecture Design

Moving up again, we arrive at the Service-Oriented Architecture Design level, which is a conceptual component that we will discuss in great detail shortly. Let's briefly summarize it as a design that implements applications as a small series of building blocks, each of which performs a discrete step or function. These blocks are then combined using another software component to create a complete application. By building this solution in a Java Enterprise toolkit it is possible create a solution that is based upon vendor neutral standards, has the potential to interoperate with other applications, and can exploit Grid Computing to its best potential.

Middleware and Applications

Now we move up the diagram to the Oracle-specific layers. First is the Fusion Middleware, which is a collection of products that run in, or alongside, the application server to provide the remaining infrastructure needed for the Fusion Applications. The Middleware forms the technical foundation that we will need to learn the most about in order to implement and support the forthcoming solution. The Application Server is just one piece of the Fusion Middleware suite of products. There are many other components that make up the Fusion Middleware suite including the SOA Suite and the Business Intelligence family of products.

The Acronyms

No architectural or technical discussion is truly complete without the use of acronyms. Perhaps that's due to the origins of these topics amongst software engineers who are highly technical and more comfortable with acronyms than should be permitted. Or perhaps it's because we all want to seem a little more expert than we are by casually throwing around words only meaningful to others that are "in the know". This discussion is certainly no exception to that rule, but we are presented with a double edge sword. On the upside we only have a couple of acronyms to deal with - which is always a pleasant surprise in any modern technology discussion - but on the downside, the abbreviations represent complex, but extremely important, concepts that will require some discussion to master. After all, we'll need to be able to deal with more than a superficial conversation if we're going to get any pride from our new knowledge.

Service Oriented Architecture (SOA)

The importance of Service Oriented Architecture cannot be overstated when discussing the Fusion environment. It drives not only the architecture of Fusion, but also much of what is seen in the technology's business value.

Let's start by defining Service Oriented Architecture (SOA for short). First, SOA is not a product that you can buy. An approach to applications design and development has these characteristics:

> A collection of programs (Services) in which each perform a unit of work and that are orchestrated together to construct a complex application that performs a business process.

The primary idea of SOA is that software is best described as a related set of smaller, discrete components. Each Service is a distinct unit that has a formal interface for how it must be invoked, and what it must return. Think of Services as building blocks that each do one thing, and are connected in a particular sequence to implement a business process.

Figure 166 illustrates this concept by showing some details of a process used to bring a new employee into an organization. Each step in the process is implemented as a Service, each with its own distinct inputs and outputs. The overall process is then managed by a separate component that does what SOA architectures refer to as "orchestration".

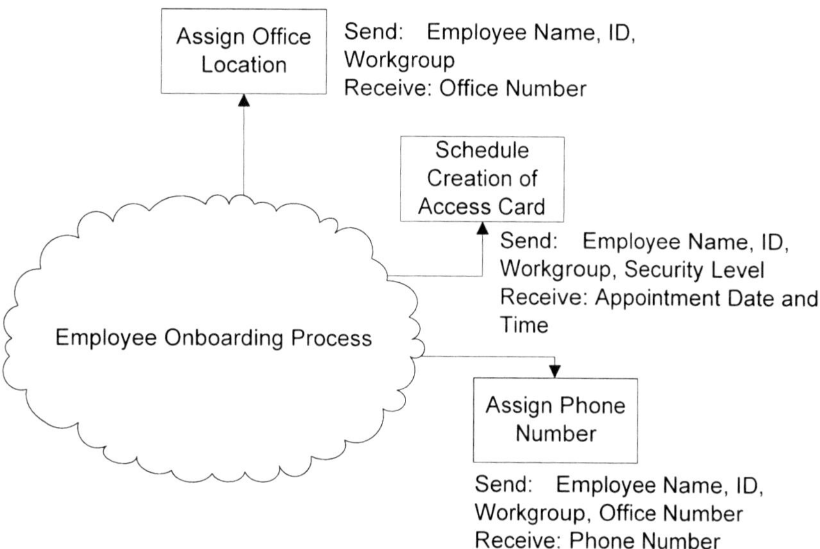

Figure 166 – Employee Onboarding Process

To make use of these Services it is necessary to have some form of glue to connect the individual Services into a structure and allow them to perform a business process, also known as an orchestration of Services. In SOA implementations built around XML, this glue is commonly provided by the Business Process Execution Language or BPEL for short. BPEL is a language for creating workflows to invoke and manage the execution of Services.

Implementations of BPEL typically have a modeling environment to create the process flow and a runtime engine to perform the work as needed. These tools also provide ancillary functions, such as monitoring the progress of the workflow, collecting data needed to perform process reporting and analysis, and notifying the appropriate people of problems. When combined, SOA and BPEL create an environment where a business process can be mapped to a Service flow, and can adapt quickly as that business process changes over time.

To put the idea of SOA into proper perspective, consider your traditional application design where components do not have rigidly enforced separation into Services, each with its own input and output contract. Instead of loosely-coupled, the logic of the application is "tightly-coupled" and highly dependent. In this environment, any component can technically be making calls to any other. Also, the same data may be treated differently in different components, meaning that a piece of data as simple as an order line entry may need to be translated into another format before it can be manipulated. These facts mean that alterations to the business process must go through a lengthy design process, potentially complex coding, and then a rigorous testing phase. And it is easy to introduce bugs to the environment by improperly translating the data, or not properly understanding all of the components that will actually be affected by a change.

By contrast, in a SOA application the alteration might require either modification of an existing Service or creation of brand new Services. As modifications are made, new "versions" of a Service are introduced. Older versions can still remain in use, allowing backward compatibility. Because SOA requires Services to be "registered" when they are installed and they have clearly defined interfaces, it is relatively easy to tell what components are using the Service and will therefore be affected by modifications to it.

For the creation of new Services, work begins by clearly defining what the Service needs to do, and then integrating it into the workflow. Because the Service's input and output requirements are clearly defined, it is practical to create a testing procedure that feeds various data into the Service and verifies that the correct output returns.

One final aspect of SOA that is worth discussing, without delving too deeply into the technologies involved, is the physical invocation of the Services. For a traditional application living within a business' infrastructure, the invocation mechanism would be a networked communication's protocol. This protocol would provide a reasonable level of security to prevent unauthorized access to Services. The data flowing through the network would be able to move messages between different programming languages and operating systems while ensuring their integrity, and would provide some means of storing messages for later delivery should a Service not be running when a process attempts to invoke it. This requires one or more centralized components to perform all of this work, with the actual BPEL and Service processes running in separate server components, potentially distributed around the environment.

If you're thinking that all of this sounds remarkably similar to how the Internet works, then you've hit upon an important concept. While internal applications can make use of a wide variety of protocols for moving Service invocation and result messages around, internet facing applications generally make use of a smaller subset of these protocols. So, a Service that is accessible from an intranet or even the internet, using a protocol such as the HTTP standard used by web browsers, is called a Web Service.

SOA, with its ability to present and use Services within a business, across networks and even via the Internet makes it far more flexible than traditional application designs. But SOA is not without its price, as technology standards dictate the use of extra components for locating and securing access to Services, and for packaging their input and output data from transmission over the network.

Event Driven Architecture (EDA)

The ability to have business processes invoked when specific events take place in the application is a natural offshoot of SOA. This capability is commonly referred to as Event Driven Architecture (EDA for short), and it is complementary to the greater SOA environment.

In the Oracle Applications, you've probably become familiar with Oracle Alerts. EDA builds on this concept to generate events and notify others by extending it outside the application.

Consider a business process such as bringing a new employee onboard within a company. In addition to all of the tasks that HR must perform, many small tasks must occur, ranging from entering the new person into the building security system to delivering some company swag ("stuff we all get") to their new desk. Many of these processes can be performed as the HR process progresses, but this can become cumbersome not simply from a technology perspective, but also from the idea that one of these steps must be added to the larger HR processes' workflow, and must therefore go through formal change management procedures. A much simpler solution would be for the HR process to generate Events, which would be sent to an Event Dispatcher, which in turn would invoke workflows for any processes that have registered to receive these Events.

In simpler terms, Event Driven Architecture inverts the flow of control, and instead allows the outboard processes to be notified whenever an event that they are interested in happens. In this instance, the HR processes would be designed to trigger a specific event when the onboarding is complete. In turn, the swag shipping process flow would be configured to receive this event and beginning its processing (see Figure 167). This inversion of control makes the SOA and EDA applications much more flexible and opens new possibilities for integration, providing business analysts a much needed mechanism for customization.

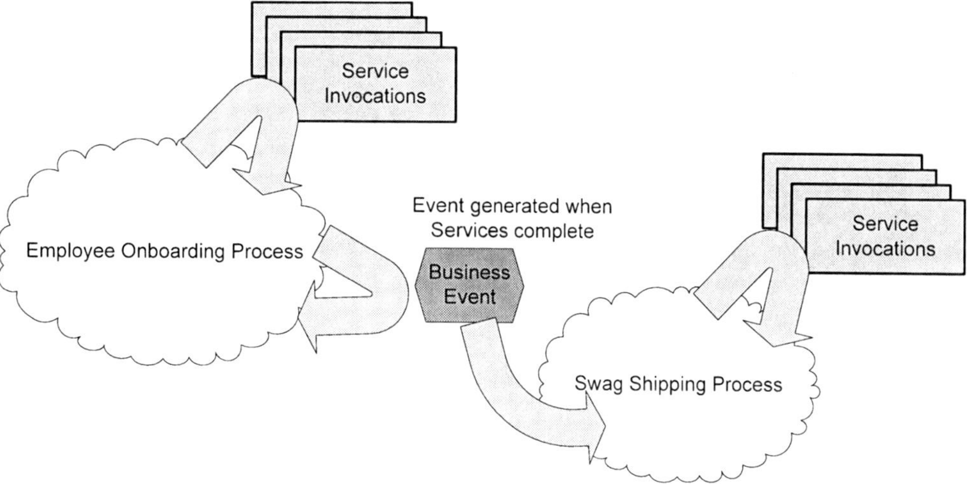

Figure 167 – Event Driven Architecture

The Business Value of SOA and EDA

The larger discussion of the business value that SOA and EDA bring is well beyond the scope of a book like this, but it can be summarized into several key points. Having a full SOA-based infrastructure can bring benefits to a broad swath of enterprise applications, and facilitate a new level of near real-time business information gathering. But let's keep this conversation focused on Fusion architecture, and the benefits it will bring.

1. Business needs the agility to react to ever changing environments: labor shifts from country to country, new regulatory requirements, and new technologies changing the way everyday tasks are performed. This requires IT tools that are equally flexible, and able to support the changes on a timely basis. SOA based applications take a large step towards providing this agility.

2. Reduced Total Cost of Ownership (TCO), and quicker Return on Investment (ROI) for new projects due to the ability to reuse Services in many cases. This can be achieved by reducing the need for additional design, coding and testing effort required to build tailored services and events thereby creating "reusable" components.

3. Use of industry standard technologies and components, making application integration easier, and making development skills less vendor specific. By using common industry standards, the need to build "custom" solutions is reduced, which also reduces the impact of subsequent maintenance and software upgrades.

THE TECHNOLOGY

Now that we know what Fusion is, and what SOA and EDA are all about, let's look at its technical components, namely the middleware layers that it will use. Again, we want to remind our less technical readers not to panic; this discussion will remain fairly high level simply because it is much too early on the Fusion Roadmap to have a detailed technology discussion. There are far too many things that *have not been* announced for us to go into much detail as of this writing.

Fusion Middleware

The Fusion Middleware is a broad group of products ranging from infrastructure components, such as the Application Server, to business tools such as BPEL. Not only are these products currently on the market, some are part of the Release 12 E-Business Suite. Others are bundled into standalone packages such as the SOA Suite, for enterprises developing custom applications. Let's start with an overview of Fusion Middleware and then we can look in more depth at some of the components that will play a key role in implementing Fusion in your organization.

The Big Picture

First, we need to understand that Fusion Middleware consists of over forty individual software products. While most of them are designed to work cooperatively, most organizations will not install every product in their environment. One reason for this is that not everyone will need the functionality and another reason is that you can't just buy Fusion Middleware and get everything included. Instead, these products can be purchased individually or in Suites. So which ones make sense for your situation? That's the challenge!

With such a large group of products, even Oracle has struggled in communicating to customers how to get started, what the benefits are, and what products are best to consider.

With that challenge in mind, let's look at the big picture. Figure 168 shows key product areas addressed by the Fusion Middleware products:

Application Server	Business Integration	Business Intelligence
Business Process Mgmt	Coherence IN-Memory Data Grid	Collaboration Suite
Content Management	Data Integrator	Developer Tools
Event Driven Architecture Suite	Identity Management	Master Data Management
Middleware for SMB	Middleware for Applications	Portal
Service Delivery Platform	Service Oriented Architecture Suite	WebCenter

Figure 168 - Product areas addressed by Fusion Middleware

Here are the key things to note about this table. Some of these have the word "Suite" in their name. That indicates that they include a bundle of products designed to tackle a specific technology area. The second thing to note is that all of these products are "outside" of the Release 12 Application. That means that they are able to interact with the Application and outside of it. This independence from the Applications makes these products very powerful. The last thing to note is that they are all enabled by the Application Server, which we will discuss now.

Application Server 10*g*

The Oracle Application Server is at the heart of Fusion Middleware. Commonly referred to as OAS10*g*, the current version as of this edition of this book is Release 3. The current release is a significant enhancement to the core of the service-oriented-architecture platform.

OAS10*g* is designed to provide a robust, standards-based platform that can support mission-critical processing. It offers High Availability features to address data failure, human error, software failure, hardware failure, and site disaster. Some of the high-availability features are derived from the underlying use of Oracle Database 10*g* and grid technologies.

The Oracle database provides Fast Undo, secure backup/recovery and Data Guard. OAS10*g* extends this by offering enhanced clustering and expanding the ability to do hot deployment of new components. Clustering allows multiple copies of OAS10*g* to be hosted on multiple servers, which can provide increased availability and/or scalability, depending upon the design of the application that is being run. The hot deployment features of OAS10*g* allow application components to be installed and patched without having to shutdown the entire application server and all of the other applications running in it.

In complex environments, you may see configurations that include five layers in the topology. These would include the database layer, the OAS10*g* layer, the HTTP layer, the Load Balancer layer and finally, the client layer. This division of resources is used not only to increase scalability, but also to increase security by isolating resources from each other on separate servers.

Within OAS10*g*, you will find support for Java Enterprise Edition (Java EE, formerly J2EE) in the Oracle Container for Java (OC4J). OC4J supports JavaServer Pages (JSP's), Servlets, Enterprise JavaBeans (EJB's), Java Message Service (JMS), and more. If your eyes are beginning to glaze over because of the acronyms, just remember that OC4J is where Java programs execute within the Application Server.

The Application Server can be managed, like most Oracle products, either from the command line or by using a graphical user interface via the browser. The Application Server Control (ASC) allows the administrator to configure and monitor the Application Server. Here's a sample screen shot (see Figure 169) of the ASC:

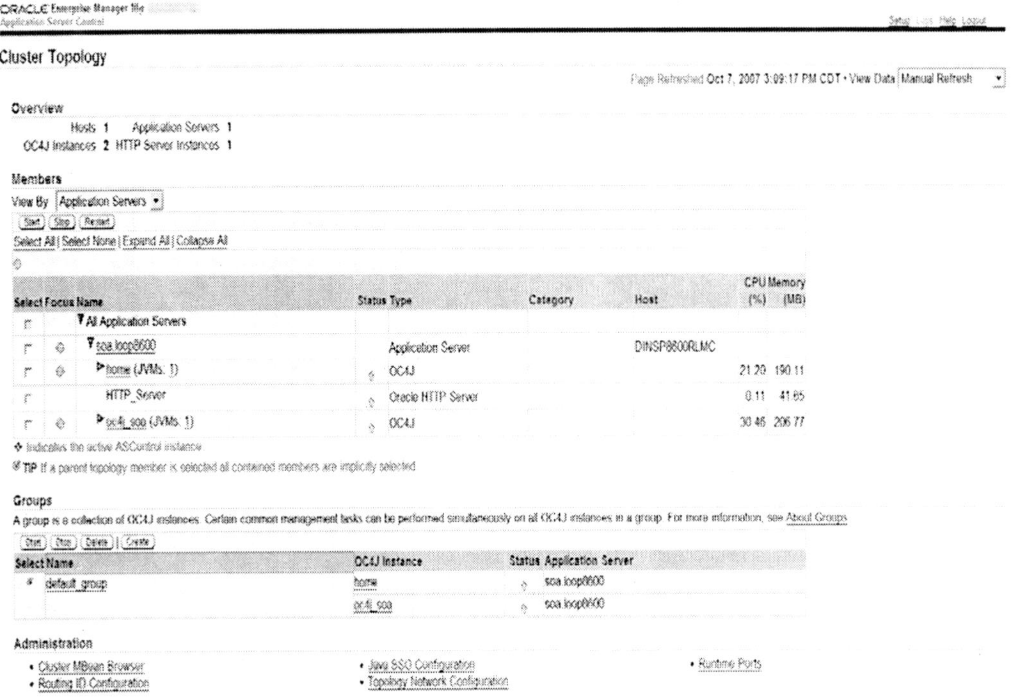

Figure 169 – The Application Server Control (ASC) screen

If we narrow down our view of OAS10*g* and focus on the components commonly used by Service-Oriented Architecture (SOA), there are four we need to consider. They are Oracle Business Rules, BPEL Process Manager, Enterprise Service Bus and Web Services Manager. There are also some supporting Fusion Middleware products that we will look at, including JDeveloper, Service Registry, Business Activity Monitor and the BI Publisher.

We will start with JDeveloper because we will refer back to it several times. Then we'll look at the four SOA components, and then explore the last three Fusion products.

Even if you never plan to write a single line of code, it is good to know something about JDeveloper. You never know when you might be trapped in an elevator with a Java wizard, so here's a quick overview.

JDeveloper

As one of the products in the developer tools area, JDeveloper is important to know about. The first thing you need to know about JDeveloper is that it is a free product from Oracle. What? Free? Yes, it's amazing and it's true. Oracle wants to encourage developers to use their products, and one of the best ways to do that is to offer it as a no-cost product. Also, some of Oracle's competition offers a free product as well.

JDeveloper is an Integrated Development Environment (IDE), which means that once you fire it up, you can do just about anything you need to do as a developer. You can write Java programs, edit XML, look at data in a database, and develop SQL queries. And that's just the beginning.

The whole idea of an IDE is to simplify software development, which is why several companies offer similar products. Microsoft provides an IDE called "Visual Studio" and Sun Microsystems calls theirs "Java Studio Creator".

JDeveloper provides a graphical interface that improves programming productivity. Figure 170 shows a sample of the JDeveloper screen.

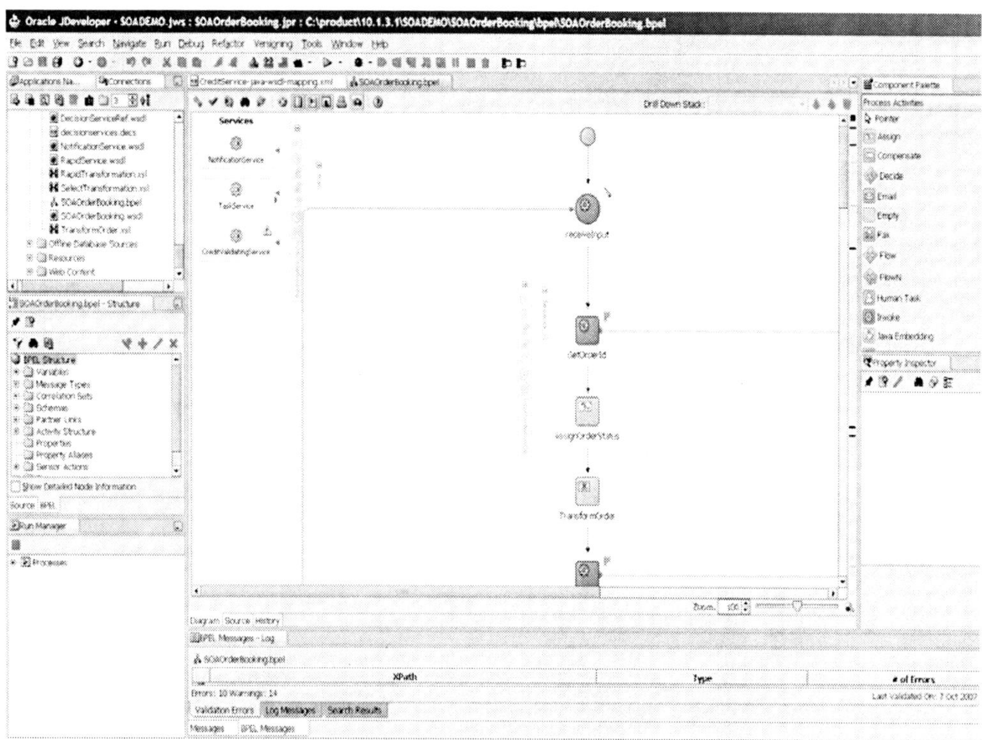

Figure 170 – A Sample JDeveloper screen

Without getting too deep here's what you should notice. First it has a center area where the work is actually done. On the left side are various pieces of software code that can be selected. On the right side are new components that can be added into the software. And along the bottom are places for messages and information to be displayed. For a developer, using a tool like this can dramatically improve the speed and quality of the software code they create. The business benefit is lower costs and faster development.

Application Developer Framework (ADF)

Another product in the area of Developer tools is the Application Developer Framework (ADF). Those of you who are not application developers are probably wondering why we're including a product for software developers. The answer is both deceptively simple and relevant to all of you. ADF will help you understand better how Java technologies are used for creating an application's plumbing and most importantly the user interface. So if you are using the Applications you should know something about ADF and the changes it will bring.

Let's start by clearly defining a few things, so that this discussion can be taken in the proper context. Both Release 11*i* and Release 12 are built out of the Oracle *Application* Framework toolkit (OAF, not ADF), which makes use of some older Java technologies for performing their work, and creating the Applications user interface. These early standards include only a small portion of the features that the Java Enterprise Edition offers to developers. That is why Oracle Forms are created in the form of a Java applet instead of in the form of a true HTML interface. This use of applet technology makes the Oracle forms only a few lines of code away from being a natively installed desktop application. This design is also a result of the fact that the Java and HTML user interfaces were not that mature when the Release 11*i* E-Business Suite was written. At that time, HTML was far from where we see it today, with so-called Web 2.0 sites being the shining example of what can now be done with HTML. To see what we mean by Web 2.0, try using Google's online spreadsheet or Yahoo's new email products. Then take a moment to remember what the first web pages you ever viewed looked like. There's a world of difference, is there not?

Oracle has stated that the Fusion Applications will be built with ADF, which employs many new Java standards, and builds upon much of the wisdom gained by writing applications in the Oracle Applications Framework (OAF). While we have not seen examples of the Fusion Applications at this time, it is fair to assume that their user interface will be much more sophisticated than what we are used to. We can in fact rest assured that this is true for one simple reason: Oracle has stated that the current Forms technology will be replaced with HTML and JavaServer Pages (JSPs).

So, what will ADF bring to those of us who are not developers? We can be certain that a more sophisticated user interface will be present, although that alone is rarely worth an upgrade, let alone a technology migration. But more importantly, we can already tell that our developer staff will have to learn a variety of new Java toolkits, and all of the associated acronyms: Java Server Faces (JSF), ADF Faces, Enterprise JavaBeans (EJBs), and so many more.

Business Rules

Every organization has rules that guide their business decisions. Some business rules are commonly known, while others are often assumed so we don't even consciously think about them. These rules are an important part of Business Process Management (BPM) because they affect how business processes make decisions.

For example, businesses usually have rules requiring approvals for Purchase Orders over a certain amount. If it is less than a certain amount, it can be approved at one level of management but as the amount increases, it requires higher levels of approval. In Human Resources there are rules about who can sign off on promotions, paid time off and raises. These business rules ensure that your company stays profitable and retains its customers. And these rules are what contribute to making each company unique.

In the Fusion Middleware, Oracle provides a way to ensure that business rules are followed by including automated processes in the Application Server. Oracle provides a Business Rule Author, Rule Repository, and a Rules Engine.

The Business Rule Author is browser-based software that provides business owners with the ability to define and change the rules using a graphical user interface. These defined business rules are then stored in a Rule Repository. Interestingly, the Rule Repository is not in the database, but stored in a "flat" file in a directory. This is because industry standards expect it to be that way. The Rules Engine runs as part of the Application Server and when directed to do so, reads the rules and interprets them, returning the appropriate decision. Using this information the software can process accordingly.

The power of Oracle Business Rules is that it simplifies the process of defining and changing rules outside of the computer code. And it makes it easier for software developers to include them in their logic. In many older systems, the developer would include the logic for the business rules hard-coded into their programs. That made it difficult to change when the rules changed. Now that problem can be avoided and everyone's life is easier.

Now let's look at the BPEL Process Manager.

BPEL Process Manager

The heart of Business Process Management in Fusion is the Business Process Engine often called the BPEL Process Manager.

As we begin, it would probably be helpful to define the acronym BPEL. BPEL, or Business Process Execution Language, is an industry-standard markup language that supports Services orchestration (control of how Services process). If you remember our discussion on Services, we mentioned that it takes many of them to make up an application. BPEL allows Services to be managed as a group.

So what is a "markup language"? If you have ever seen XML documents or the HTML that underlies a web page, then you have seen a markup language. The last two letters in XML stand for "Markup Language" and the first letter is meant to communicate "extensible".

BPEL not only controls the order in which Services process but is also used to handle error conditions that Services encounter, notify others of progress, and make sure everyone gets along.

With this in mind, the BPEL Process Manager is a Java component in the Application Server than reads and executes the commands that are defined in a BPEL file. Those commands tell the Application Server which Services to execute and provide the structure of the overall process.

A portion of a BPEL document is shown in Figure 171. As you can see it is readable (sort of) and it has many angle brackets. This is a common syntax for all markup languages.

```
<process name="BatchOrderProcessing"
targetNamespace="http://xmlns.oracle.com/BatchOrderProcessing"
xmlns="http://schemas.xmlsoap.org/ws/2003/03/business-process/"
plext:wsdlloc="http://loop8600:8888/orabpel/default/OrderBooking/OrderBooking?wsdl"/>
  </partnerLinks>
  <variables>
   <variable name="Receive_FileIn_Read_InputVariable" messageType="ns2:PurchaseOrder_msg"/>
   <variablename="Invoke_OrderBooking_initiate_InputVariable"
messageType="ns3:OrderBookingRequestMessage"/>
  </variables>
  <sequence name="main">
   <receive  name="Receive_File"  partnerLink="FileReadAdapter"  portType="ns2:Read_ptt"  operation="Read"
variable="Receive_FileIn_Read_InputVariable" createInstance="yes"/>
   <assign name="AssignFileReadOrder">
    <copy>
     <from variable="Receive_FileIn_Read_InputVariable" part="PurchaseOrder"/>
     <to variable="Invoke_OrderBooking_initiate_InputVariable" part="payload"/>
    </copy>
   </assign>
   <invoke      name="Invoke_OrderBooking"      partnerLink="OrderBooking"      portType="ns3:OrderBooking"
operation="initiate" inputVariable="Invoke_OrderBooking_initiate_InputVariable"/>
  </sequence>
</process>
```

Figure 171 – A BPEL document

If reading BPEL "looks Greek to you", you will be pleased to know that by using JDeveloper you can view this same set of commands in a graphical view, which is much clearer. An example is shown in Figure 172.

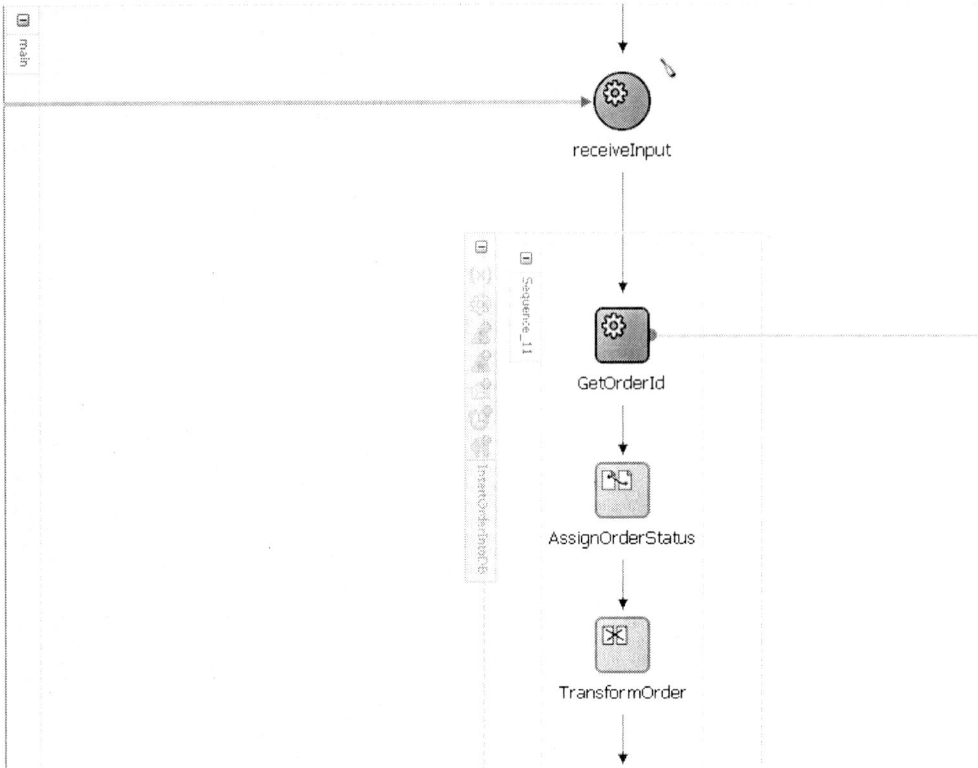

Figure 172 – A graphical view of BPEL

Each icon shown here can be opened with a click and modified by simply responding to prompted requests. That reduces the possibility of the developer typing in the wrong thing and having to find it later. Each icon is linked to another icon showing the progression of steps that will occur as the BPEL processes from start to finish.

All of these examples have focused on using BPEL to manage Services, but Oracle's version of BPEL also has the ability to interact with manual steps using Human Workflow. This new capability can be used to add steps in the business process where human approval or review is required. When this happens, the process will pause and wait for the manual steps to complete before proceeding. To make the process simple, the BPEL notifies the appropriate person(s) and provides an interface for them to respond to the event.

The important things to note are that BPEL manages Services and Human Workflow to complete a business process. This is made possible by the BPEL Process Manager (or BPEL Engines) which is the environment where BPEL is executed.

Now you may have wondered how BPEL is deployed into the BPEL Manager environment on the Application Server after it has been developed in JDeveloper. Our old friend JDeveloper provides this ability, along with the capability to edit BPEL, as we've noted previously.

With BPEL behind us, let's take a short ride on the Enterprise Service Bus.

Enterprise Service Bus (ESB)

We are still in the area of Business Process Management as we talk about the Enterprise Service Bus (ESB). Just like the BPEL Process Manager, the ESB is a Java component that executes in the Application Server.

In technology, a "bus" refers to a communication path, and that's what it means here. The Enterprise Service Bus provides Services with a way to communicate outside of the Application Server. Why would they want to do this?

Well, a Service might need to query a database or connect to a vendor's system and access the inventory stock levels, or check someone's credit limit on their credit card. Each of these situations requires sending information across the network and possibly even the Internet.

Even more importantly, the ESB helps support the clustering of Application Servers.

The ESB allows these connection paths to be pre-defined outside of any one Service, ensures that information is securely transmitted and even provides the ability to convert the data into different formats. These conversion or "transformation" capabilities ensure that everyone receives the message information in the format they expect without either party of the conversation needing to do that work.

With ESB, connections between Services can be developed, implemented and changed without low-level programming. This dramatically simplifies changes to applications. So if you like concepts, think of the ESB as a predefined secure phone line that Services can use to talk across long distances.

Web Services Manager (WSM)

The name of this product seems rather straightforward but it's a trick! The Web Services Manager (WSM) is really used to enforce security policies and track service level agreements for Services. Why security policies? Here are several reasons why Services require security.

When organizations start using Oracle Enterprise Service Bus (ESB) to perform data integration services the Web Services Manager is a requirement. This is because in an Oracle ESB environment, data elements are shared on a shared "bus" with the goal being to share data elements for efficient re-use.

Services may need to be restricted so that only certain security roles, like an administrator, are allowed to execute them. A good example is a Service that returns payroll information. If anyone could execute that Service, it would be a real problem.

Services sometimes need to hide or obscure the information in the messages they are sending to other Services. Using encryption, the passed information is only readable by the receiving Service.

There are also situations where a Service needs to confirm who sent it the message. This requires confirming the "signature" attached to the message.

Finally there is a need to ensure that Services perform as advertised based on their Service Level Agreement (SLA). An SLA is a published agreement, and with regard to Web Services, it specifies how quickly they will process. This guarantee is necessary to ensure that the speed of Service processing is not impacted.

Like Business Rules, definition of the security policies with Web Services Manager does not require any coding changes, allowing security changes to be made in real-time.

The Web Services Manager is an important part of protecting information and ensuring Services execute efficiently. It is designed to implement security standards like SSL, XML Encryption, XML Signature, WS-Security and the Security Assertion Markup Language (SAML). Figure 173 is a sample screenshot showing the Web Services Manager in action as depicted within the Oracle Enterprise Manager product.

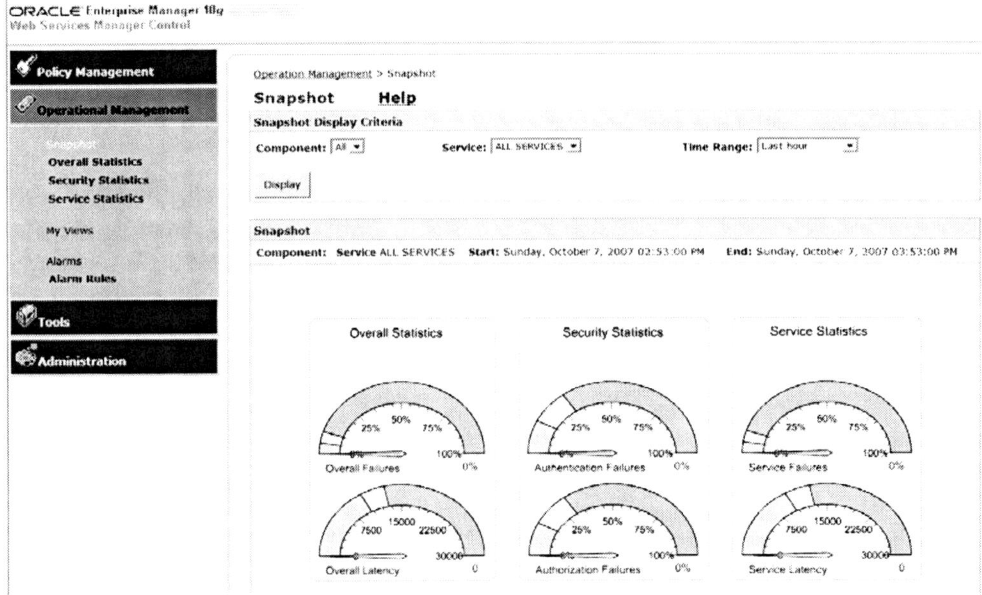

Figure 173 – The Web Services Manager

This screen shows how an administrator can monitor key performance indicators related to the security and reliability of the Services that have executed recently.

In the last few pages we've taken a look at JDeveloper and the four major components that enable Business Process Management and that are also included in Oracle's SOA Suite that are executed in the Application Server. In the next sections, we will look at several more Oracle products that are commonly used in SOA environments. Let's start with the Service Registry.

Service Registry

In the world of Services, it is important for everyone to know who's who, since each Service does something a little different. And when you have a system where there can literally be thousands of Services available for use, there is a real need for organization. What we are talking about is the Service Registry, where eligible young Services share their secrets hoping to get that special call. Well, maybe that's stretching it a bit but there are some analogies to a good singles dating service or the traditional phone book.

The Service Registry provides "published" information about what Services exist and how they work. That allows System Architects, and even running Services, to locate the right Service and access its capabilities. That encourages "reuse", which is an important part of

SOA. Reusing existing Services reduces software development and makes it simpler to change the system functionality by going to just one place for the change.

The Service Registry is a Java application that keeps its directory of Services in the Oracle database. With the Service Registry, administrators can manage a Web Service through its lifecycle. What's a Service's lifecycle? Well, we're glad you asked.

First, a Service is created and deployed. It has a Name, Version, Service Level Agreement, Messaging Parameters (what it expects to receive and what it will return) and other characteristics. The Service Level Agreement describes how fast the Service responds to requests, how often it is scheduled for downtime and provides an estimate for how often it might fail.

Over time, new versions of the Service are created and older versions are retired. The word "retired" almost gives you a picture of a group of older Services hanging out at the golf club reminiscing about their many jobs. Retired Services are retained for some defined period in case their functionality needs to be extracted. Eventually the Service is either not needed or is replaced completely with something new.

The Service Registry categorizes Services and provides an easy way for searching to find the right Service that will provide needed functionality. It shouldn't surprise you that there are standards already defined for how a Service Registry should work. The Oracle Service Registry adheres to these standards and can even operate with other Application Servers by third-party vendors. That's the value of relying on industry standards, right?

Business Activity Monitor (BAM)

This next product is considered part of the Business Process Management but also has similarities to some of the Business Intelligence products.

The Business Activity Monitor (BAM) is a configurable solution for creating real-time dashboards that display business operations information. A dashboard, in this case, is a rich browser-based user interface that graphically displays key performance information and allows the user to drill down for more details. Figure 174 is a sample BAM dashboard.

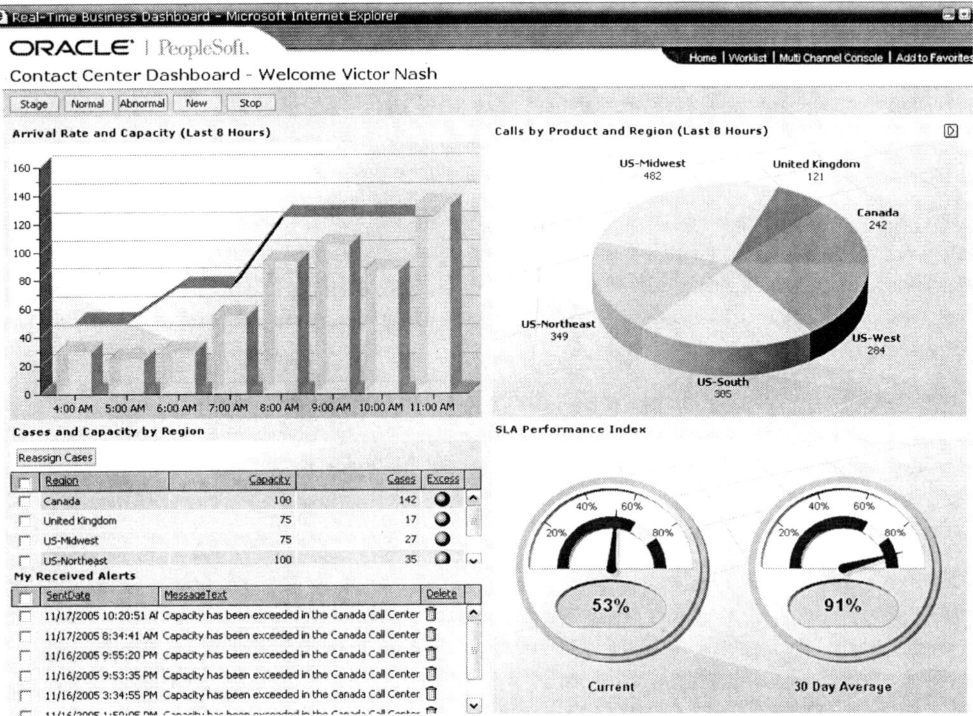

Figure 174 – The Business Activity Monitor (BAM) dashboard

BAM can display information in various formats including graphs, pie charts, and gauges, as well as traditional spreadsheets. The benefit of BAM is that it can be configured without programming skills and provides information in seconds rather than hours or days.

The secret to BAM is that it is built on a message-based, event-driven, memory-resident architecture designed for the needs of real-time analytics and reporting applications. This architecture allows it to process up to tens of thousands of messages per second!

BAM provides a way for business users to monitor business transactions and processing from the Application Server. Inside the Application Server, the BPEL language is used to provide real-time updates of what Services are doing. The BPEL Process Manager passes these notifications on. Using BAM, the Service activity can be monitored. Here's a common example:

Every company receives Orders and then processes them by shipping goods or delivering services. If the Order Management system were comprised of Services and those Services provided notifications, then a custom BAM dashboard could be created to monitor the number of Orders, Types of Orders, Speed of Processing and other Order events.

While most users would use BAM in their browser, Oracle provides the BAM Active Studio for power users, along with the BAM Architect and BAM Administrator tools for those who design and manage the environment.

For simplicity, we have skipped over a lot of the technical details about BAM and focused on how it works and the benefit it offers. Those benefits are the reason we believe that more and more organizations will be using BAM to monitor their operational information.

BI Publisher (BIP)

This next product is part of the Business Intelligence products. If you are familiar with Oracle reporting products, the BI Publisher was formerly known as the "XML Publisher". BI Publisher (BIP) reduces the costs of developing, customizing and maintaining business documents. In Release 12, BIP is used extensively and it is expected to replace the traditional Oracle Reports product within the next several years.

One of the ways BIP reduces costs is by allowing users to design their document templates in tools they are familiar with like Microsoft Word or Adobe Acrobat. That lowers the learning curve for getting started with BIP.

BIP works with XML as both input and output, so it is simple to integrate with databases, services, and other applications.

BIP is so flexible it can be used to print financial reports, invoices, purchase orders, government forms, tax forms, business reports, marketing materials, contracts and sales orders. At current count, it can work with over 185 languages and deliver content to a printer, via an email or to a web page. It can also generate PDF files.

BIP is a Java application so it can be run in any Java environment, including the Oracle Application Server.

The Rest of the Story

As you can see, we've only covered a few of the many products in Fusion Middleware and we've had to learn a lot of new concepts just to get to this point. As we wrap up, Figure 175 shows many of the products we have discussed and others that are part of Oracle's SOA Suite.

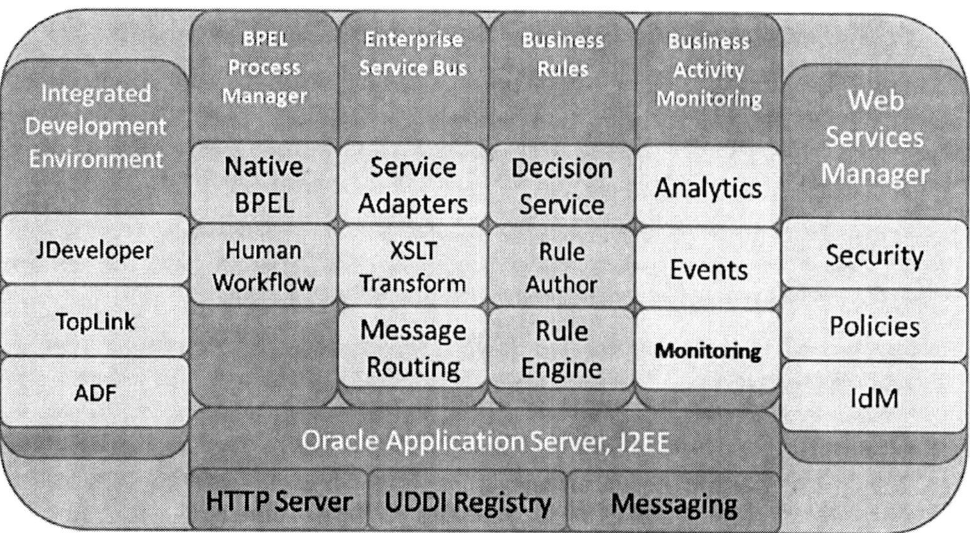

Figure 175 – Oracle's SOA Suite

Please note that Figure 175 does not include all of the products in Fusion Middleware, just those used for SOA.

Since this book is designed to be a primer, not an exhaustive in-depth study of Release 12, we will have to wrap up our exploration of Fusion Middleware at this point. If you are interested in the other products we encourage you do further reading on Oracle's website.

We recommend you start by taking a good look at the products and capabilities of

- Business Intelligence
- Identity Management
- Master Data Management
- Business Process Analysis

These other products are being used effectively by hundreds of organizations today and will likely benefit your organization as well.

With that thought in mind, let's focus back on the business issue and leave this area of technology behind.

What Does Fusion Mean to Me Today?

It isn't hard to see that even before the Fusion Applications are released, the technology that they are being built with will begin to influence new versions of the E-Business Suite. Some of these effects will come in the form of new products and technologies being added to the E-Business Suite. These changes are the most relevant to us.

So even if you're not considering the move to Fusion Applications in the near future, you'll find that Fusion's underlying technologies are becoming more and more a part of the entire Oracle ERP Applications Line. This includes the latest version of Siebel, JD Edwards, PeopleSoft and the E-Business Suite. As Oracle will often note, most of their customer are already using Fusion technologies but haven't yet seen the applications leverage all of it.

This change is clear with the Oracle Application Server 10*g*, which is a huge leap from what JServ offered several years ago. And there are components of the Fusion Middleware being promoted for use against Release 11*i* and Release 12 environments in the form of the BI Publisher, Application Integration Architecture (AIA) and the BPEL "workflow" tools.

As more of these middleware components are put forward for use against the existing software suites, the applications technical community will inevitably face the technical challenges, and new learning curves, associated with any technology shift.

One way to help ease the migration to Fusion, and certainly the best way, is to begin exploiting the capabilities of Fusion Middleware now rather than later. For instance, your organization can begin using BI Publisher both for new reports and migrating existing reports into it. Or it could begin doing integration using SOA products in the Fusion Middleware. Early adoption of these tools will help to flatten out the learning curve by letting organizations learn them now at a more relaxed pace while their use is not mandatory.

Another way to ease the pain of migration is to ensure that your current implementation is well documented, particularly in the area of customizations and external interfaces. Because of the changes in the underlying technologies, it is clear that some customizations will have to be reimplemented, and the first step in that process is having a clear understanding of what the code does, and why.

In fact, while reviewing and enhancing this documentation, it is worthwhile to compare the customizations to the current functionality in the latest release of E-Business Suite. You may find that a particular piece of custom code can in fact be replaced with functionality that is now in the Applications as delivered by Oracle!

The last recommendation is critical. Work with your organization to ensure you are up-to-date on the latest patches and releases for your Applications. This will help you benefit the most from Oracle's Lifetime Support policy as you navigate toward the future.

SUMMARY

Time marches on inexorably and with it come future promises about amazing solutions for our everyday problems. For all of us who work with the Oracle E-Business Suite on a regular basis, the future holds a simple promise. It is the promise that Oracle Applications are being re-architected to ensure that they can better adapt to meet our business needs, allow better integration with other systems and better communicate business insight.

While this promise won't let us fly over traffic on our daily commute, it should let us move more readily through the ever changing landscape that is business in the 21st century.

The future direction of Oracle Applications has been revealed for us if we look in the right places. Understanding Fusion Middleware and following the changes to the most current Applications including E-Business Suite Release 12, PeopleSoft 9.0, Siebel 8.0, JD Edwards Eon 8.12 and JD Edwards World A9.1 provides a clear roadmap to follow. Your challenge is to prioritize how you will leverage it to the best benefit of our organization.

THE BIG FINISH

So you've finished reading our Release 12 Primer. **Congratulations!** Now here's our question for you: Did you read it cover to cover, or did you skim a bit? Maybe you were thinking, "*Hey, I'm a technical guy, I don't need to know this functional stuff*", or "*Hey, that Fusion stuff is way off in the future, why worry about it now?*" Or maybe you're a functional user and figured the technical material was just for your IT organization?

If you've skipped or skimmed, the Release 12 Team recommends that you head back and read some more. Our concern, quite frankly, is founded in the book's preface. It took 17 writers plus 20 reviewers to create this simple little Primer for you. That's 37 big brains… we're of the opinion that the more you know about what lies ahead, the better you'll be at deciding the important questions:

- Should you upgrade to Release 12?
- What should you do to prepare for Fusion?
- If you're new to the Applications, should you start with Release 12, or go with Release 11*i*?

If you understand the nuances of Release 12 and Fusion, we think the decision making process will be that much easier. Remember, we are always available to answer your questions.

Good Luck!

The Release 12 Team

Your Trusted Advisor

Release12Team@solutionbeacon.com

Index

Printed in the United States
154637LV00001B/18/P

9 780615 238449